Timetable and Checklist for Preparing Your Research Paper

TOPIC/SUBJECT

☐ My subject meets the criteria of the assignment. (pp. 3–5; 15–20; 42–44)

☐ I have decided on an approach. (pp. 49–55)

☐ My instructor has approved the subject.

	Date Due	Date Completed

SEARCHING FOR INFORMATION

☐ I followed a search strategy. (pp. 59–63)

☐ I looked for primary sources. (pp. 57–58)

☐ I looked for secondary sources. (p. 58)

☐ I found information in books. (pp. 73–76)

☐ I found information in periodicals. (pp. 78–85; 87)

☐ I found nonprint sources of information including those outside a library. (pp 97–105)

☐ I found electronic sources, including InfoTrac. (pp. 88–97)

☐ I made preliminary citation cards as I searched. (pp. 63–72)

RECORDING INFORMATION   Date Due | Date Completed

☐ I am aware of plagiarism and how to avoid it. (pp. 106–13)

☐ I evaluated each potential source. (114–18)

☐ Each note is on a separate card. (pp. 118; 119)

☐ The source is completely identified on each card. (pp. 113–14; 129)

☐ I followed the conventions of writing the note cards. (pp. 118–20; 121; 128–33)

☐ I made accurate summaries of information for some note cards. (pp. 122–23; 126–27)

☐ I used paraphrases on some note cards. (pp. 123–24; 126)

☐ I have direct quotations on some cards. (pp. 125; 126–27)

☐ Some note cards contain my personal comments, ideas, opinions, and/or queries. (pp. 126–27)

ORGANIZING IDEAS   Date Due | Date Completed

☐ I reevaluated my notes and selected those that allow me to take a stand on my subject. (pp. 137–38)

☐ I wrote a useful thesis statement. (pp. 138–42)

☐ I considered the best way to organize my information. (pp. 144–49)

☐ I prepared an outline in correct form. (pp. 141–49; 151–57)

☐ Every item in the outline relates directly to the thesis statement. (pp. 150–53)

☐ The outline shows an organized progression of thought. (pp. 157–58)

☐ I received feedback on my work thus far. Yes _____ No _____

WRITING/DRAFTING THE PAPER

- ☐ The opening of my paper leads the audience into the subject. (pp. 164–70)
- ☐ My writing is coherent. (pp. 170–71)
- ☐ Transitions connect ideas smoothly. (p. 173)
- ☐ All assertions are adequately supported. (p. 172)
- ☐ My writing is specific. (p. 173)
- ☐ My writing style suits my subject. (pp. 162–63; 172–73)
- ☐ Every quotation is essential to the text and is properly presented. (pp. 180–85)
- ☐ Resources, references, and quotations are integrated with my own writing in the text. (pp. 173–80; 185–86)
- ☐ All sources are acknowledged and properly documented. (pp. 198–205)
- ☐ I used comment notes as necessary. (pp. 185–86; 240; 268)
- ☐ The paper ends with finality. (pp. 186–90)

REVISING/EDITING

- ☐ I have selected the most appropriate words for my ideas. (pp. 163–64; 191)
- ☐ Sentences are the best that I can compose. (pp. 170–72; 191–93)
- ☐ Spelling, punctuation, and capitalization are conventional. (pp. 193; 194)
- ☐ Documentation is accurate and consistent with the style selected. (pp. 198–214; 266–68)
- ☐ The title of the paper is specific. (pp. 195–97)

FINAL PRESENTATIONS

- ☐ I have followed the recommended typing or word processing format. (p. 237–38)
- ☐ I have included options as requested. (pp. 239; 242–43)
- ☐ Each page is numbered consecutively and accurately. (pp. 237–38; 265)
- ☐ All illustrations, charts, graphs, tables, pictures, etc. are properly labeled and relevant to the text. (pp. 239–40; 241)
- ☐ I alphabetized the Works Cited or References cards for sources I actually used. (pp. 216; 269)
- ☐ The Works Cited or References listing is complete and in the proper form. (pp. 215–35; 265–74; 274–79)
- ☐ Any additional sections or materials are completed, properly identified, and put in place. (pp. 242; 243–47)
- ☐ I have given my research paper a final proofreading and typographical errors are corrected. Yes _____ Not Yet _____

I turned in my research paper on _____ .

The Research Paper

Process, Form, and Content

Eighth Edition

Audrey J. Roth

Miami-Dade Community College

HEINLE & HEINLE

THOMSON LEARNING

Australia Canada Mexico Singapore Spain United Kingdom United States

HEINLE & HEINLE

THOMSON LEARNING

The Research Paper
Process, Form, and Content
Audrey J. Roth

Executive Editor: *Karen Allanson*
Developmental Editor: *Kim Johnson*
Marketing Manager: *Chaun Hightower*
Project Editor: *Tanya Nigh*
Print Buyer: *Barbara Britton*
Permissions Editor: *Yanna Walters/Bob Kauser*

Production: *Melanie Field, Strawberry Field Publishing*
Designer: *Jeanne Calabrese/Lisa Berman*
Cover Design: *Reuter Design*
Cover Image: *Geoffrey Nilsen Photography*
Compositor: *Thompson Type*
Printer: *Phoenix Color Corp*

Copyright © 1999 Heinle & Heinle, a division of Thomson Learning, Inc.
Thomson Learning ™ is a trademark used herein under license.

Printed in the United States of America
  4 5 6 7 8 9 10   06 05 04 03

For more information contact Heinle & Heinle, 25 Thomson Place,
Boston, MA 02210 USA, or you can visit our Internet site at http://www.heinle.com

All rights reserved. No part of this work covered by the copyright hereon may be
reproduced or used in any form or by any means—graphic, electronic, or mechanical,
including photocopying, recording, taping, Web distribution or information storage and
retrieval systems—without the written permission of the publisher.

For permission to use material from this text or product contact us:
Tel   1-800-730-2214
Fax   1-800-730-2215
Web   www.thomsonrights.com

ISBN: 0-15-506629-3

Library of Congress Catalog Card Number:
        98-39519

To the Teacher

Many years ago I wrote a series of handouts to help my students complete the departmental research paper assignment for a composition course I was teaching. Those dittoed pages evolved into a textbook and now into the eighth edition of that text. My purpose for writing is the same now as it was initially: to show students that by conscientiously and thoughtfully following a series of steps, they will be able to fulfill a research paper assignment, and to do so with self-satisfaction. Besides gaining the specific skills to handle that assignment, I hope students will be able to adapt this procedure to uses beyond school and to their future lives and vocations.

The Process

Formal research and many publications have, by now, convinced most teachers to view writing as a process. The ubiquitous computer, too, has been integrated into the process at various steps along the way. This edition of *The Research Paper: Process, Form, and Content,* therefore, also continues to treat producing a research paper as a process: searching for information in print, nonprint, and electronic sources; synthesizing what is learned with original ideas and interpretations; organizing the whole; finally writing and revising. That this is a process for nonacademic as well as for school uses continues to be shown in this edition, particularly in examples and references throughout. Once the skills this process teaches are learned in the production of a formal research paper, students will find applications for them as they move into all sorts of academic courses, as well as in businesses and professions.

The Form

Special effort has been made in this edition, as in past ones, to create a readable text, one accessible to students. Subheads and typefaces were selected to make information easy to locate by scanning. Lists appear, when possible, to help illustrate, consolidate, and preview materials. Finally, generous verbal examples as well as visual representations abound. In short, many elements that the author and designers of this edition took extra time to devise will make using the text more helpful to students.

Color printing performs two roles in this eighth edition, as it has in several previous editions. First, color draws students' attention to various parts of the text by making heads, subheads, and captions more likely to be noticed. Second, both sample research papers (Chapters 10 and 11) have margin notes in color that point out characteristics of research paper form; margin notes in black are about content. Students will find these notes to be quick guides for their own research papers.

The Content

The principal content change in this edition, compared to previous ones, is the greater attention paid to electronic sources and the uses students can make of them in preparing research papers. Increasingly, students have access to computers that continue to hold more information than ever before, even as their sizes shrink surprisingly—and as the whole world becomes computerized, more materials are becoming available to students.

Some information already considered "standard," based on previous editions, is transposed or augmented in this edition. I have also been attentive to changes in student work habits and to the resources that can now be accessed in libraries. As in earlier editions, text examples and appendices have been kept up to date.

Because most instructors in English and humanities courses prefer the MLA style, this book is still dominated by the conventions of documentation recommended by the Modern Language Association in the *MLA Handbook,* 4th ed. (1995), which that organization believes most appropriate for undergraduates preparing research papers. However, I have also consulted Joseph Gibaldi's *MLA Style Manual,* 2nd ed. (1998) in an effort to give students the most up-to-date thinking on documentation.

Realizing that not all students are in the humanities when they are assigned to write research papers, I have included as Chapter 11 a student-written research paper in APA style as well as other examples and materials based on the *Publication Manual of the American Psychological Association,* 4th ed. (1994). Further, to prevent confusion, examples of APA reference forms and citations are separated from the MLA style. Other documentation systems are probably not used frequently by students who will study from this book, but they are incorporated so students will know about them.

Those elements of earlier editions that both students and teachers have said are particularly useful have been retained. There continues to be emphasis on audience, from selecting a subject to incorporating that knowledge into writing and revising the paper. As before, students are shown how to avoid even inadvertent plagiarism from note taking through final writing. Persuasive writing continues to be stressed, because that seems to be the mode most requested by teachers, so many examples and the two full sample papers are persuasive ones. "Managing Your Time" and a "Search Strategy" form appear again, as does the "Timetable and Checklist," a long-time feature that serves as additional guidance to students.

Inexperienced writers seem to find a continuing problem in integrating resources into the text of their own research papers. Doing so smoothly requires practice to maintain the author's tone and style, so this edition gives many examples.

Exercises and Activities

For the last few editions of *The Research Paper, Process, Form, and Content*, I have prepared a separate Instructor's Manual of reproducible exercises and possible answers to them. This edition continues that tradition by offering a separate booklet containing both group and individual activities designed to reinforce learning from this text.

And Thanks . . .

Books take a long time to ready for publication. There is evaluation, tryout, writing, revision, editing, and more revising. But I am lucky in having so many people available to assist me.

First, of course, there are the students—mine and those of my colleagues—who have worked through this material, given thoughtful responses, and even allowed me to include their work. None of these editions would have been possible without them. I have also always had the assistance of friendly and helpful librarians; for this edition that assistance came through Laurie Hime of the Miami-Dade Community College Kendall Campus library. Finally, there are those people associated with my publisher, who include the ever-watchful Melanie Field and, for the second time, copyeditor Elliot Simon.

Thanks go, also, to the many colleagues and friends whose comments and suggestions have helped me to continue inproving this book: Peggy Brent, Hinds Community College; James Stokes, University of Wisconsin–Stevens Point; and Mary A. Fortner, Lincoln Land Community College.

For this edition, as always, I acknowledge my understanding and supportive family. I particularly would have liked to let my husband know, again, how important his contributions have been. And this time I add Joshua Ryan Aldama's name to the family list.

Audrey J. Roth
Miami, Florida

To the Student

If you spend much time surfing the Internet, you are doing a lot more research than you realize. Every time you access a Web site of interest or follow the links connected to it, you are doing research. The computer, therefore, has transformed both the meaning as well as the extent of research. What once took days of working in a library gathering information can now be obtained almost in a matter of hours seated before a computer screen. And rather than being limited to one or perhaps two local libraries, research can now extend to almost anywhere in the world.

Because so much information is so readily available, early parts of preparing a research paper have meant some changes. It is now particularly important to narrow and limit your subject, lest you be overwhelmed by the amount of material that readily comes to you. Therefore, this edition continues what so many students working from previous editions have found so helpful: discussion in Chapters 2 and 3 to help you learn how to narrow and focus ideas in deciding on a research subject. I hope you will use the varied suggestions in these chapters and explore the many possibilities open to you before making a final decision. Time and again, I have seen a hurried or thoughtless choice lead to various difficulties while a thoughtful subject choice leads to a successful research paper.

Examples and illustrations drawn from a wide variety of businesses and professions are retained in this edition, for I know that most of you are unlikely to spend the rest of your life in academe. And even though research paper assignments are often given in English classes, you will find many examples from other academic disciplines.

Chapter 4, "Searching for Information," has been augmented in this edition to incorporate the many current ways to find content for your research paper.

Although the emphasis throughout this eighth edition is on MLA [Modern Language Association] conventions, you will also find here, as in the last edition, a chapter on the format recommended by the American Psychological Association [APA]. This format is used for writing about the social sciences and even for writing about research in the humanities. Many of the natural science conventions are close to those of the APA, so you can readily make required changes should instructors in those disciplines ask you to follow them. If you keep this book, you will have a good guide to research papers required of you in other courses—and a valuable addition to your own permanent library.

"Managing Your Time" has proved helpful to many students because it addresses the common problem of researching information, drafting, writing, and citing sources for a resesearch paper—all while you are keeping up with other courses, jobs, and family or other personal obligations. The "Search Strategy" has helped keep my own students on track, as has the "Timetable and Checklist" at the front of the book. Even students who initially feel that the "Process Log" is time-consuming agree that it is a helpful device to let them see their own progress and is satisfying to look back on after the research paper is completed. Therefore, these elements from the previous editions are updated and incorporated into this eighth edition.

Finally, the publisher and I have tried to make the design and typography of this edition easy to use and helpful in finding what you need. Use the **index** as a reference source for the many ideas within the book. See how the **illustrations** are coordinated with the text for clarity and how the many **subheads** help you scan for specifics. The great number of **lists** point up key information to help you find it most readily. Look carefully at the **marginal notes** in the two sample research papers, those **in color,** which call attention to forms you need to follow in your own research paper, and those in **black type,** which are about the content and can serve as guides to writing your own paper.

This book doesn't guarantee a magic formula that makes preparing a research paper easy. It *does,* however, offer a procedure to follow and a framework to use for such a paper, and it guides you through many skills basic to both academic and nonacademic tasks. It also encourages you to make discoveries about yourself and about knowledge beyond textbooks and libraries.

I hope this book will enable you to make research a useful part of your education and preparation for the future. As you learn increasingly to work on your own and to trust your own abilities, you will continue to learn what going to school is all about.

A.J.R.

Contents

TO THE TEACHER   v
TO THE STUDENT   viii

CHAPTER 1
Starting the Research Paper   1

KINDS OF RESEARCH   1
DIFFERENCES AMONG A REPORT, A DOCUMENTED PAPER, AND A
  RESEARCH PAPER   2
WHAT A RESEARCH PAPER *IS*   3
WHAT A RESEARCH PAPER *IS NOT*   4
LENGTH OF RESEARCH PAPERS   6
FIVE STEPS TO A RESEARCH PAPER   6
  Step 1. Choosing the Subject   6
  Step 2. Collecting Information   7
  Step 3. Evaluating Materials   7
  Step 4. Organizing Ideas   8
  Step 5. Writing the Paper   8
WHY A RESEARCH PAPER IS IMPORTANT   9
WHO READS RESEARCH PAPERS—AND WHY   10
MANAGING YOUR TIME   10
KEEPING A PROCESS LOG   11

CHAPTER 2
Choosing a General Topic   15

THE TERMS "TOPIC" AND "SUBJECT"   15
QUALITIES OF A GOOD TOPIC   16
TOPICS TO AVOID   18
ASSIGNED TOPICS   20

FIELD-OF-STUDY TOPICS   20
1. Take Stock of What You Already Know   21
2. Make Use of Printed and Electronic Aids   21
3. Build From Your Own Interests   29
4. Surf the Internet   31
FREE-CHOICE TOPICS   31
LIBRARY CATALOGING CUSTOMS   33
Classifications of Books   33
Contents of the Online Catalog   37
Individual Catalog Entries   37
Alphabetizing of Books and Periodicals   38
AN ADDENDUM: DOUBLE SUBMISSIONS   40

CHAPTER 3
Narrowing the Topic   42

SOME LIMITATIONS YOU WORK WITHIN   42
1. Length   42
2. Materials Available   43
3. Audience   44
FOCUSING ON A SUBJECT TO RESEARCH   44
Freewriting   44
Free Association   44
Clustering   45
Subdividing   46
The Five Ws   46
Combined Method   49
FINDING AN APPROACH   49
DECIDING ON AN APPROACH BEFORE BEING WELL INFORMED
 ABOUT YOUR SUBJECT   49
Examining or Analyzing   51
Evaluating or Criticizing   52
Comparing and Contrasting   53
Relating   53
Arguing or Persuading   54
WORDING YOUR APPROACH   55
A Word of Caution   56
CHOOSING A RESEARCH PAPER TITLE   56

CHAPTER 4
Searching for Information   57

PRIMARY AND SECONDARY SOURCES   57
Primary Sources   57
Secondary Sources   58

THE WHAT, WHERE, AND HOW OF FINDING INFORMATION   58
DEVISING A SEARCH STRATEGY   59
  Print-on-Paper Resources   60
  Electronic Resources   60
  Nonprint Resources   61
  The Search Strategy Record   61
CONVENTIONS FOR MLA-STYLE PRELIMINARY (AND FINAL)
  CITATIONS   63
  General Conventions   63
  Conventions About the Author Unit   64
  Conventions About the Title Unit   65
  Conventions About the Publication Information Unit   66
CITING SPECIFIC SOURCES   72
FINDING AND CITING PRINT-ON-PAPER RESOURCES   73
  Encyclopedias   73
  Bibliographies and Reference Books   74
  Handbooks   76
  Indexes   76
  Government Publications   85
  Other Sources of Print Information   86
  Microforms   87
FINDING AND CITING ELECTRONIC RESOURCES   88
  Computer Connections   89
  Online Catalogs for Books   89
  The Internet   90
  Computer Databases   91
  CD-ROMs   93
  Electronic Journals and Newsletters   95
  Discussion Groups, Chat Lines, and Bulletin Boards   97
FINDING AND CITING NONPRINT RESOURCES   97
  Three Units of Information in a Nonprint Preliminary Citation   97
  Radio and TV Programs   98
  Interviews   99
  Lectures and Speeches   100
  Questionnaires, Surveys, and Polls   101
  Films, Filmstrips, and Slides   102
  Videocassettes, Laser Discs, and DVDs   103
  CDs, Audiotapes, and Other Audio Recordings   104

CHAPTER 5
Recording Information   106

WRITING NOTES   106
PLAGIARISM—AND HOW NOT TO COMMIT IT   106
  Of Words and Ideas—and Plagiarism   107
  How *Not* to Plagiarize   108

Notes That Plagiarize   108
Notes That *Don't* Plagiarize   110
COMMON KNOWLEDGE   112
READING TO TAKE NOTES   113
Previewing   113
Skimming   114
Scanning   114
EVALUATING SOURCE MATERIALS   114
Before You Read, Look, or Listen   115
When You Read, Look, or Listen   117
QUALITIES OF GOOD NOTES   118
Legibility   118
Accuracy   119
Completeness   120
KINDS OF NOTES   121
Summary Notes   122
Paraphrase Notes   123
Direct Quotation Notes   125
Personal Comment Notes   126
Combination Notes   126
NUMBER OF NOTE CARDS   127
CONVENTIONS FOR WRITING NOTES   128
1. Quotations   128
2. Words Omitted from a Quotation   131
3. Interpolations or Commentaries   131
4. Foreign Words and Phrases   133
5. Titles Within Quotations and Sources   133
A NOTE ABOUT PHOTOCOPIES AND PRINTOUTS   133
IF YOU USE A COMPUTER   134

CHAPTER 6
Organizing Ideas   136

RECONSIDERATION TIME   136
PUTTING THE PARTS TOGETHER   137
WHAT A THESIS STATEMENT *IS*   138
WHAT A THESIS STATEMENT *IS NOT*   139
HOW A THESIS STATEMENT EVOLVES   141
HOW AN OUTLINE EVOLVES   142
WAYS OF ORGANIZING CONTENT   144
Time   145
Known to Unknown or Simple to Complex   145
Comparison and Contrast   145
General to Particular or Particular to General   146
Problem to Solution or Question to Answer   146
Cause to Effect or Effect to Cause   146

RELATING ORGANIZATION TO OVERALL APPROACH   147
VISUAL ORDERING—CLUSTERING AND MAPPING   147
OUTLINES   149
   Content of Outlines   150
   Forms of Outlines   153
CONVENTIONS FOR OUTLINES   154
REVISING OUTLINES   157
COMPUTER AIDS TO OUTLINING   158
A FINAL CHECK   158

CHAPTER 7
Writing Your Paper   160

REPRISE OF WRITING PREPARATION   160
WHAT "DRAFTING" MEANS   160
WRITING STYLE   162
STARTING YOUR PAPER   164
   Good Openings   164
   Bad Openings   169
DRAFTING THE BODY OF YOUR PAPER   170
   Unity and Coherence   170
   Adequate Support   172
   Emphasis   172
   Concreteness and Specificity   173
INTEGRATING RESOURCE INFORMATION   173
   Examples of Well-Integrated Resource Information   174
   Six Ways to Integrate Documented Information into the Text of a
   Research Paper   175
RECORDING AND PUNCTUATING QUOTATIONS   180
   Short Prose Passages   182
   Longer Prose Passages   182
   Short Passages of Poetry   183
   Longer Passages of Poetry   183
   Drama   184
COMMENT NOTES   185
ENDING THE PAPER   186
   Good Endings   186
   Bad Endings   190
REVISING AND EDITING YOUR PAPER   190
   Editing for Word Choice and Sentence Structure   191
   Mechanics   193
REVISING ON A COMPUTER   193
SELECTING A TITLE   195
   Characteristics of a Good Title   195
   Kinds of Titles to Avoid   195
   Conventions for Titles   197

CHAPTER 8
Documenting Your Paper   198

WHEN, WHERE, AND HOW TO MAKE ACKNOWLEDGMENTS   198
PARENTHETICAL DOCUMENTATION: MLA [MODERN LANGUAGE
  ASSOCIATION]   199
  Conventions for Parenthetical Documentation   199
  Punctuation and Spacing in Parenthetical Documentation   200
  Identifying Sources in Parenthetical Documentation   201
DOCUMENTING VISUALS: ILLUSTRATIONS, MAPS, CHARTS, GRAPHS,
  AND TABLES   203
USING COMMENT NOTES IN ADDITION TO PARENTHETICAL
  DOCUMENTATION   205
MLA ENDNOTE DOCUMENTATION   205
  Differences Between Endnotes and Works Cited   206
  First References in MLA-Style Endnotes: Books   206
  First References in MLA-Style Endnotes: Periodicals   209
  First References in MLA-Style Endnotes: Other Print Sources   210
  First References in MLA-Style Endnotes: Electronic Sources   211
  First References in MLA-Style Endnotes: Nonprint Sources   211
  Subsequent References in MLA-Style Endnotes   213

CHAPTER 9
Preparing the Works Cited List (MLA Format)   215

WHAT TO INCLUDE   215
  Conventions to Follow   216
STANDARD FORMS FOR WORKS CITED   217
  Entire Books   217
  Portions of Books   222
  Periodicals   223
  Other Print Sources   227
  Electronic Sources   229
  Nonprint Sources   230

CHAPTER 10
Final Presentation—MLA Style   236

MANUSCRIPT PREPARATION AND PROOFREADING   236
WORD PROCESSING/TYPING   237
PAGE NUMBERING   237
FIRST PAGE OF THE RESEARCH PAPER TEXT (MLA)   238
OUTLINE   239
THE TEXT (MLA STYLE)   239
ILLUSTRATIVE MATERIALS: CHARTS, TABLES, GRAPHS, AND OTHER
  VISUALS   239

COMMENT NOTES   240
ENDNOTES   240
WORKS CITED   241
ANNOTATIONS   241
APPENDIX   242
OTHER OPTIONS: PREFACES, STATEMENTS OF PURPOSE, PROPOSALS,
  SYNOPSES, AND ABSTRACTS   243
FASTENING PAGES   243
SAMPLE RESEARCH PAPER IN MLA FORMAT   244

CHAPTER 11
APA and Other Styles   265

APA FORMAT AND PAGE NUMBERING   265
APA-FORMAT TITLE PAGE   266
CONVENTIONS FOR APA CITATIONS IN THE TEXT   266
  Quotations Acknowledged in the Text   268
COMMENT AND DOCUMENTATION NOTES   268
APPENDIXES AND OTHER MATERIALS   269
REFERENCES IN APA FORMAT   269
  Print Resources   272
  Nonprint Resources   273
  Electronic Resources   274
OTHER RESEARCH DOCUMENTATION AND REFERENCE SYSTEMS   274
  Footnotes   274
  Between-Line Documentation   275
  Full In-Text Documentation   275
  Numbering Sources   275
SAMPLE RESEARCH PAPER IN APA FORMAT   276

APPENDIX A
Selected List of Reference Works Available in Libraries   289

GENERAL REFERENCE WORKS   291
SCIENCE AND TECHNOLOGY   294
SOCIAL SCIENCES   296
HUMANITIES   299
VOCATIONAL STUDIES   302

APPENDIX B
Reference Words and Abbreviations   304

Index   307

The Research Paper

Process, Form, and Content

Eighth Edition

CHAPTER 1

Starting the Research Paper

KINDS OF RESEARCH

You may think of research as something you do for a class paper. But you actually do research for many reasons, most of them unrelated to academics. Every time you make a careful, serious, systematic investigation to find information, you are doing research. Sometimes your purpose is as simple as finding out more about a sports figure you've seen on TV or a subject you have heard about, such as pressed glass. Other times, you conduct an investigation to help you make a decision such as where to go on a vacation, whether you can do better by buying or renting a car, or which computer to buy. In fact, most research is likely to be for personal reasons.

Other people do research, too, and for a variety of purposes. Legislators gather information and make investigations before deciding how to vote on a bill. Businesspeople do research about zoning and demographics before determining where to locate a retail store or whether to expand an existing one.

The sudden boom in personal computers and the accompanying growth of the way information is handled, especially since the mid-1990s, has put a whole new light on information gathering, storage, and dissemination. Everyone who uses this electronic technology now has unprecedented access to and uses for information. What was once available only in print from libraries now can be accessed readily from the libraries and directly onto a home, business, or school computer. There are also newer sources, such as organizations (states, CD manufacturers, museums, and more), essentially advertising themselves and/or their wares. Also, other people worldwide now serve as resources through computer discussion groups.

There are five categories of research, each with varying objectives.

- **Pure research** is aimed at adding new knowledge to what people have already been able to learn, even if such knowledge doesn't seem to have any immediate or practical appplication. It may be research done in a laboratory or by a deep-space-probe vehicle.

- **Applied research** attempts to make practical application of what has already been discovered or theorized. For instance, what was discovered in laboratories about the chemical properties of various sorts of plastics has resulted in methods of recycling and in new products that have contributed to a cleaner environment.

- **Technical or business research** is a form of applied research used by people who have to make such practical decisions as deciding whether or not to seek a new CEO for a company in order to improve its sagging dividends for shareholders. Automobile design and engineering continually benefit from technical research.

- **Market research** is the study of what consumers want (or say they want) and is always undertaken before money is invested in an idea. ATM machines, drive-in prescription services, moveable shelves in refrigerators, and ever-increasing styles of portable phones are among the many new products and services developed from such research.

- **Scholarly or academic research** concentrates on gathering materials already in existence. The person or group doing the gathering may then synthesize the ideas or look at such information in new ways. Your teachers do this sort of research when they write journal articles or speeches to give at their professional organizations. You will be doing it when you use this book to help you write an academic research paper.

DIFFERENCES AMONG A REPORT, A DOCUMENTED PAPER, AND A RESEARCH PAPER

Call it a "term paper," a "library report," an "investigative report," a "documented paper," or a "research paper"—the names are often used interchangeably, though there are some differences among them. All have in common the need to locate information on a given subject and to write conclusions based on your findings.

Perhaps in elementary or high school you did some library work or even wrote a library paper. That is, you looked for facts, recorded them, and then handed in a composite of what you found. If you merely compiled such information without making evaluations or interpreting it, you were actually preparing a **report.**

Although reports are usually from one to several pages long, they may also be book length. They are very much a part of school assignments. However, reports are also used so often in business, industry, and government that college courses are given in business and technical report writing.

A good report must document its contents, acknowledging the sources of information from which it's compiled. Therefore, the term **documented paper** or **documented report** is often used in academe. To write such a report, you find and record information and present it *without* including your own evaluation, interpretation, or ideas. Although no truly unbiased work is possible, in a documented paper you should try to present the results of your research in as "objective" a manner as you can. To do so, you must take notes meticulously, render summaries and paraphrases thoroughly, and ascribe sources accurately.

Several kinds of documented papers are possible. You might *trace* the *history* of something, such as the history of beach volleyball (how beach volleyball developed, acquired professional player leagues, and eventually was accepted as an Olympic sport). Or you could *explain* a notion, such as flexible working time, perhaps illustrating the explanation with examples of how this concept has been implemented in various businesses or industries. Opportunities abound to write *comparison and contrast,* such as the relationship between Bizet's stage opera *Carmen* and its movie version, *Carmen Jones.* Or you might *examine* and report on a single subject, such as how robots are being used for difficult or dangerous jobs in the auto industry.

A **research paper** differs from a report or a documented paper in one major way: you are expected to evaluate or interpret or in some other way add to and participate in the information you gather and write about. In a research paper, then, you are expected to *develop a point of view toward your material, take a stand, express some original thought.*

You can do that by first narrowing a general area and then deciding on a specific approach to take in searching for information. Later, after you have interpreted your findings or evaluated your information, that approach will be reflected in the thesis or underlying idea of your research paper. So, although you might start with an interest in elephants, you could focus on examining how their ivory tusks became a trade item. International convention now says that ivory cannot be exported, but your research may show that this ban is not being enforced everywhere. Also, in studying the elephant ivory situation, you may discover that the animals are being killed for reasons beyond the money their tusks might bring. Study and your own imagination might then suggest ways to close present loopholes in laws or a better monitoring of exports, and your research paper could reflect these ideas.

WHAT A RESEARCH PAPER *IS*

A research paper, as the term is used in this book, is an entirely new work, one you create, one that can only be found on the pages you write. It will, therefore, have a number of qualities that reflect *you* and make it your own special creation.

1. The research paper synthesizes your discoveries about a topic and your judgment, interpretation, and evaluation of those discoveries.

Your discoveries will be mostly the knowledge and ideas, even the actual words, of people who have spoken or written about the subject you investigate. It may also include pictures. Thus, your discoveries should come from both print and nonprint sources. The special value of all that collected material is that *you weigh your discoveries and draw conclusions from them.* Thus, your involvement is evident because the entire research paper reflects your own ideas as much as those of anyone else who has dealt with the subject.

2. The research paper is a work that shows your originality.

The paper resulting from your personal processes of study, evaluation, and synthesis will be a totally new creation, one *you* originate. True, you are using many and varied sources, but in a carefully crafted research paper, your own hand and thought—your originality—are evident.

3. The research paper acknowledges all sources you have used.

The words, ideas, and visuals of others need to be recognized and documented in ways that prevent a reader from believing that the intellectual property of somebody else is, instead, yours. Doing so is only ethical. Thus, although your research paper is a new and original work, none of it would have been possible without the various sources you consulted to prepare it. Acknowledging that debt to others is only right and fair!

So basic is such acknowledgment to research writing that a whole series of customs or conventions has developed for crediting what you borrow from other people. You begin such acknowledgment when you start taking notes (see Chapter 5) and conclude when you incorporate that recognition into your own writing (see Chapter 8).

4. The research paper shows that you are part of a community of scholars.

Other people will acknowledge what you have done when you complete a research paper. In an academic setting, where your paper is going to be read by other students and by one or more teachers, the paper demonstrates your ability to be counted as one of a community that values research and original thought. Being part of such a group will bring you much satisfaction.

WHAT A RESEARCH PAPER *IS NOT*

If you accept the definition of a research paper that underlies this book—that it is a synthesis of your thought applied to materials supplied to you by others, that it is original, and that it acknowledges source material—you will never make the mistake of attempting to hand in what is certainly *not* a research paper.

1. A summary of an article or a book (or other source material) is NOT a research paper.

A summary can't fit our definition of a research paper for two reasons: (1) a single source doesn't allow you to select materials or to exercise your own judgment, and (2) the organization can't be your own because a summary must follow the structure of the original source.

Summaries of written, visual, or audio materials have their uses—and they are important ones—but substituting for a research paper is not one of them.

2. The ideas of others, repeated uncritically, do NOT make a research paper.

By definition, the research paper has to reflect something about yourself—a synthesis, an interpretation, or some other personal involvement. To repeat, uncritically, what others have said is merely to report information already available elsewhere.

3. A series of quotations, no matter how skillfully put together, does NOT make a research paper.

Quotations are certainly important in a research paper because they are the words of experts in the field you are investigating or of those who are experts in using words. But a paper assembled completely (or even mostly) from other people's words lacks the "you" of the synthesis that really makes a research paper. You yourself are not really involved in such a paper, nor does such a work give any evidence of your originality.

Furthermore, patching together dozens of quotations from different people will likely reflect the multiple styles of their individual authors and thus not create a coherent whole.

4. Unsubstantiated personal opinion does NOT constitute a research paper.

Although you are expected to inject some personal thinking into any research paper you write, you must have reasons for your beliefs and make them evident to readers. So, although individual thoughts and attitudes are valuable in certain kinds of writing assignments, the research paper is not usually one of them—unless you can support those ideas and attitudes. For one thing, the "search" aspect would be lacking. For another, a good research paper topic doesn't lend itself to opinions without extensive and factual bases.

5. Copying or accepting another person's work without acknowledging it, whether the work be published or unpublished, professional or amateur, is NOT research. IT IS PLAGIARISM.

To pass off as your own any writing you didn't actually do is morally wrong. To present such work without acknowledging the source—and therefore to let someone assume it is yours when, in fact, it is not—is plagiarism. (See more about plagiarism on pages 106–12.) Turning in as your own a research paper done by someone else is indefensible, whether you accepted it from a friend trying to help you out, bought it from a company that supplies research papers to those assigned to write them in schools, or downloaded it from an Internet site. There are laws against plagiarism, and in many schools any student involved in plagiarism (including the supplier of such a paper) is automatically dismissed.

Showing that you can base your work on that of others is one mark of an educated person. But, obviously, presenting such materials as your own is not! Students who respect themselves and their work will certainly not be tempted to copy from anyone. Instead, they will always extend proper credit to others for ideas, as well as for specific wording.

Often, only the finest line of distinction separates what must be credited in a research paper from what you can safely present without documentation. What requires crediting or documentation to avoid plagiarism and what doesn't is discussed in Chapter 5 in the section entitled "Plagiarism—and How Not to Commit It." In general, it's a good idea to credit a source if you are in doubt about the need to do so.

LENGTH OF RESEARCH PAPERS

Length has nothing to do with whether a piece of work is a report or a research paper. Approach makes the difference. Writing ten pages on the differences between bottlenose and river dolphins would be a report; writing ten pages about why bottlenose dolphins are preferable to other kinds of dolphins for training and exhibition would be a research paper.

The length of a research paper may be:

- specified in advance by an assignment
- related to an instructor's expectations for course work
- determined by the complexity of the material
- governed by a student's willingness to work
- controlled by the time a student has available

Most undergraduate college-level research pages are expected to be from 1,500 to 3,000 words (that is, six to twelve double-spaced, typewritten or word processed pages). This book is written on the assumption that you will be working on a research paper of that length.

FIVE STEPS TO A RESEARCH PAPER

Research papers are as likely to be assigned in nursing, forestry, or accounting as they are in English, history, music, or economics. Whatever the school course or subject of the paper, your **goals** will be the same:

- to learn from a study you undertake
- to present your material competently
- to earn as high a grade (and as much personal satisfaction) as possible

You can achieve these goals most readily if you **follow an orderly procedure from the time a paper is assigned until you turn it in.** Instead of looking for shortcuts (which often turn out to make your work harder), concentrate on doing each of the following steps carefully and completely. Some parts of this process may seem difficult or tedious at first, but you will soon find them easier as they become more familiar. And if some of these instructions sound unnecessary at first, remember that many people have found them the best of several possibilities.

The completed research paper, whatever its length or its subject, will be the result of your having taken only five steps.

Step 1. Choosing the Subject

Choose the right subject and you have a good chance of producing a good (or excellent) paper. Choose the wrong subject and you probably *can't* write a good research paper. This step is so important and basic to everything else you do that Chapters 2 and 3 are devoted to helping you with this task.

If you have the option of choosing your own subject, remember that specific subjects make better papers than very broad ones. "The Role of Music in Society" is impossible to work with because it could be everything—or nothing. However, focusing on "Background Music in Travel Videos" is specific enough to make a research paper for a class.

Step 2. Collecting Information

You might do most of Step 1 by yourself at your desk, but for Step 2 you need to head for a library and a computer with Internet capability. Plan, also, on going *beyond* these sources. Query people. Also think of videotapes and videodiscs, films, the radio, and your television set as valuable sources of information. Increasingly, too, other materials accessible via computer and CD-ROM are becoming available.

To complete this second step of a research paper, you will

a.   find various sources of relevant information

b.   read, look at, and listen to what the sources countain

c.   keep a record (that is, written notes) of what you learn

If you already have some knowledge of your chosen subject, certainly you can incorporate that into your paper. But you will undoubtedly have to seek out most of what you want to include in any research paper you do. Chapters 4 and 5 will help you in this second step, the one in which you will be concerned mostly with the *search* part of *research.*

Step 3. Evaluating Materials

A good research paper reflects a critical attitude toward the information you collect. Evaluating that information—that is, judging and weighing its usefulness and determining its relevance to your subject—takes place as you formulate your own ideas about your investigation and develop an approach toward what you've been learning.

Some of the information you get may not even be sufficiently reliable to incorporate into your work. For example, reading entries of a computer news or chat groups will certainly put you in touch with people who share your interest. Many who post messages may well be experts in the subject, but they tend to be "interested amateurs" who do not publish in the field and are unavailable through more traditional research methods. A great advantage of reading such notes and comments is that you can probably reach the authors either by personal e-mail or through the news group and initiate other dialogs. Others who post notes on a news group are simply computer users anxious to send their opinions to lots of other people, and you should be aware of biases they represent that you may not want to reflect in your own work.

Not every piece of information you collect is equally important. As the paper begins to take shape in your mind, you may even realize that some of your notes are no longer relevant for the track you intend to take. Or you may change your outlook about an author's veracity and find that you need to do a little more research. Chapter 5 will give you some help in this step. However, be aware that much of this evaluation takes place as you work with your subject, take notes, and aim toward the next step.

Step 4. Organizing Ideas

A collection of facts, quotations, summaries, and ideas can be either meaningless or purposeful. Much as a collection of musical notes can be either random noise or a top-selling record, the work of the previous three steps can be either a hodgepodge or the foundation of a successful research paper. The difference depends on how well you put together the materials at hand.

If what you collected and evaluated is coordinated and arranged to lead logically to a conclusion, if it all makes a point that is well supported, you will have a good research paper. Therefore, putting your notes together in an organized way, such as in an outline, before you begin writing the paper is crucial. Chapter 6 will help you organize material so you can begin writing the paper.

Step 5. Writing the Paper

In this step you finally put down on paper what you have learned and what you believe about the subject of your research paper. Writing will be easier if you have carefully and thoughtfully completed all the preparatory work of the previous four steps than if you try to plunge into writing without really being ready. That's not to say that you won't rewrite, perhaps even change the organization in some way, or decide to eliminate some ideas you planned earlier to include. Such is the nature of writing, as you have undoubtedly learned through experience and in school courses. Many of the elements of writing noted next will seem to happen simultaneously. That is, you may revise as you draft or even as you proofread.

Draft a copy of your research paper as a starting point for this step. Follow an outline or other organizing guide and the aids in Chapter 7 to write out your paper. You will find, if you don't already know, that using a word processing program on a computer is particularly helpful on this long a paper because it permits changes and variations easily.

Document your paper as you draft, and be sure to keep the documentation straight as you revise. If you are following the MLA [Modern Language Association] style, as emphasized throughout this book and explained in Chapter 8, documentation will be parenthetical and thus easy to incorporate into this early writing stage. When you finish the paper, you can prepare the list of Works Cited, as explained in Chapter 9. See Chapter 11 for APA [American Psychological Association] forms and a sample paper in that style.

Revise what you have written. Take a hard look at what you've said and how you've presented it. See if you can get a better flow of thought by changing some text, by moving words or phrases to different places, or even by eliminating some of them. If you are writing on a computer, such changes, even trying whole blocks of text in one place or another, are easy to do. Even if you're not composing on a word processor, be willing to make changes in what you've written, including cutting and pasting sections of the draft to try out rearrangements.

Research about how people write has shown that most writers do some revising as they draft; confident ones may make many changes as they write. If you are *really* revising and not just prettying up punctuation and spelling, you will want to allow plenty of time to do so. Don't ignore revision because the paper is due tomorrow. Proceed only if you're satisfied that you've said everything you want to say in the most effective way you can devise.

Edit your writing for spelling, punctuation, capitalization, and adherence to required research paper forms during the last stage of revision and before you prepare the final copy of your work in presentation form recommended in Chapter 10. The grammar checkers and spell checkers available on many computers (and as part of many word processing programs) are invaluable helpers and great time savers. But remember not to depend on them blindly; even the best of them can't know the context of what you've written and certainly not what you intended. ("Write" will be accepted by a spell checker, because it's an actual word, even when "right" is the correct word for a particular context.)

WHY A RESEARCH PAPER IS IMPORTANT

All the skills you have just been reading about in this sketch of the research paper process—making decisions about a subject, developing an inquiring attitude, gathering information, examining it critically, thinking creatively, organizing effectively, and writing convincingly—are crucial to academic success. Learn these skills now, in preparing a research paper, and you will find yourself using them again and again in many ways and in different circumstances, both in and outside of school.

Decisions about job assignments and promotions are made by one or more people using these skills. The same skills are also used by accountants, marine engineers, fashion designers, and physicians. Attorneys use them, too, in most of their work, from preparing courtroom cases to incorporating businesses.

Teachers don't assign research papers capriciously. In addition to sharpening the skills noted, the following are reasons for the popularity of the research paper assignment.

1. **You will follow this same procedure in your various future writing assignments,** even if you never become a professional writer.

2. **You will probably become a better reader** of nonfiction articles, instruction manuals, and books when you know the process by which they were developed. Being familiar with how main ideas and their support are presented is key to effective studying as well as to better reading.

3. **You will have a sense of achievement** when you work *independently* to pursue a task and fulfill the goal of completing a research paper. You will also take satisfaction in a job well done.

4. **You will become well informed about a subject** of interest to you. If you have a free choice of subjects for the research paper, you may even have the chance to investigate something that will be helpful in your present or future job.

5. **You will learn how to use the resources, including the electronic ones, of your school and community.** The experience of working through a research paper will give you insight as well as confidence.

6. **You will establish yourself as an individual,** even in large classes. An instructor reading your paper concentrates entirely on you and your work.

7. **You will exercise *critical thinking*** as you go through the process of preparing the research paper. That is, you develop the ability to weigh words, to discriminate among ideas, to separate fact from opinion or assumption, to find and select relevant materials, to draw conclusions, to synthesize results—all skills that are embodied not only by critical thinking but also by all of education.

WHO READS RESEARCH PAPERS—AND WHY

Before beginning your research paper, you should know who is going to read it. Will it be just the instructor for whose class you are writing the paper? Will other students in the class be reading it? And even if classmates don't read the paper, will you be presenting its key ideas to them orally? Will your visiting relatives want to read it? What about your boss who is contributing to your school tuition so you can upgrade your skills? Smart writers know in advance for whom they are writing so they can **choose a subject that interests the reader and write so as to get their information to the reader.**

Be less concerned about whether the reader will be interested initially in the subject you select than in being interested in it yourself. Choosing the right subject for yourself and pursuing good and thoughtful work will make your paper interesting to others; what you care about leads others to care too. Also, don't make assumptions about what someone, especially your instructor, will want to read. Most teachers are glad to read about any topic, providing the research is solid and the paper is well written.

Finally, think about *why* you are going to write this paper. For a grade, of course. But others may want to read it: future teachers, friends, even people who give scholarships. Some students have found that a paper written in one course can serve as the basis for further study or a springboard to new ideas and perspectives in another course. You may even decide that you want to write a research paper simply to inform yourself about a particular subject!

MANAGING YOUR TIME

Again and again students have cited time management as their biggest problem in completing a research paper assignment. You can, however, take advantage of several aids to overcome this difficulty.

1. **Use the Timetable and Checklist for Preparing Your Research Paper** at the very beginning of this book to keep you on track and on time during the research and writing process. If your instructor doesn't give you due dates for the various steps listed there, set your own schedule—and stick to it!

2. **Don't procrastinate!** Work put off is often work never done. Or else it may be work done sloppily and hastily. Instead of delaying what you need to do, get the work done on time—and then take a break or give yourself a reward.

   Allow yourself concentrated time, even after you have all the notes you want. Thinking through organization, no less than drafting and redrafting, can't be postponed until the last minute; these steps take time to work through successfully.

3. **Utilize available fragments of time.** Walking between classes or from the car or bus to the library may not take very long, but if you use such segments of time for thinking, planning, even jotting down notes, you will be surprised at how much you can move your work ahead.

4. **Try to have a regular work place and time.** Try to find a working place where you can keep your research paper materials without constantly having to move them. Gathering them together takes time, and reorganizing them can be distracting. Even if you can't find permanent space in which to work through this research paper process, at least try to locate one with minimum distractions. You will probably find that a quiet place allows you to work with the sustained concentration demanded by the research paper, even though you may customarily do other homework with the radio or TV on. If you can't find a quiet place to work in your home, consider the writing center or library at school.

   A regular time to work on your research paper, if not necessarily on your other school work, will also help you to manage time better. Some people are very productive for an hour or two in the early morning, others work better at night. Try to get in the habit of setting aside a regular working time for your research paper so the task will proceed regularly and be easier for you.

5. **Don't try to fight every distraction.** The child in your home who needs attention is more important than any school paper; just be sure to get back to the work at hand when you've taken care of the domesticity. Even drowsiness that interferes with your concentration should be part of your work plan: change what you are doing, or take a nap so you can come back to your research paper refreshed and ready for work again.

6. **Discipline yourself.** Chances are that the course for which you need to prepare a research paper isn't the only one you are taking. You may even have more than one research paper to write during the same term. Juggling that assignment along with responsibilities toward family and job means you need to plan for the wise use of your time—and then stick to the plan! Rather than working sporadically on your research paper, do it regularly and unspectacularly.

KEEPING A PROCESS LOG

A *log* is a record of what has happened and when. A Process Log is a record of the process you follow through the five steps that result in your research paper. However, the Process Log you keep should include a bit more. In addition to noting what you do and how long you spend doing it, your Process Log ought to include some brief, personal comments as you record the progress of your research paper. Even if you make your entries short, one look at the Process Log will show you (and your instructor) what you have accomplished and where you are in the research process. When your paper is finished, you will have a memento of your work—something on which you can look back proudly!

Here are some kinds of entries you can put in your Process Log.

- **Thinking time.** This is really working time, because you need to think before as well as during your work.

- **Study time.** Record even the time you spend reading assignments in this book, for it certainly helps you to prepare a successful paper. Also, a brief summary of what you accomplished during each study period will be a memory aid to you.

- **Reminders to yourself.** Note a follow-up you want to make or a source you want to check so that you can relate that information to what you have already done.

- **Difficulties you encounter.** No sustained work is without its problems. If you encounter a problem, such as all the books on your subject are out of the library or a microfilm is damaged or your computer stops working just when you are at a crucial information-gathering time on the Internet, you should record those difficulties for an accurate picture of your working process.

- **Solutions to problems.** Don't be afraid to toot your own horn. If you solve a problem, write about it in your Process Log!

Begin keeping your Process Log **now.** Copy the format into a notebook, repeating it as you need additional pages. Or make a master page from which to make photocopies. Or set your master page on a computer program, and simply print pages as you need them.

Date	*Time*	*Entry*
Write the date of the entry	Record the time you began **and** ended each activity.	Tell what you did that was part of the research paper process. Be detailed and specific.

Check with your instructor about whether your entries should be in complete sentences or whether fragments will be acceptable.

Use as examples the following entries in the Process Log of the author of the MLA-style sample research paper at the end of Chapter 10. (You'll also find the Process Log format repeated on the inside back cover.)

EXAMPLE

RESEARCH PAPER PROCESS LOG

Date	*Time*	*Activity*
Sept. 9	6:30-7:30 p.m.	I tried playing around on the computer to find a subject. No luck. There's just too much available.

Sept. 13	8:30-8:40 a.m.	I saw an article in the newspaper recently about how fishermen look for ways to get around the no-netting laws for dolphin. These are mammals, so they have to come up out of the water to breathe air. But when they get tangled in the long nets set out for fish and then get dragged by commercial fishing boats, many are killed every year. Tonight I opened a can of tuna for dinner and saw on the label that it is "dolphin safe," which means that the fish in these cans was caught in nets that don't also catch and kill dolphins. I think finding out more about dolphins would be interesting.
Sept. 14	2-2:05 p.m.	Last time I went to the Seaquarium, which was a long time ago, I remember seeing dolphins perform. I can't just write about training them. The paper has to be persuasive, so I'm not sure what aspect of dolphins I can research. I was talking about them to Pat, but got to thinking that keeping them on display was not so good. There are plenty of dolphins around where I live. I have also seen them out in the ocean or when I've been on the beach. Maybe I can find some people to interview.
Sept. 19	1-4 p.m.	I went to the Marine Sciences Library because I figured there would be lots of scholarly articles there and I need to include some as a requirement of the research paper. The librarian was very nice and saved me hours of work by helping me look in some of the databases and then find

		some complete articles in bound volumes right there. Already I have more information than I can possibly use, so I can see that the subject needs to be limited even more before I go back to that library.
Sept. 20	5-6 p.m.	I started checking some of the search engines on my computer. "Dolphin intelligence" doesn't work out right. It's a fact that people can't see, so I don't see how I could write anything persuasive on that subject. It's obvious that I will have to do still more narrowing before I can move ahead.

Choosing a General Topic

THE TERMS "TOPIC" AND "SUBJECT"

In this book, the word *topic* refers to a broad range or general field of interest. The word *subject* indicates a part of a topic, one that is narrow enough to investigate and write about. Because a good topic is the beginning of a good research paper, the rest of this chapter is about selecting a topic you can research. Then Chapter 3 shows you how to narrow a topic into a subject suitable for an effective research paper.

EXAMPLE

"Literature" is a topic.

"Differences among best-seller lists" is a subject.

The subject is derived by narrowing the topic. It is still in a general stage, however, because the author has only decided on what to investigate and not yet determined an approach; nor, without reading on the subject, can the author write the thesis statement that must underlie every coherent piece of writing.

Decide on your research paper topic as soon as possible after receiving the assignment so you will have plenty of time to gather information, mull over ideas, write your paper, and revise it several times before turning it in. If you are given interim due dates for various parts of the process, write them on the **Timetable and Checklist for Preparing Your Research Paper** at the very beginning of this book. If your instructor doesn't give you such dates, set them for yourself as a time management aid.

The assignment to write a research paper will be one of three kinds:

1. **Assigned Topics** are developed by an instructor and presented to you; they usually appear as an actual list of writing subjects (rather than topics) to choose from.

2. **Field-of-Study Topics** are those that you may select but where the assignment stipulates that the topic (and subsequent subject) must relate in a specific way to the course for which the research paper is assigned.

3. **Free-Choice Topics** give you broad rein to investigate any area you choose.

Sometimes topic and subject selections seem to telescope so the two processes meld into one. But in the explanations later in this chapter and in the next, they are considered separately. However, before you consider the topic itself, you ought to have some notions of what will work as a research paper topic and what to avoid.

QUALITIES OF A GOOD TOPIC

Because a good topic choice sets you on the right track for a good research paper, it ought to meet the following eight qualifications:

1. The topic will enable you to fulfill the assignment.

Be sure that what you propose will do what you've been asked to do. Can you find enough information to meet the specified length? If you are choosing a Field-of-Study Topic, is it really related to the course for which you are writing? If your instructor will deal with the topic in class, how will your research supplement what is included in the course?

If you aren't sure about a topic choice, check with your instructor, even if such approval isn't required.

2. The topic interests you enough to work on it.

You commit yourself to spending a lot of time and energy when you start a research paper. If you don't think you are sufficiently interested in a topic to expend both or don't feel committed to it, don't even start on it. Choose another one!

3. The topic will teach you something.

A research paper isn't busywork. You should be able to learn something new from the topic you are investigating. If you don't think you will learn, choose another topic.

4. The topic is of manageable scope.

Narrowing an initial topic choice is the ultimate key to manageability. Even at the first stages, a research paper isn't the only demand on your time, so you can (and should) impose your own limitations on the topic. Though the topic you choose may be broad, you still have the step of limiting it before you finally select the subject to investigate.

5. You can bring something to the topic.

You have already read (Chapter 1) that a research paper "synthesizes your discoveries about a topic and your judgment, interpretation, and evaluation of those discoveries." That is, you put something of yourself and your ideas into the research paper together with the material you discover. A good topic lets you do that.

6. Enough information on the topic is available to you.

With so many sources of information available to you, it may be surprising that you can still find yourself short on information. If you've keyed a subject into a computer search and you get back a message that there are 1,256 entries under that wording, the notion that there may not be enough information available may seem absurd. But as you begin to narrow that topic, you may, indeed, discover that what you were aiming to investigate is an inadequate choice.

Much of the information for your research paper will probably come from print sources—either what you can locate in a library or the databases housed in one. Even the materials that come to you so quickly on a computer screen originate almost entirely in print that is also stored in libraries. So as a way of making a "rough cut" to choose a research topic, you might go to a library, especially one that offers you direct access to book and periodical shelves, and ascertain whether there will be enough information available on the topic you are thinking about selecting for your research paper.

If you choose a topic recently in the news and are required to use both books and periodicals as reference sources, you may have to change the proposed topic because no book on it is yet available. There is an informational time lag. Although daily and weekly periodicals are timely, the editors of less frequently published journals and magazines (which are often monthly or quarterly) usually select the contents many months in advance. Books take even longer—a year from submission of a completed manuscript to its publication is not unusual. Therefore, while books may supply the background for current newsworthy topics, their usefulness may be limited. Or there may be nothing available in any book on a very current topic.

Be aware, also, that libraries select their purchases to serve a particular constituency. A community library will tend to have holdings that reflect the interests of its users and therefore contain general, rather than scholarly, sources. You may have to change libraries or change topics.

7. The topic is suitable for your audience.

Because you are writing this research paper for one or more readers, knowing that audience's reading ability, concerns, age, educational background, and perhaps even leanings or beliefs should enter into your decision about the suitability of a topic. For instance, a specialized technical topic may be suitable for your teacher in that field, but not for beginning students in it, should they be your designated audience.

8. The topic lets you demonstrate all your abilities that a research paper is meant to show.

A topic too broad, too restrictive, too mundane, or too esoteric might not let you show off the extent of your ability to develop ideas, find information, evaluate and organize it, make reasoned judgments, present them convincingly, and support your statements. Be sure that the topic you decide to research will let you demonstrate all those skills.

TOPICS TO AVOID

To avoid wasting time and effort, you should know that certain kinds of topics are unsuitable for research papers. The following eleven items (some of which are the obverse of the good qualities you read about in the preceding section) are a guide to help you avoid potential problems when choosing your own Field-of-Study or Free-Choice Topic.

1. Do not choose a topic for which a single source will provide all the information you need.

Only if you consult several information sources can you develop an individual viewpoint, use investigational skills, evaluate materials, and organize your findings in an original way. In short, you can follow the procedures for scholarly research only if you read and study widely. Working from a single source allows only for parroting or summarizing.

2. Do not reuse a paper you have written for another instructor.

Repetition doesn't produce new learning. Besides, to pretend you have done new work when, in fact, you have not is dishonest.

However, some instructors are willing to let you *continue* studying something you have already investigated, provided the topic warrants further research. Or they will let you examine another aspect of a topic about which you have already written a paper. Neither of these situations is the same as handing in a paper you've already presented to someone else. Should you want to use a previously submitted research paper as the basis for a new one, the safest procedure is to discuss the matter frankly with your present instructor.

3. Do not choose a topic on which you do not plan to do all the work yourself.

Any other person who researches or writes all or part of your assignment is preventing the work on it from being your own; the paper is, therefore, not acceptable. Using material of any sort from someone else without proper and adequate acknowledgment is **plagiarism!**

4. Do not choose a topic that is too broad for a research paper.

Any topic that is the title of a book or a subject in a database or index may be a starting place, but it is not a stopping place; you must go on to the second step, which is to narrow the topic. After all, if a published writer needs a whole book to deal with a topic, you surely can't say much of substance about it in ten or fifteen pages. Nor can you undertake to solve a problem that is seemingly insoluble— hunger, homelessness, tax reform—in a dozen pages.

5. Do not choose a topic about which your conclusions will be irrelevant.

A paper on how the Ford Motor Co. should have designed the Edsel (an automobile Ford manufactured only briefly in the 1950s) is not fruitful, because it doesn't matter now. Shift your thinking. If the Edsel is really a love of your life, another sort of investigation about the car might have some value. Or the subject might be relevant to special kinds of design or marketing courses or to collecting particular makes of autos.

6. Do not start work on any topic unless you think it will hold your interest long enough to complete the paper.

Research is a difficult enough assignment in itself. If you have to fight boredom with your own topic along the way, it becomes impossible.

7. Be wary of choosing a topic so neutral that you cannot express an attitude toward it.

Unless you plan a documented report, not a research paper, you will need to express some views or opinions about your material. For this reason, many teachers discourage biographical papers because, unless the author has created a work of art or an invention, initiated a business practice, or done something else about which you can get firsthand (that is, primary source) information, as explained in Chapter 5, a biography easily becomes just a compilation of what others have written.

8. Do not pursue a topic that seems to go nowhere for you.

If you have trouble narrowing a topic to a manageable subject or finding an approach (both are explained in the next chapter), perhaps that topic will prove unproductive for you. Consider dropping that topic and go on to something you can really work with. Another person might be able to narrow that topic and make it workable; but if you can't, you are better off making a complete change and starting something more productive.

9. Consider avoiding a topic that has been particularly popular among students.

Unless you can give a unique slant to the study or you have a special interest in pursuing such a topic, your teacher (and others who make up the audience) may be just plain bored reading yet another paper on abortion or drugs or other over-examined topics. Check with your instructor if in doubt about the advisability of researching a particular topic. Or consult a research librarian; such a person receives requests for help constantly and thus knows what topics many other students have been working on.

10. Consider avoiding a highly controversial or emotional topic unless you think you can bring something new and special to it.

You may find that time and length limitations on the research paper won't let you find or present sufficient material to cover adequately a controversial topic, such as health care reform. Similarly, avoid choosing a topic to which you have a deep emotional commitment, such as a particular religious belief, because you might not be able to be sufficiently objective or critical toward it to produce a good research paper. If you have any doubts about the advisability of working on a topic, discuss the matter with your instructor.

11. Do not choose a topic unsuited to your audience.

Some topics may offend the sensibilities of the instructor or other readers. For example, reading about various ways to investigate gory murders may not be the way your audience wants to spend its time. Writing for an audience means that you conform in some way to that audience's expectations or interests. So no matter how clever or sensational you think a topic is, don't hesitate to abandon it—or change the way you plan to treat it—if you suspect the topic might not suit your intended audience.

ASSIGNED TOPICS

An Assigned Topic is not stifling, and you should not view it as one to avoid because it is limiting. Rather, consider that it makes your beginning work easier while providing you with many opportunities for personal expression. You will have the leeway to develop a project that depends heavily on what you can discover and say on a subject.

Often an "Assigned Topic" is really a subject—an idea that has already been narrowed for you by someone else (usually the instructor) and is ready for investigation. Examples of such topics (or subjects) are: *lie detector tests as a prerequisite for employment* and *how environmental activists can achieve their goals by nonviolent means.*

FIELD-OF-STUDY TOPICS

If the broad field for which you have to write a research paper is familiar to you, finding a topic to write about will be easier than if the field is entirely new. Even if the field is unfamiliar, you can cope by using one or more of the following methods, as explained in the subsequent sections.

1. **Take stock of what you already know.**
2. **Use printed aids to help you (including those delivered electronically):**
   your textbook
   other course materials
   encyclopedias
   online catalogs and databases
   computer search engines
   periodical indexes and CD-ROMs
3. **Build from your own interests.**
4. **Surf the Internet.**

1. Take Stock of What You Already Know

If you have taken a course prerequisite to the one for which you have to write this research paper, you already know something about this field of study. If the field is new to you, think about what the instructor has said in giving you an overview of the course. Maybe you know something about the field from talking with friends about the class or its content. You can use all that prior knowledge as a starting place.

List some of the broad categories of information in this field of study that you already know. Suppose you have to work within anthropology. If you already know that archaeology is a branch of anthropology or that one unit in the course is about cultural anthropology, you have a good beginning.

Or write down some of the information that particularly interested you in a prerequisite course. Don't worry about organizing what you write, and don't worry about spelling and punctuation; just get the ideas down on paper. In doing so, you use one method of taking stock of what you already know, and you will get a start at choosing a Field-of-Study Topic about which to write your research paper.

2. Make Use of Printed and Electronic Aids

Using Your Textbook

The most convenient place to begin looking for a Field-of-Study Topic for your research paper is your class textbook. Make use of its many parts as aids to finding a topic.

The table of contents   as in Figure 1, will tell you a lot about the course and give you an overview of the field, even if you won't be studying the entire text in one term. Look over the contents, keeping alert for ideas that might interest you, and circle those you think might be interesting enough to pursue, as in Figure 2.

The index   of a textbook gives specific page locations of key ideas in the book. If you see a topic of interest listed in the index, circle it for possible Field-of-Study research, as in Figure 3 on page 24. (In some textbooks, you may find that the index is combined with the glossary.)

A glossary   lists and defines key terms used in a book. From the words listed (as in Figure 4 on page 25), you can get a great deal of information about what's important in a course, even before you take it, so you can get a head start on your research paper by selecting one such term.

The bibliography   of a textbook is another place to look. In this listing of resources an author has used or recommends, you may find the title of a book or periodical article intriguing enough to encourage you to look further at that particular subject. Books that have "Further Reading" lists at the ends of chapters can help as much as any other bibliography.

CONTENTS

CHAPTER 2

EXPLORING THE FAMILY   27

Theoretical Perspectives on the Family   28
  The Family Ecology Perspective   28
  The Family Development Perspective   30
  The Structure-Functional Perspective   30
Case Study 2.1 The Family as a Child-Rearing
  Institution   33
  The Interactionist Perspective   35
Box 2.1 Marriages and Families Across
  Cultures   36
  Exchange Theory   37
  Family Systems Theory   38
  The Conflict/Feminist Perspectives   39
  There Is No Typical Family   40
Studying Families   40
  The Blinders of Personal Experience   41
  Scientific Investigation: Removing
    Blinders   41
Box 2.2 A Closer Look at Family Diversity:
    Studying Ethnic Minority
    Families   42
  The Application of Scientific
    Techniques   47
In Sum   47
Key Terms   47
Study Questions   48
Suggested Readings   48

CHAPTER 3

OUR GENDERED IDENTITIES   51

Gendered Identities   52
  Gender Expectations   52
  Gender Expectations and Diversity   53
  Cultural Messages   53
  To What Extent Do Individual Women
    and Men Follow Cultural
    Expectations?   54
Case Study 3.1 An Inside View of
  Masculinity   55
  Male Dominance   57

Is Anatomy Destiny?   60
  Genetics-Based Arguments   61
  Society-Based Arguments   61
  The Interaction of Culture and
    Biology   63
Gender and Socialization   64
  The Power of Cultural Images   65
  Theories of Socialization   65
  Girls and Boys in the Family   66
  Play and Games   68
  Socialization in Schools   68
Gender in Adult Lives   70
  Gender and Stress   70
  Gender and Personal Change   71

Fig. 1. A table of contents page. Source: Mary Ann Lamanna and Agnes Riedmann, *Marriages and Families: Making Choices in a Diverse Society* 6th ed., Wadsworth, 1997: xii.

The preface or introduction   of a textbook is more than just a summary of contents; it is usually the author's way of leading you into the subject of the course or book. Read it and you may be able to use some of the ideas it contains to suggest a topic for research.

Appendices   are supplements to the basic book that are printed after the text so as not to interrupt it. They contain relevant but often peripheral information, so they may also be of help to you in finding a topic.

CHAPTER 13

WORK AND FAMILY   389

The Labor Force—A Social Invention   391
> *The Labor Force in Postindustrial Society*   391
The Traditional Model: Provider Husbands and
Homemaking Wives   391
> *Husbands and the Provider Role*   392
> *Wives as Full-Time Homemakers*   394
Women in the Labor Force   397
> *Women's Market Work*   397
Two-Earner Marriages—Newer Provider-Caregiving
Options   400
> *Two-Career Marriages*   400
> *Self-Employment*   401
> *Part-Time Employment*   401
> *Shift Work*   401
> *Leaving the Labor Force and Reentry*   402

Fig. 2. A detail of a table of contents. Source: Mary Ann Lamanna and Agnes Riedmann, *Marriages and Families: Making Choices in a Diverse Society*, 6th ed., Wadsworth, 1997: xx.

Authors included in an anthology bear looking at, for they suggest people whose work might be investigated for a Field-of-Study Topic.

Using Course Materials

Some courses are taught from several assigned or recommended books rather than from a single text. Or you may receive a suggested reading list containing both books and periodicals. Perhaps such nonprint materials as films are also included. You can use any of these sources in the same way you can use your textbook to help you choose a broad Field-of-Study Topic.

If you are given a course syllabus (whether or not the course has a textbook), look through it as well at the beginning of the term and draw information from it about what the course will cover. Use the syllabus as an additional start in deciding on a topic for your research paper.

Skimming Encyclopedias

Both **general encyclopedias,** the kind you are probably most familiar with, and **subject encyclopedias** have a great deal to offer as prompts in selecting a research paper topic. With some exceptions, the very inclusiveness of most encyclopedias makes their entries tend to be more attuned to overviews (and therefore

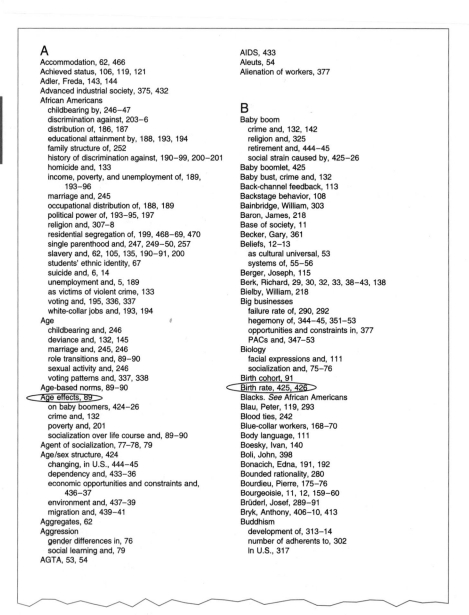

A

Accommodation, 62, 466
Achieved status, 106, 119, 121
Adler, Freda, 143, 144
Advanced industrial society, 375, 432
African Americans
    childbearing by, 246–47
    discrimination against, 203–6
    distribution of, 186, 187
    educational attainment by, 188, 193, 194
    family structure of, 252
    history of discrimination against, 190–99, 200–201
    homicide and, 133
    income, poverty, and unemployment of, 189,
        193–96
    marriage and, 245
    occupational distribution of, 188, 189
    political power of, 193–95, 197
    religion and, 307–8
    residential segregation of, 199, 468–69, 470
    single parenthood and, 247, 249–50, 257
    slavery and, 62, 105, 135, 190–91, 200
    students' ethnic identity, 67
    suicide and, 6, 14
    unemployment and, 5, 189
    as victims of violent crime, 133
    voting and, 195, 336, 337
    white-collar jobs and, 193, 194
Age
    childbearing and, 246
    deviance and, 132, 145
    marriage and, 245, 246
    role transitions and, 89–90
    sexual activity and, 246
    voting patterns and, 337, 338
Age-based norms, 89–90
Age effects, 89
    on baby boomers, 424–26
    crime and, 132
    poverty and, 201
    socialization over life course and, 89–90
Agent of socialization, 77–78, 79
Age/sex structure, 424
    changing, in U.S., 444–45
    dependency and, 433–36
    economic opportunities and constraints and,
        436–37
    environment and, 437–39
    migration and, 439–41
Aggregates, 62
Aggression
    gender differences in, 76
    social learning and, 79
AGTA, 53, 54

AIDS, 433
Aleuts, 54
Alienation of workers, 377

B

Baby boom
    crime and, 132, 142
    religion and, 325
    retirement and, 444–45
    social strain caused by, 425–26
Baby boomlet, 425
Baby bust, crime and, 132
Back-channel feedback, 113
Backstage behavior, 108
Bainbridge, William, 303
Baron, James, 218
Base of society, 11
Becker, Gary, 361
Beliefs, 12–13
    as cultural universal, 53
    systems of, 55–56
Berger, Joseph, 115
Berk, Richard, 29, 30, 32, 33, 38–43, 138
Bielby, William, 218
Big businesses
    failure rate of, 290, 292
    hegemony of, 344–45, 351–53
    opportunities and constraints in, 377
    PACs and, 347–53
Biology
    facial expressions and, 111
    socialization and, 75–76
Birth cohort, 91
Birth rate, 425, 426
Blacks. *See* African Americans
Blau, Peter, 119, 293
Blood ties, 242
Blue-collar workers, 168–70
Body language, 111
Boesky, Ivan, 140
Boli, John, 398
Bonacich, Edna, 191, 192
Bounded rationality, 280
Bourdieu, Pierre, 175–76
Bourgeoisie, 11, 12, 159–60
Brüderl, Josef, 289–91
Bryk, Anthony, 406–10, 413
Buddhism
    development of, 313–14
    number of adherents to, 302
    In U.S., 317

Fig. 3. Section of an index. Source: Jean Stockard, *Sociology: Discovering Society*, Wadsworth, 1997: 562.

to topics) than to details and specifics. Such broad perspectives may well help you to come to a topic idea for your research paper. Thus, skimming an encyclopedia can be very helpful. But beware of relying too heavily on a general encyclopedia as a source for the kind of detailed content that the research paper itself will require.

perforin   A type of protein, produced and secreted by cytotoxic cells, that destroys antigen-bearing targets.

pericycle   (PARE-ih-sigh-kul) [Gk. *peri-,* around, + *kyklos,* circle] Of a root vascular cylinder, one or more layers just inside the endodermis that gives rise to lateral roots and contributes to secondary growth.

periderm   Of vascular plants showing secondary growth, a protective covering that replaces epidermis.

peripheral nervous system   (per-IF-ur-uhl) [Gk. *peripherein,* to carry around] Of vertebrates, the nerves leading into and out from the spinal cord and brain and the ganglia along those communication lines.

peristalsis   (pare-ih-STAL-is) A rhythmic contraction of muscles that moves food forward through the animal gut.

peritoneum   A lining of the coelom that also covers and helps maintain the position of internal organs.

peritubular capillaries   the set of blood capillaries that threads around the tubular parts of a nephron; they function in reabsorption of water and solutes back into the body and in secretion of hydrogen ions and some other substances in the forming urine.

permafrost   A permanently frozen, water-impenetrable layer beneath the soil surface in arctic tundra.

peroxisome   Enzyme-filled vesicle in which fatty acids and amino acids are digested first into hydrogen peroxide (which is toxic), then to harmless products.

PGA   Phosphoglycerate (FOSS-foe-GLISS-er-ate). A key intermediate in glycolysis and in the Calvin-Benson products.

PGAL   Phosphoglyceraldehyde. A key intermediate in glycolysis and in the Calvin-Benson cycle.

pH scale   A scale used to measure the concentration of free hydrogen ions in blood, water, and other solutions; pH 0 is the most acid, 14 the most basic, and 7, neutral.

phagocyte   (FAG-uh-sight) [Gk. *phagein,* to eat, + *kytos,* hollow vessel] A macrophage or certain other white blood cells that engulf and destroy foreign agents.

phagocytosis   (FAG-uh-sigh-TOE-sis) [Gk. *phagein,* to eat, + *kytos,* hollow vessel] Engulfment of foreign cells or substances by amoebas and some white blood cells by means of endocytosis.

pharynx   (FARE-inks) A muscular tube by which food enters the gut; in land vertebrates, the dual entrance for the tubular part of the digestive tract and windpipe (trachea).

phenotype   (FEE-no-type) [Gk. *phainein,* to show, + *typos,* image] Observable trait or traits of an individual; arises from interactions between genes, and between genes and the environment.

pheromone   (FARE-oh-moan) [Gk. *phero,* to carry, + *-mone,* as in hormone] A type of signaling molecule secreted by exocrine glands that serves as a communication signal between individuals of the same species. Signaling pheromones elicit an immediate behavioral response. Priming pheromones elicit a generalized physiological response.

phloem   (FLOW-um) Of vascular plants, a tissue with living cells that interconnect and form the tubes through which sugars and other solutes are conducted.

Fig. 4. Detail of a glossary. Source: Cecie Starr, *Biology: Concepts and Applications,* 3rd ed., Wadsworth, 1997: n.p.

In addition to the various entries, many encyclopedia articles have **cross-references** (that is, listings of related articles in the same encyclopedia). Some of them may be topics you want to look into—or that suggest still other ideas to you. (See Figure 5.)

Another way to use an encyclopedia article to help you find a topic for research is to consider the major divisions of an entry as a starting place. This is exemplified by the outline of an encyclopedia article in Figure 6.

Finally, a **bibliography** at the end of an encyclopedia entry (as in Figure 7) will introduce you to still more ideas. Some of the books and articles listed, or others by the same authors, may be in the library you are using or can be obtained through an interlibrary loan system. Or they can quickly be obtained through a computer online search of the Internet. Either use the titles in a bibliography as topic ideas, or use the books as additional sources, drawing ideas from their tables of contents, introductions, indexes, or other features.

Other related articles

Computerized instruction
Curriculum
Educational psychology
Elementary school
Fulbright Scholarship
Grading
Guidance
High school
Junior high school
Kindergarten

Learning
National Defense Education Act
Nursery school
Reading (The teaching of
    reading)
School
Special education
Study
Testing
Universities and colleges

Fig. 5. Listing showing cross-references in an encyclopedia. Source: "Teaching." *The World Book Encyclopedia,* 1997.

Outline

I. A teacher's duties
  A. Preparing for classes
  B. Guiding the learning of students
  C. Checking student progress
  D. Setting a good example for students
  E. Other duties
II. Teaching as a career
  A. Teacher-training programs
  B. Certification of teachers
  C. Job opportunities
  D. Employment practices
  E. Rewards of teaching
  F. Continuing education
  G. Teachers' organizations
III. Current Issues in U.S. teaching
  A. The effectiveness of teaching
  B. The effectiveness of teacher training

Fig. 6. Major divisions of an encyclopedia entry in outline form. Source: "Teaching." *The World Book Encyclopedia,* 1997.

Online Catalogs and Databases

The library you are using for your primary print research may no longer have wooden card catalog drawers; those have been mostly retired, especially in academic libraries, in favor of the more up-to-date computer catalogs. Furthermore, the computer catalogs usually give you access to far more than the holdings of a single library; they often tie together materials from throughout a county library system or even the libraries of all the postsecondary institutions in a state. From a

Bibliography

General works: For an introduction to the major theories of ethics, the reader should consult RICHARD B. BRANDT, *Ethical Theory: The Problems of Normative and Critical Ethics* (1959), an excellent comprehensive textbook. WILLIAM K. FRANKENA, *Ethics,* 2nd ed. (1973), is a much briefer treatment. Another concise work is BERNARD WILLIAMS, *Ethics and the Limits of Philosophy* (1985). There are several useful collections of classical and modern writings; among the better ones are OLIVER A. JOHNSON, *Ethics: Selections from Classical and Contemporary Writers,* 5th ed. (1984); and JAMES RACHELS (ed.), *Understanding Moral Philosophy* (1976), which places greater emphasis on modern writers.

Origins of ethics: JOYCE O. HERTZLER, *The Social Thought of the Ancient Civilizations* (1936, reissued 1961), is a wide-ranging collection of materials. EDWARD WESTERMARCK, *The Origin and Development of the Moral Ideas,* 2 vol., 2nd ed. (1912–17, reprinted 1971), is dated but still unsurpassed as a comprehensive account of anthropological data. MARY MIDGLEY, *Beast and Man: The Roots of Human Nature* (1978, reissued 1980), is excellent on the links between biology and ethics; and EDWARD O. WILSON, *Sociobiology: The New Synthesis* (1975), and *On Human Nature* (1978), contain controversial speculations on the biological basis of social behaviour. RICHARD DAWKINS, *The Selfish Gene* (1976, reprinted 1978), is another evolutionary account, fascinating but to be used with care.

Fig. 7. Part of a bibliography at the end of an encyclopedia entry. Source: "Ethics." *Encyclopaedia Britannica, Macropaedia,* 15th ed., 1997.

computer in your own home, your dormitory, or a library you may also be able to look through the holdings of large and famous libraries in other cities or in well-known universities.

Use a computer catalog as you would any list of topics written on catalog cards: go through the headings, as already suggested in the preceding section on using your textbook as a source of ideas.

Don't overlook the potential of "See also" catalog listings to help you even more. They refer you to related subject headings where you can find even more books to consult; use them as just described to help you find a topic.

Computer Searches and Web Sites

You can use a computer to find research paper ideas through search engines and Web sites. Search engines do the drudge work in locating information but are especially useful if you launch them with some idea of a topic, because then you are likely to have a search term to input at the start. Many of the search engine names are probably familiar to you: Yahoo, Alta Vista, Infoseek, and Lycos. They are often consulted by students at several steps along the way in writing research papers.

General Sociological Web Sites

American Sociological Association Home page: http://www.asanet.org/

Socioweb: http://www.socioweb.com/~markbl/socioweb/

Research Engines for the Social Sciences: http://www.carleton.ca/~cmkie/research.html

Sociological Data from the U.S. Government

Federal Web Locator: http://www.law.vill.edu/Fed-Agency/fedwebloc.html

Statistical Abstract of the United States: http://www.census.gov/stat_abstract

United States Census Bureau: http://www.census.gov/

Department of Labor: http://www.dol.gov/

National Institute on Aging: http://www.senior.com/npo/nia.html

Centers for Disease Control and Prevention: http://www.cdc.gov/

National Institute of Health: http://www.nih.gov/

National Science Foundation: http://www.nsf.gov/

Nongovernment Organizations with Sociological Data and Analyses

American Society of Criminology: http://sun.soci.niu.edu/~asc/

Russell Sage Foundation: http://www.epn.org/sage.html

The Center for the Future of Children: http://www.futureofchildren.org

International Sources of Data and Analyses

Population Reference Bureau: http://www.prb.org/prb/

United Nations: http://www.un.org

World Bank: http://www.worldbank.org/

Information on Obtaining Grants

The Foundation Center: http://fdncenter.org/

Money for Contracts and Grants: http://pages.prodigy.com/V/R/A/VRNF46A/money.html

Nonprofit Resource Catalog: http://www.clark.net/pub/pwalker/

Nonprofit Resource Center: http://www.igc.apc.org/npo.html

Fig. 8. Listing of some sociology-related Web sites. Source: Jean Stockard, *Sociology: Discovering Society*, Wadsworth, 1997.

Directories of Web sites continue to grow, and you can access them for various purposes. With a computer modem and a browser program such as Netscape or a commercial Internet provider such as America Online or CompuServe, you need only enter the URL (uniform resource locator) of a Web location. Figure 8 shows some of the sociology-related Web sites you can readily call up to begin finding information to research in that field.

Periodical Indexes, CD-ROMs, and Databases

Many million more words are printed in periodicals than in books, so you will find such regularly published magazines, journals, and newspapers helpful in choosing a Field-of-Study Topic for research. Each discipline has many specific indexes; some of them are listed in Appendix A, "Selected List of Reference Works Available in Libraries." *Education Index, Chemical Abstracts,* and *Book Review*

Index are just a few that are widely used by students deciding about research. There are also general indexes such as the *New York Times Index* and the familiar *Readers' Guide to Periodical Literature* that will help you find topics to write about. Consult the principal headings or divisions, but don't overlook the "see also" listings in many indexes as a source of additional ideas for a Field-of-Study Topic.

Look at several volumes of an index, and check related topics in a volume to be sure you get a broad range of ideas to work with.

Much information that used to be printed and bound biweekly or monthly for currency now appears initially on a CD-ROM (compact disc read-only memory), a disc imprinted with information that can be readily accessed by computer and read on a monitor. Its great advantage is that great amounts of material can be stored very compactly, just as much music is held on the familiar CDs.

CD-ROMs are updated periodically, as are computerized databases now in libraries or available through a home computer, such as InfoTrac. They are especially convenient to use, and will work fine to give you broad categories you may want to investigate. Realize, however, that bound indexes in print are likely to give you greater scope because they cover more time and, sometimes, more details.

3. Build From Your Own Interests

One of the most satisfying ways of selecting a Field-of-Study Topic is to relate the field for which you have to write a paper to what you already know or have special vocational or avocational interests in. Then you can study something you already care about or you may find useful.

A Personal Inventory

Begin by making a Personal Inventory. That is, draw four vertical lines for columns on a piece of paper and put one of the following headings at the top of each. Then, under each heading write as many individual items as you can.

Know and Care About (Include hobbies, clubs, special events, scouting badges earned, favorite kinds of music, previous school courses, and so on.)

Special Concerns (List things you think about, ideas that intrigue you, and more.)

Vocational Interests (Include a satisfying job you now have or careers you are considering.)

Like to Learn About (Give free rein to your imagination for this listing.)

EXAMPLE

Know and Care About	Special Concerns	Vocational Interests	Like to Learn About
fashion design auto racing	child care air pollution drinking laws gun control	aviation medicine banking	computers weather forecasts sailboats destruction of rain forests

Be honest with yourself on these lists; they're for your own use. Make each list as long as you can, but don't make choices at first. Use memories, free association, whatever techniques you can in order to add items to each of the four lists. Naturally, you won't be able to use many of the items, nor will they all make sense with the next step you should follow. But this sort of listing will be useful for other courses, other writing assigments—and for a résumé when you look for a job!

Making Relationships

Use your Personal Inventory as a starting point to arrive at a Field-of-Study Topic for your research paper by writing the name or the field or course at the top of a blank sheet of paper. Draw a vertical line down the center of the page and on the right side of it write a word from one of the lists you just made. On the left side of the line write words related to the course for which you need to write the research paper. (If you aren't familiar with the terminology, look in the table of contents of the textbook for your course.) Now you are ready to start making relationships to help you arrive at a Field-of-Study Topic.

E X A M P L E

LITERATURE   [course for which you will write this research paper]

[literature-related words]

1. authors
2. novels
3. nonfiction
4. plays   [special interest]
5. eras   aviation
6. poems
7. countries
8. adventures

By combining each word in the left column with the word on the right, you can arrive at related ideas that will serve as general topics for a research paper.

E X A M P L E

1. authors + aviation = pilots who have written books
2. novels + aviation = fiction books about flying
3. nonfiction + aviation = books about the history and development of the aviation industry or about special-purpose aircraft
4. plays + aviation = plays or movies about flying or flyers
5. eras + aviation = flight in the mythology of ancient cultures
6. poems + aviation = poetry about flying or by pilots

7. countries + aviation = stories about flying, true or fictional, from different countries

8. adventures + aviation = written records of such adventures as speed or altitude records or aviation under adverse conditions

If the relationship you're looking for doesn't work out for a particular word, try another from one of the lists in your Personal Inventory. Be creative, be inventive, be imaginative in making relationships!

4. Surf the Internet

Much as we may think of computers as being the latest in communication resources, information from them is delivered almost entirely in print form—that is, in writing on a monitor screen. The Internet and the World Wide Web offer potential researchers an embarrassment of riches—far more ideas than a single person can use. Even though there is probably more potential in electronic resources for narrowing a topic to a workable subject than for finding a topic, don't overlook this source of ideas for locating a topic.

FREE-CHOICE TOPICS

If you have free choice of a topic, suddenly all of human knowledge is open to you! The trick is to pinpoint just one part of it to work with, and the best way to do that is to examine several possibilities systematically before choosing what is most appealing to you. Here are eight possibilities to help you make that choice.

1. Expand a familiar area.

Choose a topic or area about which you already know something but would like to know more. Instead of breaking completely new ground, you will then have a chance to increase your learning in an organized way.

EXAMPLES

- You studied the Aztecs in a history course but would like to know more about them.

- A few years ago you did a paper on cryogenics and now you wonder if there have been any developments in the process or in official attitudes toward it since then.

2. Look to an area new to you.

EXAMPLES

- You saw a TV program about the mummy of a young girl found high in the Andes and want to know more about the customs that led to its being there.

- Grimmelshausen is the name of the author of a book you saw in a bookstore. It's such an unusual name. Who is or was that person?
- You've always meant to find out about the history of jazz.

3. Try a textbook.

Look through a textbook you own or one in the library on some subject you care about or that holds special interest for you. Look through the table of contents, index, glossary, bibliography, appendices, and preface. Apply the same methods described earlier in the chapter for choosing a Field-of-Study Topic.

4. Work from your strengths.

Take stock of your strengths and abilities and use one of them as the basis for your research paper. If you haven't already read the earlier section on making a Personal Inventory, do so now and create such an inventory. Use the following listing for your categories:

- what you know and care about
- special concerns or intriguing ideas
- vocational interests
- what you want to know more about
- outstanding or significant personal experiences
- things you do well

List words and phrases. Don't stop to compose complete sentences or to evaluate as you write; just get the ideas down on paper.

Every item on each list represents a personal strength because each is prompted by you. Use the items as starting places to find topics you care enough about to study further for a research paper.

5. Become a browser in the library.

Walk around and see what's available to you. There are books, of course, and you can get some ideas by looking at the Library of Congress and Dewey Decimal classifications listed a little later in this chapter. However, many ideas are available if you will look at magazines and academic journals that may be on open shelves in your library; scan the titles of articles in them for topic ideas. If *Ebony, Omni, Ms,* or *Car and Driver* are already familiar, try looking through titles that are new to you, such as *American Crafts, Modern Healthcare, Changing Times, Journal of Atmospheric Sciences,* or *Mental Retardation.* In them, you may find articles that suggest topics you will want to investigate.

Another kind of purposeful browsing is to take a cue from the "Selected List of Reference Works Available in Libraries" (Appendix A). The library you are working in may not have all the works listed there, but you can check off the titles that seem of interest; if the volumes are available, you can skim through them, on the lookout for topics you care to investigate further.

6. Try brainstorming.

Make a list of all sorts of names, subjects, places, events, or whatever else comes to mind. Perhaps even enlist the aid of a friend and, together, bounce words back and forth for a list. Even better, turn on a tape recorder to record the list of words and ideas both of you say, without having to bother to write them down. When you play back the tape, don't make any judgments or attempt any decisions— just check off likely research prospects on your written list or write down research possibilities. Narrow the list to two or three topics before heading to a library or a computer to find reference works on them.

7. "Get inside" the library catalog system.

To understand most completely the riches available to you in a library—and therefore available to you as Free-Choice Topics—you should understand the cataloging systems used to make books and periodicals accessible to you. Such conventions are explained in the next section of this chapter.

For now, begin with books on the open shelves in the library where you are doing your research. Start looking through a particular section of books until you find a topic that strikes your fancy for research. (If the library doesn't have open shelves, you will have to do your browsing for interesting-looking titles in the catalog and then request books that seem likely prospects for topic ideas.)

You could also consult either a general or a specialized periodical index (see some titles in Appendix A), many of which are now on CD-ROM for easy access. Be aware, however, that if you are required to use books as a reference source in your research paper, some entries in a periodical index may be so new or current that there are no books yet on that specific topic.

8. Explore computer links.

Just as there are "See also" designations in library catalogs and indexes, so are there "links" for many computer topics. Once you key in a word or phrase on the computer, related words or phrases are called to your attention, either by on-screen color designation (usually blue print) or by wording. Following such leads may give you even further topic ideas, if you need them, or will help you begin to focus on narrowing a topic to a workable subject.

LIBRARY CATALOGING CUSTOMS

Classifications of Books

All the book holdings in a library are arranged either by the **Library of Congress** classification system or by the **Dewey Decimal** classification system. Because the books—and, thus, knowledge or possible research topics—are divided into broad categories, you can focus on general areas to think about. Each category is then subdivided into progressively smaller or narrower groups for the convenience of those who designate and shelve books (while at the same time helping you to narrow a too-broad research topic).

The Library of Congress Classification System

[Note that there are only twenty-one groups in this system; the letters I, O, W, X, and Y are omitted.]

A General works and polygraphy	M Music
B Philosophy and religion	N Fine arts
C History and auxiliary sciences	P Language and literature
D History and topography (except America)	Q Science
	R Medicine
E *and* F America	S Agriculture and plant and animal industry
G Geography and anthropology	
H Social sciences	T Technology
J Political science	U Military science
K Law	V Naval science
L Education	Z Bibliography and library science

The Dewey Decimal Classification System

[Note that each class is identified by a three-digit number in this system devised by Melvil Dewey.]

000–099 Generalities

100–199 Philosophy and related

200–299 Religion

300–399 The social sciences

400–499 Language

500–599 Pure sciences

600–699 Technology (Applied science)

700–799 The arts

800–899 Literature and rhetoric

900–999 General geography and history

Each classification system is further divided. In the Library of Congress system, the second subdivision is indicated by a letter added to the primary letter. An example of second-level classifications is presented in Figure 9. Further subdivisions are given a numerical range.

In the Dewey Decimal system, each division is subdivided into groups of ten numbers (see Figure 10), and each of those is further divided to accommodate books of greater specialization.

Even at the third level of these classifications, all you can get is a large selection of Free-Choice Topics for research. For example, "South American History" and "Reptiles and Birds" are fine topics for books, but not for student research papers. Whatever topic you choose from these classifications will have to be narrowed further into a suitable subject, as explained in Chapter 3.

C (Auxiliary sciences of history)

C   Auxiliary sciences of history (general)
CB   History of civilization
CC   Archaeology (general)
CD   Diplomatics, archives, seals
CE   Technical chronology, calendars
CJ   Numismatics
CN   Inscriptions, epigraphy
CR   Heraldry
CS   Genealogy
CT   Biography (general)

D (History, general and Old World)

D   History (general)
DA   Great Britain
DAW Central Europe
DB   Austria, Liechtenstein, Hungary, Czechoslovakia
DC   France
DD   Germany
DE   The Mediterranean region, the Greco-Roman world
DF   Greece
DG   Italy
DH   The Low Countries
DJ   Holland
DJK Eastern Europe
DK   Soviet Union, Poland
DL   Scandinavia
DP   Spain, Portugal
DQ   Switzerland
DR   Balkan Peninsula
DS   Asia
DT   Africa
DU   Australia, Oceania
DX   Gypsies

E-F (History, America)

E   Indians, United States (general)
F   U.S. local history, Canada, Mexico, Central and South America

G (Geography, anthropology, recreation)

G   Geography (general), atlases, maps
GA   Mathematical geography, cartography
GB   Physical geography
GC   Oceanography
GF   Human ecology, anthropogeography
GN   Anthropology
GR   Folklore
GT   Manners and customs
GV   Recreation, sports, leisure

H (Social sciences)

H   Social sciences (general)
HA   Statistics
HB   Economic theory, demography

Fig. 9. Library of Congress second-level classification. Source: George M. Eberhart, *The Whole Library Handbook, 2,* Chicago: American Library Association, 1995: 289.

Second Summary*
The Hundred Divisions

000   Generalities
010   Bibliography
020   Library & information sciences
030   General encyclopedic works
040
050   General serials & their indexes
060   General organizations & museology
070   News media, journalism, publishing
080   General collections
090   Manuscripts & rare books

100   Philosophy & psychology
110   Metaphysics
120   Epistemology, causation, humankind
130   Paranormal phenomena
140   Specific philosophical schools
150   Psychology
160   Logic
170   Ethics (Moral philosophy)
180   Ancient, medieval, Oriental philosophy
190   Modern Western philosophy

200   Religion
210   Natural theology
220   Bible
230   Christian theology
240   Christian moral & devotional theology
250   Christian orders & local church
260   Christian social theology
270   Christian church history
280   Christian denominations & sects
290   Other & comparative religions

300   Social sciences
310   General statistics
320   Political science
330   Economics
340   Law
350   Public administration
360   Social services; association
370   Education
380   Commerce, communications, transport
390   Customs, etiquette, folklore

400   Language
410   Linguistics
420   English & Old English
430   Germanic languages   German
440   Romance languages   French
450   Italian, Romanian, Rhaeto-Romanic
460   Spanish & Portuguese languages
470   Italic languages   Latin
480   Hellenic languages   Classical Greek
490   Other languages

500   Natural sciences & mathematics
510   Mathematics
520   Astronomy & allied sciences
530   Physics
540   Chemistry & allied sciences
550   Earth sciences
560   Paleontology   Paleozoology
570   Life sciences
580   Botanical sciences
590   Zoological sciences

600   Technology (Applied sciences)
610   Medical sciences   Medicine
620   Engineering & allied operations
630   Agriculture
640   Home economics & family living
650   Management & auxiliary services
660   Chemical engineering
670   Manufacturing
680   Manufacture for specific uses
690   Buildings

700   The arts
710   Civic & landscape art
720   Architecture
730   Plastic arts   Sculpture
740   Drawing & decorative arts
750   Painting & paintings
760   Graphic arts   Printmaking & prints
770   Photography & photographs
780   Music
790   Recreational & performing arts

800   Literature & rhetoric
810   American literature in English
820   English & Old English literatures
830   Literatures of Germanic languages
840   Literatures of Romance languages
850   Italian, Romanian, Rhaeto-Romanic
860   Spanish & Portuguese literatures
870   Italic literatures   Latin
880   Hellenic literatures   classical Greek
890   Literatures of other languages

900   Geography & history
910   Geography & travel
920   Biography, genealogy, insignia
930   History of ancient world
940   General history of Europe
950   General history of Asia   Far East
960   General history of Africa
970   General history of North America
980   General history of South America
990   General history of other areas

*Consult schedules for complete and exact headings

Fig. 10. Dewey Decimal second-level classification. Source: *Dewey Decimal Classification and Relative Index*, 20th ed., v. 2: x.

Contents of the Online Catalog

Every book in a library's collection is listed in its catalog. Most are now online; computer keyboards and screens now face library users instead of the former banks of drawers of 3 × 5-inch cards, with each card representing a book in the library. What appears on the computer screen is close to what you used to see on a single card. A few libraries may still have card catalogs and some may have printed catalogs, that is, bound volumes on whose pages are reproductions of the cards that would otherwise be in the traditional library drawers. However, the changeover to computers has been in the interest of speed and accessibility for users; additionally, electronic storage also represents an enormous space saver for every library.

- **Fiction books** each have two entries in the catalog: one by title and one by the author's name. Collections of short stories may also have additional entries headed by titles or authors within the book.

- **Nonfiction books** each have at least three entries in the catalog: one by subject, one by title, and one by author's name. They may also have additional screen entries headed by as many alternate subjects as seems practical. For instance, a book about trees might be listed under such subject headings as "trees," "forestry," and "ecology."

Because catalog entries are made to help you locate information, they may also be headed by a **translator's name** or an **author's pseudonym.**

Audiovisual holdings are usually represented by entries in the general catalog of a library, thus making it easier for you to find nonprint sources of information, even when this doesn't necessarily help you select a research topic. (Audiovisual and computer materials may, additionally, be cataloged in a separate area, such as one from which they may used or borrowed.)

Government documents held in a library are also listed in its catalog. They, too, may also be cataloged in a separate section, depending on the quantity of such documents that a library has. You can also get an overview of the enormous number and kind of government documents available by keying in the following URL on a computer: <http:/gpoaccess.gov>.

Individual Catalog Entries

The **author entry** is basic to the catalog and is the prime one for each book in a library. When a book is published in the United States, copies of it are sent to the Library of Congress in Washington, D.C. The author information or catalog entry is developed and put online there or by other library-supply sources; your library receives the entry from one of them.

Each library also adds a classification number or other relevant information on the computer screen by following the guidelines of whichever system it uses, the Library of Congress or the Dewey Decimal. (See Figure 11.)

"See also" entries or **"Links"** are also made at the library level; they will help you both in finding a topic and in searching out information for your research paper.

```
TITLE           Dolphin cognition and behavior : a comparative
                   approach / edited by Ronald J. Schusterman,
                   Jeannette A. Thomas, Forrest G. Wood.
IMPRINT         Hillsdale, N.J. : L. Erlbaum Associates, 1986.
DESCRIPTION     xv, 393 p. : ill. ; 24 cm.
SERIES          Comparative cognition and neuroscience.
NOTE            Papers of a conference held at the Hubbs Marine
                   Research Institute at Sea World in June, 1983.
BIBLIOG.        Includes bibliographies and indexes.
SUBJECT         Dolphins--Behavior.
                Dolphins--Psychology.
                Cognition in animals.
                Mammals--Behavior.
                Mammals--Psychology.
ALT AUTHOR      Schusterman, Ronald J.
                Thomas, Jeanette A.
                Wood, Forrest G. (Forrest Glenn), 1918-
                Hubbs Marine Research Institute.


    LOCATION              CALL NO.              STATUS
1 > Marine Lib. Stacks    QL737.C432 D65 1986   NOT CHK'D OUT
```

Fig. 11. Computer printout for a library book.

Alphabetizing of Books and Periodicals

Material in a library, whether you find it in an online catalog or on a CD-ROM, is filed alphabetically according to author, title, or subject. Here are some other uniform practices of library cataloging.

1. If the same word is applicable to a person, place, subject, or book title in a dictionary catalog, the entries follow that same order.

E X A M P L E

Lincoln, Abraham   (the person)

Lincoln Center for the Performing Arts   (the place)

Lincoln Finds a General   (a book title)

Obviously, this practice can be applicable only to a dictionary catalog (which lists all holdings in alphabetical order according to entry headings) and not to a divided catalog (where authors, titles, and subjects are in separate groups).

2. Abbreviations, such as "St.," "Dr.," "U.S.," and "19th cent." are filed as if they were spelled out: "Saint," "Doctor," "United States," "Nineteenth century," and so on.

If you were looking for the book *St. Thomas and the Future of Metaphysics* and didn't know the author, you would look for "Saint Thomas . . ." in the catalog.

3. Listing is alphabetical, word by word and letter by letter to the end of each word.

It is *not* simply letter-by-letter listing in either an online catalog or a periodical index.

EXAMPLE

Actual Catalog Order	*Incorrect Order*
South Carolina	South Carolina
South Dakota	South Dakota
South Wind	Southern Women Writers
Southern Women Writers	Southwest Pacific
Southwest Pacific	South Wind

4. Names or words beginning with *Mac* or its variations—such as *Mc* or *M'*—are listed as though they began with *Mac.*

EXAMPLE

Proper Catalog Order
Mach
McHale
MacHenry
Machiavelli

5. Foreign prefixes with names (such as "de," "van," or "von") are not used in alphabetizing.

Instead, the listing is by last name, with the prefix following.

EXAMPLE   Beethoven, Ludwig von

English names beginning with "De" or "Van" are listed by that prefix.

EXAMPLE   DeWitt, John

Spanish names are listed by the patronym (father's family name), although they often include the mother's maiden name.

A place name also sometimes is added to an individual's name, according to Spanish custom, but it is not used for alphabetizing.

EXAMPLE   Cervantes Saavedra, Miguel de

6. Titles that begin with "A," "An," or "The" are alphabetized by the second word.

Although these three articles are ignored for alphabetizing purposes, they are shown following a comma at the end of the title.

EXAMPLE   *Adventures of Huckleberry Finn, The*

7. Acronyms appear before words that are spelled out.

Thus, "OPEC" will be listed before "oil" in catalogs and periodical indexes.

8. Subjects—except history—are subdivided in alphabetical order.

EXAMPLE

Songs   [subject]
  Ballads
  Carols
  Children's songs
  Drinking songs   [subdivisions]
  Folk songs
  Madrigals
  Popular songs

9. History is subdivided according to eras or time.

EXAMPLE

Gt. Brit.—History (By Period)
  Roman Period, 55 B.C.–A.D. 449
  Anglo-Saxon Period, 449–1066
  14th Century
  War of the Roses, 1455–1584

AN ADDENDUM: DOUBLE SUBMISSIONS

If you have two research papers assigned in the same term, you may want to consider choosing a topic suitable for both of them. For example, a paper for a psychology class may be on a topic that is also acceptable for an education course; one prepared for an English class might be on a topic suitable to fulfill a research assignment in electronics or art history. You may even find that both teachers will permit the same paper to be submitted to them, in the belief that a top-notch job on one paper is preferable to a half-hearted or hurried job on two of them. Or, with the permission of both instructors, you could choose the same topic and perhaps use the same sources—but tailor the papers differently for each course.

If you consider a dual submission of either sort, consult the instructors involved, explain your reasoning, and get permission before making any final topic choices. Realize, too, that in a dual submission you may have to use different forms of documentation (depending on the conventions of the academic discipline for which you write each paper), and you will have to submit to the grading criteria of two different people—all the more reason for planning ahead with your instructors.

Narrowing the Topic

SOME LIMITATIONS YOU WORK WITHIN

After deciding on the topic that will be the starting point for your research paper, you should narrow it down to a **specific subject** in order to start gathering informaton effectively. In making that determination of specificity, bear in mind three limitations that are the "givens" within which you must work:

1. the required length of the paper you will write
2. the source material available to you
3. the audience that will read your paper

1. Length

Many assignments specify a minimum (or optimum) length for the research paper; if yours doesn't, you will need to exercise your own judgment. Be guided by the sort of work you expect of yourself, the time available to fulfill the assignment, and the importance you and your instructor put on the individual research paper. (As you already read in Chapter 1, this book assumes you are working on a research paper of 1,500 to 3,000 words, or about six to twelve double-spaced typewritten or word processed pages. Use your judgment, based on time and expectations, for papers of other lengths.)

The subject you decide to research should have sufficient range and depth to show you are a serious student and that you can deal adequately with whatever you select. Just don't choose a subject so broad that you will have to be superficial in order to treat it in the required length. For instance, a research paper on the film director John Ford would have to be too long or too general; better to limit the study to how Ford used Monument Valley as a setting in his films.

Although many people seem to have trouble limiting the range of a subject, it's also possible to choose one so specialized or esoteric that you need to devote several pages of background information to prepare the audience before you can begin to write about the subject. Such imbalance doesn't leave you enough space to say anything substantial in your paper.

2. Materials Available

You must be able to locate, conveniently, enough information for a paper you want to write. School libraries try to have materials for the work of their students, so the library is probably your best beginning source of information. However, budgets always limit a library's acquisitions. For example, if you attend a school where engineering and natural science courses are primary, you may not find enough materials on art or music to make possible extensive research on those subjects.

Computer searches are likely to elicit more sources of material than you have time (or even inclination) to work with. For example, databases will sometimes give you over a thousand titles of books or articles to choose from, even for a fairly limited subject. Because she was living in Florida, the author of the sample research paper at the end of Chapter 10 was able to go to a university marine biology library to find materials; she figured, rightly, that she was likely to find there the full texts of many articles that, on the basis of the titles in the databases she consulted, seemed to be helpful.

Print Materials

Before you decide definitely on a subject for your research, go to the principal library you plan to use. If you haven't already used its facilities to arrive at a topic for research, you should now look through the online catalog or even some of the databases it subscribes to and make sure information is available. Also, look at relevant periodical indexes. Both books and periodicals will give you ideas of how to narrow a topic. In the periodical indexes, as well as in the databases you consult, check to be sure that the library has some of the items listed that may be needed for research on the subject you plan to work with or that you can download complete articles.

If you have trouble finding information in a library, check with a librarian; each is a specialist in helping students locate materials. If you still can't find the right kind of information, adjust the scope of your proposed subject.

In general, you should consider any materials you obtain from databases and other electronic sources as print materials. True, as computer technology has become increasingly sophisticated, you can obtain visuals and hear sound on many computers; however, they transmit information primarily as words to be read.

Nonprint Materials

Investigate the availability of nonprint materials before you make a final decision on your subject. As explained in Chapter 4, not all research sources are in print or in a library. Unless you are asked to do just a library search, most instructors are happy to have you demonstrate your ability to find and work from varied sources. Interviews may be useful. What you hear on radio or see on television may be relevant. You may even plan to write letters of inquiry to promising sources if you have enough time to wait for answers or can supply your return e-mail address to which they can reply. Videotapes in libraries or in private collections may be useful. Traditional or interactive computer programs may also be counted among nonprint sources of information.

3. Audience

You already know that from the very beginning of the research paper process you must consider who will read what you write (see "Who Reads Research Papers—and Why" in Chapter 1). Even the earliest considerations of narrowing a topic to a workable subject should be done with your readers in mind: who they are, what they know, what they'd be interested in knowing, and how they will respond to what you write.

In some classes, students work collaboratively at various stages or make oral presentation of their final research paper. If yours is such a class, you can probably get responses about subject choice from classmates at this point, because they will be your audience.

FOCUSING ON A SUBJECT TO RESEARCH

Occasionally, the topic you choose will bring to mind immediately a specific subject, a part of that broad category you want to investigate. If that happens, you're lucky. Most people have to narrow the topic, and many have trouble limiting it to workable proportions. Yet finding a specific subject is crucial to a successful research paper. If you have trouble limiting or focusing on a subject, try one (or all) of the five methods explained here:

- freewriting
- free association
- clustering
- subdividing
- the five Ws

Freewriting

Sit down with a blank sheet of paper in front of you, take a pen or pencil in hand (or sit before your typewriter or computer keyboard), and start writing whatever comes into your head about the topic you selected. Don't plan or try to think ahead. Most especially, don't stop to worry about spelling or punctuation. Just write without stopping. That's freewriting. Later, read what you've written and either a subject will become evident or your writing will coach you toward one.

Free Association

People call upon free association in many problem-solving situations—and narrowing a topic to a subject suitable for research is certainly a problem to be solved. Free association (sometimes also called *brainstorming* when you do it orally and with other people) consists of writing down words or phrases that occur to you at the time they come to mind and without regard to order, spelling, usefulness, applicability, or any other matter of judgment.

Begin by writing down the topic you selected, and underneath it list everything that comes to mind. Make the list as quickly as you can, just by letting your mind rove over every idea the topic suggests.

EXAMPLE

Oceans

coral reefs	scuba diving
pollution	marine mammals
edible fish	overfished species
for travel	Costeau
usefulness to people	Pacific rim volcanoes
international conference	

From this list you could choose a subject, but it might be too broad. So another listing made by free association is in order. This time, begin with one of the words or phrases from the first list.

EXAMPLE

Marine mammals

whale agreements	tuna labeling
research about	trained dolphins
exploitation	big variety

The student whose research paper appears at the end of Chapter 10 followed these two procedures. Finally, several of the items in the preceding list led her to a subject decision. She had recently seen a TV ad for a water park that showed a trained dolphin performance. Earlier she had learned about how dolphins who get tangled in drift fishing nets set to catch fish commercially can die from lack of air, and since then she had made it a point to buy canned tuna fish that was labeled "dolphin safe." The day before making the list, the student had bought such a can of tuna. So she decided to research marine dolphins. At this point, however, she still wasn't sure what she might focus on for a suitable research subject.

Therefore, the student took a logical next step. With the "almost" subject of marine dolphins in mind, she went to the library and browsed through some periodical indexes. She might also have called up the subject on a computer search engine or on a CD-ROM in the library. (Any of these sources will give you something more specific than will an online catalog of book titles.)

Clustering

In clustering, you write down your ideas in a way that shows their relationships. (See Figure 12.) Begin by writing your topic in the center of a page and enclosing it in a small circle. Then, start your imagination or "stream of consciousness" working. As ideas occur to you, arrange them in relation to one another, with more circled words and more lines showing which ideas stem from which others.

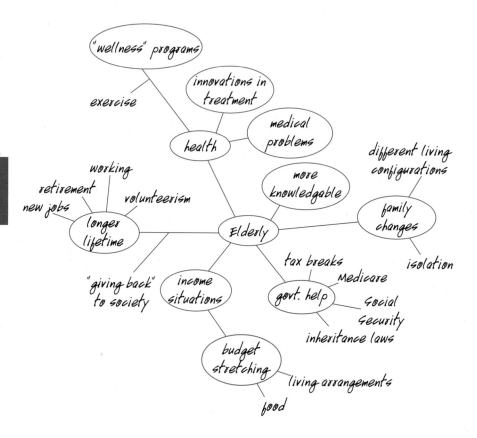

Fig. 12. Example of clustering.

Subdividing

Figure 13 shows another organized way to narrow a topic: divide it into progressively smaller units. Continue subdividing the topic until you reach a subject
you're sufficiently interested in (or that is limited enough) to research. Sometimes
possibilities for a research paper emerge only after a few levels of subdividing.

Subdividing looks—and is—somewhat more structured than clustering. With
clustering you can move anywhere at any time. Subdividing, however, requires a
more orderly thinking process as you write down possibilities. Also, remember that
nothing can be divided into just one part; you must have at least two parts in order
to make a subdivision.

The Five Ws

Asking questions—"What about . . . ?" or "What if . . . ?" or others—is still
another way of narrowing a topic to a subject you can work with. You might simply
ask yourself (or write down) those questions that occur to you about the topic you

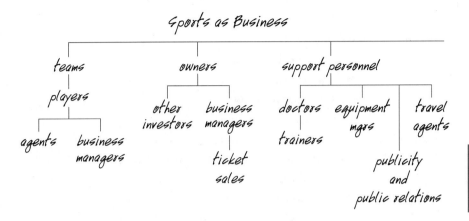

Fig. 13. Example of subdividing.

start with. You could assume the role of someone who knows nothing about the topic and ask questions to elicit information you'd like to have.

Or you can develop questions in an organized way by adapting the journalist's tradition of good reporting, which means covering the five Ws of a story: **who, what, where, when,** and **why.** These key words lead a reporter to cover a subject completely, so if you use them as guides, they can help you arrive at a topic useful for a research paper.

Who?	people
What?	problems, things, ideas
Where?	places
When?	times (i.e., past, present, future)
Why?	causes, reasons, results, conditions

To use these five Ws as an aid in finding a subject, write your topic at the top of a page. Under it write each of the five W words as headings and fill in appropriate words and phrases. Or, as in the following example, write down the questions and leave room to list writing subject ideas that respond to each question.

EXAMPLE 1

Television [the broad topic]

Who?	producers
	stars
	talk show hosts
	Oprah Winfrey
What?	advertising
	home videotaping of programs
	sports

	``unbiased'' news
	violence
	children's programming
Where?	via satellites
	studio productions
	public-access channels
When?	commercial beginnings
	possible future technical developments
Why?	education
	public dependence on
	homogenization of thought
	entertainment medium

Some of the topics listed in Example 1 are still too broad for a ten-page paper and need further narrowing. Use the same five Ws method again, but this time begin with one of your "answer" words from the first level of response.

EXAMPLE 2

Television Violence   [from the "What?" list]

Who?	audience responses
	characters in shows
	tell-all guests
What?	graphic
	suggestive
Where?	specials
	police shows
	news
	cartoons
When?	daytime
	prime time
	Saturday mornings
Why?	realism
	voyeurism
	``bloodthirstiness''
	psychology

On the basis of this further narrowing, you might decide to investigate the psychology of audiences wanting to see violence on television programs. Or you might decide to study ways in which violence in cartoons works to desensitize young people to the effect of the reality of violence in real life.

Combined Method

You may already have noticed that the five methods for focusing on a research subject are not exactly "pure" categories. That is, free association is probably used in the five Ws, and brainstorming may be what yields clusters that result in workable research subjects.

The student who wrote the sample research paper at the end of Chapter 10 actually arrived at her subject by combining the methods you have been reading about. She started with a Free-Choice Topic of interest—animals—and narrowed it in several steps: First she decided that a study of marine dolphins would be interesting. Then she discovered that bottlenose dolphins are not only superior and willing performers in captivity, but also prove their usefulness to people in various kinds of research. The thrust of her paper evolved as she began to consider the extent to which studying and working with this species of dolphins was "cost effective." (See Figure 14.)

FINDING AN APPROACH

Deciding on an *approach* to your subject doesn't mean deciding on a thesis statement before doing the research! To do that would mean you'd already decided what to say and therefore didn't expect to learn anything from this whole process. Rather, the early choice of an approach is a way of focusing your energy and ideas on what will be most useful for your final paper. Thus, you can do good work with greater ease, make intelligent decisions during the information-gathering process, and read what will be most useful to you.

Sometimes the approach will be defined for you by the assignment. For instance, if the instructor specifies that you produce a persuasive or argumentive paper, the decision about an approach is made for you. But if the choice is up to you, make it at this stage and you will have three advantages:

1. **You will be able to use your critical thinking abilities to select information more carefully.** That is, having an advance idea of what information needs to be included in your paper will set you to looking for it without wasting time on nonessentials.
2. **You will have a good idea of the kind of support you need for the materials you choose to include.**
3. **You will start to develop some notions of how to present your information.** That is, you will begin early to get a feel for how to organize your paper.

DECIDING ON AN APPROACH BEFORE BEING WELL INFORMED ABOUT YOUR SUBJECT

How, you might well ask, can you decide what information to look for if you don't know much about your subject? How can you evaluate the quality of what you find if you are just learning about the subject? And how can you know whether

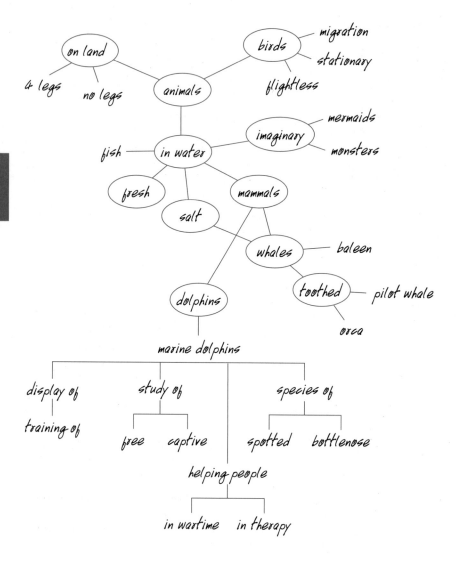

Fig. 14. Combined clustering and subdividing for sample research paper in Chapter 10.

or not you're being original when you don't know what others have studied or written about this subject that may be new to you?

These are valid questions, the answers to which will be found in part by consulting two readily available print sources. First, get a quick overview of your subject by reading about it (or one similar to it) in an encyclopedia—and possibly in a specialized rather than a general one. Also, look at titles of periodical articles on the Internet or in a popular database related to your subject within InfoTrac College Edition. (A librarian can be helpful in directing you to these materials quickly.) The periodicals will give you an idea of what people in the field are thinking and writing about. You might also be able to visit a computer chat group, if you can find one or more of them that is closely related to your chosen subject.

Skim, but don't read these sources closely yet. (The skill of skimming for ideas is explained in Chapter 5, in the section on "Reading to Take Notes.") When you have this fuller sense of what you will be working with, you can make an intelligent choice of approach. Choosing one of the following approaches will be helpful.

Five Possible Approaches to a Research Subject

1. **Examine or analyze the subject,** looking at various aspects of it and viewing it from more than one perspective.

2. **Evaluate or criticize the subject,** thus making a judgment about some quality of it.

3. **Compare and contrast things or ideas,** showing how both similarities and differences exist or are evident when someone looks closely at the subject.

4. **Establish relationships among ideas,** showing how they may have drawn from each other or are related in other ways to each other.

5. **Argue for or against something** and try to persuade the audience to agree with you.

As you will note in the following explanations and examples, it's not always possible to make clear-cut distinctions among the five ways of approaching a subject. A paper concerned with *examining* may also involve some *comparison. Comparison and contrast* are essentially types of *relationships.* However, if you decide on a primary approach to your research subject at the outset, you will find it easier to work with purpose and to gather only potentially usable material, thus saving yourself time and effort.

Examining or Analyzing

Examining a subject is like putting it under a microscope so you can see its details and look at them individually. You can examine anything, from a single event to an entire political system or scientific theory.

Analyzing something means looking at it closely enough to see what its components are and how it is put together. Thus, when you examine a subject, you are almost always also analyzing it.

Remember, also, that the examination or analysis you perform should involve your own ideas, filtered through your own perceptions, not just a report of the notions of others. Here are some kinds of examinations or analyses you might undertake as approaches to researching a subject:

- **Stylistic devices,** such as in a work of art

  EXAMPLES

  - Chinese elements in Mayan art
  - political satire in *Gulliver's Travels*

- **Intellectual, scientific, or sociological background** of a person or a historical period

  EXAMPLES

  - economic considerations in the European common market
  - emergence of women as presidents in South American countries
  - appeal of the Society for Creative Anachronism

- **Variations or revisions,** especially of a work of art or a philosophical idea

  EXAMPLES

  - changes in the character of Carmen from story to opera to film
  - major changes in the idea of Communism, from Marx to Mao
  - abolition of amateurism as requisite for participation in the Olympics

- **Evolution** of a business practice

  EXAMPLES

  - changing concepts of "the workplace" in light of electronic developments
  - blurring lines between information and advertising

If you decide to examine or analyze a subject for your research paper, don't fall into the trap of just enumerating information, thus ending with a report rather than a research paper. Instead, as discussed in Chapter 1, you need to bring your own thoughts to what you learn through research.

Evaluating or Criticizing

An *evaluation* is a judgment about a subject after it has been studied. *Criticism* means weighing or judging the quality of something, and should include both positive and negative commentary. (Contrary to widespread popular belief, criticism is *not* just finding fault.) Some kinds of evaluative or critical approaches you might take are:

- **Evaluate individuals, works, or ideas** in order to make judgments about them.

  EXAMPLES

  - changes in automobile air bag regulations
  - effectiveness of the death penalty as a deterrent to crime
  - computer games as early childhood learning tools

- **Criticize works or ideas**

  EXAMPLES

  - the rush to local incorporation within an urban area
  - ethics of assisted suicides

Comparing and Contrasting

To compare is to find similarities; *to contrast* is to find differences. The two verbs define different approaches, but they are generally used together to give a fuller view of a subject than either can provide alone. Also, the two verbs are usually linked because some similarity between elements must be established before a contrast is possible. For instance, though the Democratic and Republican party platforms differ during national election years, they can be compared and contrasted because both will deal with many of the same national and international issues. Comparison and contrast usually involve, but are not limited to, two elements. Some examples of comparing and contrasting approaches are these:

- **Works of art,** either with similar works or with the same one in different times or different media

  EXAMPLES

  - *High Noon* and *Shane* as archetypal western films
  - views of the novel *1984* when it was published and in the year 1984
  - *Pygmalion* by Shaw and the film *My Fair Lady*

- **Views of an individual**

  EXAMPLES

  - Jimmy Carter's diplomatic leverage as a sitting president and as a past president
  - Eleanor Roosevelt as the president's wife and as his widow

- **Ideas**

  EXAMPLES

  - government by mayor and by city manager
  - nutritional values in three popular diets
  - male and female attitudes toward the gender of a personal physician

- **Events**

  EXAMPLES

  - an auto race viewed by participants and by spectators
  - public reactions to moon landings

Relating

People learn by establishing relationships between what they already know and what is unfamiliar. Therefore, if you decide to undertake a research project that establishes (or explores) relationships, you will need to show how something the audience knows is related to something you presume is new to it. In fact, if you think back over what you have just read about comparison and contrast (and, to a lesser degree, about examining and evaluating as approaches), you will see that the ability to perceive and establish relationships permeates much of what you do in deciding on any sort of approach to a research paper assignment.

If you set out to approach your subject specifically as a matter of establishing relationships, you might select one of the following kinds of relationships:

- **A theory and its practical application**

  EXAMPLES

  - medieval beliefs about numerology and their influence on European church architecture
  - fiber optics as applied to computer communication

- **A person's work or thought and life**

  EXAMPLES

  - Arthur Ashe as a role model for youths, African Americans, and sports players
  - The Beatles as pivotal in popular music
  - Alfred Nobel's influence on economics

- **Specific events or attitudes**

  EXAMPLES

  - influence of the American Revolution on the French Revolution
  - how the Challenger space shuttle accident affected American space flight appropriations

Arguing or Persuading

Whenever you try to get someone to believe or act in a particular way, you are arguing or persuading. (The terms are usually used interchangeably.) One school of thought is that as soon as you take a stand on a subject—as you must to involve yourself in a research project and determine an approach toward a subject—you automatically begin persuading your audience.

Although all good writing supports the points it makes, in argument and persuasion there is usually more emphasis on logical support using evidence. ("Logic" is reasoning without fallacies—that is, without errors.) Evidence of your own critical thinking ability is that you can convince a careful reader by choosing what you need to include in an argument and then unfolding the material in an orderly way.

Although you will probably not take a position in deciding on the specific elements or on an argumentive or persuasive approach until *after* you've done some research on a subject and know where you stand on it (or what you believe you can successfully convince your audience about), you should know that several kinds of possibilities exist. You could:

- **Defend a position** that has already been taken.

  EXAMPLES

  - attempted cleanup of biological weapons after Desert Storm
  - required return of native American tribal artifacts

- **Justify an action.**

  EXAMPLES

  - federal government regulation of auto leasing contracts
  - improving air transportation standards
  - need for year-round public schooling

- **Prove or support a belief.** In order not to make a decision about what stand you will take before doing research on the subject, you might consider phrasing an approach by beginning with an "if."

  EXAMPLES

  - if election campaign funding will ever really change
  - if nonacademic "scholarships" ought to be called by another name
  - if battery-powered autos are likely to become widespread in the next five years

WORDING YOUR APPROACH

When you find an approach to your subject, you are focusing on a principal idea that you might develop in your research paper. Rather than depend on recalling the wording hours later, **write it out and put it in front of you when you sit down to work.** It's easy to forget details because there are so many demands on your time and thoughts, even during the several steps of the research process. But you'll stay on track if you write out your approach so you can look at it from time to time.

Word your approach as a two-part phrase, with the narrowed subject to research as one part and the approach as the other.

EXAMPLES

Approach	*Narrowed Subject*
examine ways performers can overcome	stagefright
argue for or against spending public funds to assist private	job retraining
compare and contrast the novel and film versions of	David Copperfield
analyze the effectiveness of TV in providing intellectual content in	children's programming

Note that **none of these sample subjects or approaches is in the form of a question.** You will have plenty of questions to ask yourself as you begin collecting information, and you should save questions until then so you can try to answer them through your research. Therefore, if you find yourself thinking in terms of a question, simply rephrase it as a statement.

EXAMPLE

Question	Rephrased as a Statement
How have filmmakers depicted Romeo and Juliet?	Romeo and Juliet as presented in films of different decades (approach: comparison and contrast)

You wouldn't know before finding information on this subject whether that depiction was similar or different, so the wording of this approach would have to remain general.

A Word of Caution

Even if you've taken the time to perform all this part of the research process, including skimming some related print materials (as described in Chapter 5), you *may* find you've chosen an approach that you can't work with. Or you may find that, once you start collecting information, the approach you expected to use isn't feasible. Rather than stick with something that won't work out well, don't hesitate to find another approach based on your early information gathering or on a conference with your instructor. There's no need to commit yourself to a direction that will prove unproductive.

CHOOSING A RESEARCH PAPER TITLE

Sometimes the wording you select for your approach will sound very much like the title for a paper. It may even end up as the title. However, don't be too quick to choose the title; that is a decision you need not make until the end of your writing.

If you do feel more comfortable working from a title than from a subject stated as an approach, then by all means write one down so you don't forget it. Many professional writers, in fact, say they work best when they start writing from a title.

Titles for research papers don't have to be clever or provocative. In fact, since your paper will be an academic one, and since most academic writing uses descriptive titles, you should probably follow suit. The advantage of a descriptive title for this sort of paper is that it immediately signals the audience as to what to expect.

CHAPTER 4

Searching for Information

PRIMARY AND SECONDARY SOURCES

To whatever extent possible, you should try to include both primary and secondary sources in searching out information for your research paper. Primary sources, desirable as they are, may not always be available. Or the limited time you have for some research assignments may make obtaining them difficult or impossible. On the other hand, there is danger in relying too heavily on secondary sources, especially if you ignore the materials on which they are based or the possible slanting they reflect. (See "Evaluating Source Materials" in Chapter 5.)

Primary Sources

Primary sources come straight from the people or works you are researching and are, therefore, the most direct kinds of information you can collect. Rely on them when they are available, because they are firsthand observations and investigations. Examples of primary sources include Dr. Shannon Lucid's report of experiments during her record-setting time aboard the Russian space station Mir, and a juror telling about how a decision was reached in a trial. Primary sources of information include the following:

- **Diaries, notes, journals, and letters**
- **Interviews**
- **Autobiographies**
- **Works of art you are writing about,** such as novels, poems, short stories, plays, films, paintings, sculpture, librettos, and musical scores
- **Spoken or written works by someone who participates in an event or discovery,** such as a recording of a president's television address or the observations of an astronomer
- **Many public documents,** such as the *Congressional Record* or statistics from the U.S. Bureau of the Census.

Use your ingenuity to locate primary sources for your research subject. For instance, to find out about the psychological strain of living with someone suffering from Alzheimer's disease, primary sources might include interviews with their caregivers.

Secondary Sources

These are one step removed from the original source and are often an examination of a study someone else has made on a subject or an evaluation of, commentary on, or summary of primary materials. Some examples of secondary sources are:

- **Critical (i.e., evaluative) reviews or commentaries**
- **Biographies**
- **Second-person reports**

EXAMPLES

About Abraham Lincoln

Primary Sources: Lincoln's letters and speeches

Secondary Sources: Carl Sandburg's books on Lincoln

About Carl Sandburg

Primary Sources: Sandburg's books on Lincoln; Sandburg's letters and journals

Secondary Sources: a biography

About misuse of government funds

Primary Sources: reports and records of disbursements

Secondary Sources: newspaper stories about the issue

Check secondary sources carefully by going back to their original (or primary) sources if possible. View materials skeptically and critically. And never, *never* rely solely on anyone's review of a film, record, book, or play without watching, listening to, or reading that work yourself!

THE WHAT, WHERE, AND HOW OF FINDING INFORMATION

Our era is rightfully dubbed "the information age." Never before has there been so much information available or so many ways to disseminate and retrieve it. Even as you read this, new Web sites are being developed, books and newspapers pour from printing presses, satellites send sound and pictures for academic edification as well as for entertainment. New ways of storing sounds and images are even now being developed that will soon make obsolete much of how we can access information today. As someone working on a research paper, you need to know:

1. **What** kind of information to look for
2. **Where** to find it
3. **How** to cite or acknowledge it

What you need to look for depends on the subject you are studying and how much knowledge you bring to it. The more selective you have been in choosing a subject and an approach, the more focused your search will be and thus the more likely you are to hone in on information that will be useful to you. Also, know in advance what sources you are expected to use. Will it be periodicals as well as books? Nonprint as well as print? Primary as well as secondary sources?

Where to look for the information will not be overwhelming if you organize your search and follow an orderly pattern. To that end, the section that follows, called "Devising a Search Strategy," is divided according to where you will find needed source materials: traditional print-on-paper resources, electronic resources, and nonprint resources. Then use the "Search Strategy Record" presented later in the chapter to keep a record of your activities.

How to record what you find is actually done in two steps. First, you should make preliminary citation cards that show all the possible sources of information, even though you probably won't use all of them. After writing your research paper, you will be able to draw from that group of cards those works you actually cited and, if you follow the conventions explained in this chapter, you will already have recorded them in the proper format. The MLA [Modern Language Association] style of citing sources is used predominantly in this book; however, the APA [American Psychological Association] style and other standard styles are explained and illustrated in Chapter 11.

Follow the conventions detailed in this chapter's section on "Conventions of MLA-Style Preliminary (and Final) Citations." They serve as guides to the many conventions your preliminary citation cards are expected to adhere to. But don't be daunted by them! Nobody expects you to memorize *all* these conventions; just know where to locate the explanations and models this book contains.

DEVISING A SEARCH STRATEGY

Given the wide array of print, electronic, oral, and visual resources available to you for research, you need to be organized and selective in order to accomplish your task. Smart researchers set up **a strategy to discover what resources are available.** While making such a search, you will also discover whether or not your subject and approach will yield the required information. If you find at this early stage that they won't, you can make a change or variation before you've invested a lot of time and energy.

The record to keep for each resource you locate while following your search strategy is called a **preliminary citation card.** It is "preliminary" because each card records potential, though not necessarily ultimately usable, information. Some materials you locate during this initial search will not be available to you, and some will not be relevant to what you seek or, eventually, incorporate into your paper. **Preliminary citations contain information about the author, title, publication, and *location* of each potential source of information.** They will be used for three purposes:

1. To locate and consult the resources you've identified and want to read or view or listen to in order to take from them information for your paper

2. To simplify documenting the text of your research paper

3. To prepare the Works Cited list at the end of your paper

Start your information search at either a library or a computer, depending on which is more immediately accessible to you. If you have a computer available off campus, you may want to start on it; otherwise, use school facilities.

Involve a librarian at an early stage of your search strategy. Nobody knows more about the resources of a library than the people who have been specially trained to help students use them. In fact, at most colleges and universities the librarians have faculty status, thus attesting to their function as teachers.

At this stage, don't plan on reading the sources you locate, except perhaps for skimming encyclopedia articles for overviews while you already have the proper volumes open. Rather, concentrate first on locating the resources.

Print-on-Paper Resources

The most effective search strategy usually begins in the most traditional way: finding general reference information and later moving to more specific materials. Usually, that means starting in the reference room or section of a library, though you will undoubtedly need to go to other sections. Include as many of the following print-on-paper resources as you can:

- **Encyclopedias,** for the overviews they offer
- **Bibliographies and reference guides,** to find books and other sources, sometimes unexpected, on your subject
- **Handbooks,** to give you additional general information
- **Indexes (including those for subjects and for periodicals—magazines, journals, and newspapers),** for sources of up-to-date as well as retrospective information on your subject. (Many of these are now available on CD-ROMs and will be noted in the next section, on electronic resources.)
- **Government publications,** especially in libraries designated as repositories
- **Dictionaries, almanacs, maps, atlases, directories, biographic references, and more** (such as PAIS)
- **Microforms,** the originals of which were probably print on paper

Electronic Resources

These resources are likely to be ever more wide-ranging. Some will be in the general catalog of a library or in specific collections, arranged by medium (as for films) or by department (such as music).

- **Online (or card) catalogs,** to locate relevant films and books and, from descriptions of them, to get an idea of their contents
- **Internet and Web sites**

- **CD-ROMs,** especially those containing encyclopedias and indexing periodicals
- **Computer databases,** often for access to periodical information, but also for books and newsletters
- **Abstracting services,** to find many sources not easily accessed elsewhere
- **Computer programs and interactive videos,** listed either in a general catalog or at a media or computer center.

Nonprint Resources

These may be listed in the general catalog of a library, but often they're cataloged only at a media center.

- **Radio and TV programs**
- **Videos,** whether tapes or discs
- **Films**
- **Filmstrips or slides**
- **Audiotapes, CDs, other audio recordings**
- **Interviews**
- **Lectures and speeches,** some of which may be recorded

Those sources that you originate, such as **telephone or in-person interviews** or **questionnaires** that you develop and administer, will of course not be accessible to or replicable by others.

The Search Strategy Record

Use the following record sheet as a guide to what you might want to consult and what you have already accomplished. (You will, of course, also be recording what you do in your Process Log.) Fill in the "Dates checked" and make preliminary citation cards (following the samples for each category of source in this chapter) whenever you find materials that seem as if they'll be useful. Then use your record for the following purposes:

1. **To make sure you have fulfilled the requirements of the assignment.** For instance, if you were supposed to include both magazines and journals as resources and didn't locate any journals, be sure there are none with relevant contents. Otherwise, you can either rectify the problem or consult with your instructor about it.

2. **To share your preliminary citation cards with classmates who are familiar with the contents of this book and with your assignment.** That way, you can get an outside view of your research paper work as it progresses.

3. **To ascertain that you are ready to move ahead to the next step in the research process.**

RESEARCH PAPER SEARCH STRATEGY RECORD

SUBJECT: _____

AUDIENCE: _____

POSSIBLE SOURCES   *Date checked*

Print-on-Paper Resources

    Encyclopedias   _____

    Bibliographies and reference guides   _____

    Handbooks   _____

    Indexes (subject and/or periodical)   _____

    Government documents   _____

    Dictionaries, almanacs, etc.   _____

    Microforms   _____

    Other   _____

        (names) _____

Electronic Resources

    Online catalogs   _____

    Internet and Web sites   _____

        (names) _____

    CD-ROMs   _____

        (names) _____

    Computer databases   _____

        (names) _____

    Abstracting services   _____

        (names) _____

    Computer programs, interactive videos   _____

        (names) _____

Nonprint Resources

    Radio and TV programs   _____

    Videotapes/videodiscs   _____

    Films   _____

    Filmstrips/slides   _____

    Audiotapes/CDs/discs   _____

    Lectures and speeches   _____

    Interviews   _____

      Appointments made: Yes ___ No ___

Questionnaires, surveys, polls   _____

    Plans made: Yes ___ No ___

Other Resources:

    (names) _____

POSSIBLE PRIMARY SOURCES *(list below):*

_____

_____

CONVENTIONS FOR MLA-STYLE PRELIMINARY (AND FINAL) CITATIONS

Well-written preliminary citation cards keep you from retracing your steps or spending additional time as you move ahead in the research process. Use the same care in writing them as you use in all other academic and scholarly work. You may set up a matrix for entering the preliminary citation cards or carry a laptop computer into a library with you on which to write information, but once you begin searching electronic sources, using the computer may be awkward. Therefore, the most convenient way to record the citations is **in ink on 3- × 5-inch cards.**

All preliminary (and final) citations record author, title, and publication information about sources, though there are slight variations depending on the medium—all of which will be detailed later in the chapter. You will also be expected to adhere to some general conventions, especially about punctuation and spacing, that are given in the next section. If you don't find an example here of citation information you need to record, check the specific examples in Chapter 9 or use the index of this book to locate a description that covers what you want to find.

General Conventions

1. **Use hanging indentation,** but also allow both a left and a right margin between your writing and the edges of the card. That is, the first line of each entry begins at the left margin and continues to the right margin you set. Each succeeding line is indented five spaces from the left margin and continues as far as needed to the right margin.

   EXAMPLE

   ```
   Hanging indentation looks like this. It is the opposite of
       normal paragraphing and it makes the first word of a
       citation easy to read or to find in a list.
   ```

2. **Each unit of a citation—author (beginning with last name), title, and publication—ends with a period.** However, if an author uses any initials in place of a full first and/or middle name, the period after the last initial

substitutes for the period that concludes the unit. If a title ends with a question mark or exclamation mark, let it substitute for the period.

EXAMPLES   **Goldman, Emma.**

Auden, W. H.   [Comment: This poet usually uses just initials for his given and middle names.]

"How Fair Are Airline Fares?"   [Article title ending with a question mark]

<u>**Wonderful to Behold!**</u>   [Book title ending with an exclamation mark]

3. **Spacing after punctuation is the same as in typing text.** That is, allow two spaces after a period (or other end mark), and one space after any comma or colon.

EXAMPLE   <u>**The Research Paper: Process, Form, and Content, 8th ed.**</u>

4. **Long poems appearing in book form, such as *Paradise Lost* or *The Rime of the Ancient Mariner*, are treated as books.**

5. **The Bible and the names of books within it are not underlined.** The King James Version is assumed as the reference, unless you state otherwise in your paper.

Conventions About the Author Unit

1. **The author's surname appears first, followed by a comma, then the given name(s) and a period. Record the information exactly as you see it in the source from which you take the preliminary citation.** Some listings give an author's complete name, including all given names, even when the person ordinarily uses initials for all but the surname. Periodical indexes usually show only initials for given names. Later, if you consult that source, correct the preliminary citation card to conform to the author's choice of name usage in print or film. Newspaper article authorship may appear as a by-line (but never as simply a wire service); if there is none, omit it on the citation card and begin with the title (i.e., the headline) of the article.

EXAMPLE   **Barber, Elizabeth Wayland.**

Roth, A. J.   [on preliminary citation card, later corrected to: **Roth, Audrey J.** as shown on the title page]

2. **If there are *two authors*, only the name of the first person shown is reversed; the other is written in normal first-name then last-name order.** The names are joined by the word "and," preceded by a comma.

EXAMPLE   **Altshuler, Thelma, and Richard Paul Janaro.**

3. If a work has *three authors*, put a comma only between the first and second persons' names; the comma plus "and" are placed after the second person's name.

EXAMPLE　　　Bauermeister, Erica, Jesse Larsen, and

Holly Smith

4. If a work has *four or more authors*, record only the first person's name and use the Latin abbreviation "et al." (meaning "and others") **to signal that there are additional authors.** The period that shows abbreviation of the second word becomes the period at the end of the author unit.

EXAMPLE　　　Maimon, Elaine P., et al.

Conventions About the Title Unit

1. **Titles of books, pamphlets, magazines, newspapers, radio or television programs, videotapes or -discs, full-length films, plays, operas, TV series, and computer software are underlined.** When you type any of the titles in a Works Cited list, you either **underline** them or use **italics.** Subtitles (that is, wording following a colon) are considered part of the title.

EXAMPLE　　　**Women's Work: The First 20,000 Years**

2. **Titles of poems, short stories, essays, articles in newspapers or magazines or journals, chapter titles within a book, individual radio or TV episodes in a series, songs, lectures, and speeches are enclosed in quotation marks.** Put the period ending the title unit *within* the quotation marks. If the title already contains wording in quotation marks, use single quotation marks where the double marks appear in print.

EXAMPLES　　　''The Killers.''　　[title of a story]

"'Look at Me When I'm Talking to You!':

Cross Talk Across the Ages."

[title of a chapter in a book]

"The Scapegoat in 'The Lottery' and in

Life."　　[title of a short story within the

title of an essay]

3. **The headline of a newspaper article is treated as if it were the title.**

4. **Capitalize the first letter of each word in a title (except articles, conjunctions, or prepositions) when you write them,** even if all letters appear as all capitals or all lowercase in the information from which you get the title.

EXAMPLE

Title Appearing in the Index　　　*Title as You Should Record It*

Airbags and auto safety　　　"Airbags and Auto Safety"

5. **Special cases of titles:**

a. *If a book is a revision or has a numbered edition or some other variation,* end the underlining at the last letter of the title, put a comma, and then abbreviate (but do not underline) the special information. Some common designations, used alone or in combination as required, are: rev. (revised), alt. (alternate), ed. (edition). Remember that the period after the abbreviation suffices as the period to end the title unit.

E X A M P L E   <u>The Research Paper: Process, Form, and</u>

<u>Content</u>, 8th ed.

b. *If the title of a book contains the title of another work that is usually underlined,* underline the title of the book, but neither underline nor put quotation marks around the second title.

E X A M P L E   <u>Focus on Rashomon.</u>

[*Rashomon,* the title of a feature-length film, is normally underlined, but here it is the subject of a book for which it's also part of the title]

c. *Titles normally put in quotation marks are so recorded if they appear within titles that are underlined.*

E X A M P L E   <u>Sourcebook for ''Snows of</u>

<u>Kilimanjaro.''</u>

[The book title, underlined, is about the short story in quotation marks]

Conventions About the Publication Information Unit

Expected in publication information are the name of the publisher and the date of publication (or copyright year). Beyond that is a wide range of variations depending on the medium being recorded. For instance, if you are recording information about a book, the location of the publisher is needed (see section A, which follows). If the information is in a periodical, its title must be given (sections B and C that follow). Electronically transmitted sources need to note the publication medium and vendor (section D), and nonprint sources must note comparable information (section E). In short, one purpose for recording publication information on a preliminary citation card (or in the Works Cited listing of your research paper) is to give enough information about a source that someone wanting to replicate your search or check some aspect of your work on the topic can do so easily.

A. Book Publication Information

1. **For the place of publication:**

a. Record the city (but not the state) where the publisher is located, followed by a colon.

E X A M P L E   **Belmont:**

b.   Add an **abbreviation for the name of a foreign country,** except **Canada, which is identified by abbreviating the province** in which the publisher has its main office.

EXAMPLES

Fr.   [for France]

Alb.   [for Alberta, Canada]

c.   If you can't find a place of publication (either for the preliminary citation card or for the final Works Cited list), **write "n. p." (for "no place") where the city name would ordinarily appear.**

d.   If several cities appear for a publisher's location, **use the first one or the featured one** on the list (often shown by being printed in boldface or in a larger type size).

EXAMPLE

The source lists: • San Diego • New York • Chicago • Austin • London • Sydney •

Tokyo • Toronto

You write: **San Diego**

2.   **For the name of the publisher:** In the interest of streamlining publication information, both the MLA [Modern Language Association], on whose conventions this book is primarily based, and the APA [American Psychological Association] adopted the following as standards to record the names of publishers.

a.   Record only the **first word of a company name.**

EXAMPLES

Publisher's Name	*Record as:*
Farrar, Straus & Giroux, Inc.	**Farrar**
Bedford Books of St. Martin's Press	**Bedford**
St. Martin's Press, Inc.	**St. Martin's**
Pocket Books	**Pocket**
The Free Press	**Free**
Houghton Mifflin Co.	**Houghton**

b.   If the publisher's **name is that of one person** (the first and last names, or the initials and last name), **record just the last name.**

EXAMPLES

Publisher's Name	*Record as:*
R. R. Bowker Company	**Bowker**
Alfred A. Knopf, Inc.	**Knopf**
G. P. Putnam's Sons	**Putnam**

c.   **Omit business abbreviations** (such as "Co.," "Inc.," "Ltd.," or "Corp."), **articles, and descriptive words** (such as "Press" and "Publishers") that are part of the publisher's full name.

EXAMPLES

Publisher's Name	*Record as:*
Wadsworth Publishing Co.	**Wadsworth**
Clark Boardman Co., Ltd.	**Boardman**
George Allen and Unwin Publishers, Inc.	**Allen**

d. **Record university press publications as the name of the university together with the initials "U"** (for University) **and "P"** (for Press or publishers). No periods are required after the letters.

EXAMPLES

Publisher's Name	*Record as:*
Oxford University Press	**Oxford UP**
Princeton University Press	**Princeton UP**
University of Chicago Press	**U of Chicago P**
The Johns Hopkins University Press	**Johns Hopkins UP**

e. **Use standard abbreviations for words that are part of a publisher's name.**

EXAMPLES

Publisher's Name	*Record as:*
Harvard Law Review Association	**Harvard Law Review Assn.**
Academy for Educational Development	**Acad. for Educ. Dev.**

f. **Use familiar capital letter combinations** if the name of the publisher is customarily known by them. However, if you think that readers may not know the acronym or letter combination, use abbreviations.

EXAMPLES

Publisher's Name	*Record as:*
U.S. Government Printing Office	**GPO**
National Council of Teachers of English	**NCTE**
Modern Language Association	**MLA** or **Mod. Lang. Assoc.**

3. **For the date of publication (i.e., the copyright date):**

a. If several copyright dates are given (showing publication dates of several editions of the book), **record only the most recent one.**

EXAMPLE

The Source Lists:	*You Write:*
© 1996, 1993, 1987, 1984, 1980	**1996.**

b. **If no copyright or publication date is given, write "n. d."** after the comma where the copyright date is usually written. The period at the end of that abbreviation suffices as the period concluding the unit.

c.   **Do not confuse the date of a printing with the copyright date.** Some books are reprinted a number of times, and you may see something like "5th printing, 1997"; the copyright date is often a year or more earlier and is preceded by the copyright symbol, ©.

B. Magazine and Journal Publication Information

Three units comprise the publication information noted for these periodicals: the **title** of the publication, the **date of publication,** and the **pages** on which the article being cited appears. Differences between page numbering systems (whether *individually in an issue or continuous through a year*) will require some variation in the publication date form of the preliminary citation you write. You may find a volume number or an issue number of a publication as you search through sources, and these are only in the citation for some scholarly journals, as noted in subpoint (d), to follow.

Paging by issue.   This means that each time the magazine or journal is published, the issue begins with page 1 and numbering continues until the end of that issue. Most general-interest and many special-interest magazines are paged this way (such as *Time, Newsweek, Ebony, Car and Driver*); so are some academic and professional journals (such as *The Annals of the American Academy of Political and Social Science*). Later, when you look at the actual resource that you've recorded on a preliminary citation card, check to be sure your inference about the page numbering system is accurate.

Paging by volume.   This system, used frequently in academic and scholarly journals, is also called *continuous pagination* or *successive pagination.* ("Pagination" means page numbering.) It means that page 1 will appear only once during a 12-month cycle: in the first issue of the publication's volume year. Thereafter, the pagination will continue through the volume year.

E X A M P L E

Quarterly Journal Paged by Volume

Volume 22	published in January	contains pages 1 through 128
	published in April	contains pages 129 through 298
	published in July	contains pages 299 through 416
	published in October	contains pages 417 through 550
Volume 23	published in January	contains pages 1 through 115
	published in April	contains pages 116 through 254
	(and so on)	

Most publications consider a "volume" or "volume year" the same as a calendar year (that is, running from January through December), but it may also coincide with a customary academic year of September through June.

The term "volume" often means that after the individual editions of a journal are published through a year, they are bound together in a volume in order to be readily accessible on a library shelf.

a. **Record the *title of the publication and underline it,*** but put no punctuation at its end. (You will remember that the title comes after the period following the author(s) name(s) and that the article title, including end punctuation, is enclosed in quotation marks.)

b. If the publication shows a **month as its *date of publication,* record this in the customary three- and four-letter abbreviations—except for May, June, and July, which are written out in full. Double issues or those that show only a season should be recorded that way.**

    EXAMPLES

    ```
    Feb.     May     July     Sept.     Nov.
    Feb./Mar.    Summer     Summer/Fall
    ```

c. **If the publication is *paged by each issue,* write the year immediately after the month.** Put a colon after the year, to show that the next section of the citation will be page numbers. **If the publication is weekly,** as with a news magazine, **write the exact date *before* the month and year.**

    EXAMPLE

    ```
    Sept. 1996:

    19 Sept. 1996:
    ```

d. **If the publication is a scholarly journal with *pages numbered consecutively throughout a year,*** though appearing in several issues during that year, **put the volume number immediately after the journal title and then put the year in parentheses.** Omit the month or an issue number, even if one or both appears on the source from which you get this preliminary bibliography information or on the material itself when you consult it.

    EXAMPLE

    ```
    Teaching English in the Two-Year College 23 (1996):
    ```

    A **scholarly journal with pages numbered by each issue must show both the volume and issue numbers,** with a dot between them, before the year.

    EXAMPLE

    ```
    Oceanus 32.1 (1989)
    ```

    When an index always shows both volume and issue number and you have not yet seen that actual source, there is a slight problem in how to tell which form to use (that is, whether or not it is necessary to use the issue number). You may have to guess, if you aren't familiar with the publication. If the page numbers seem high (that is, more than 250), you can infer numbering throughout a year. However, be sure to check the publication itself and make appropriate changes in citing information when you consult the actual publication.

e. **Numbers following the colon show that these are *the pages on which an article appears.*** (Do not use the word "pages" or any abbreviation for it.) **If they are successive pages, record the first and last page numbers with a hyphen between.** If the article begins and ends on **three-digit page**

numbers, the first of which is the same, no repetition is needed. However, **if the first digit changes, record all of them.** A period concludes this unit.

EXAMPLES

:86-90.   :75-78.   :235-42.   :298-309.

f. **If the article is *not* on successive pages, record only the first page followed immediately by "+."** Articles that have advertising or other text separating their pages are not on successive pages.

EXAMPLE

An article begins on page 56, an ad is on page 57, and the article continues on pages 58 and 59 and then jumps to page 75.

You write: :56+.

C. Newspaper Publication Information

After the name of the author (if there is a byline) and the headline (i.e., the "title") of the article, write the publication information: **the name of the paper (underlined), the date of publication (in date, month, year order), the name of the edition, the section of the newspaper, and the page(s) on which the article appeared.** Put a comma after the year, a colon after the name of the edition, and a space after each of these parts or the punctuation mark following them. The unit concludes with a period, of course.

EXAMPLE

Miami Herald 21 Dec. 1996, final ed: B2.

1. **Omit an article that is part of the name of a newspaper, even if it appears on the masthead.**

EXAMPLE

The Title of the Paper on the Masthead Reads: *You Record It as:*

The Miami Herald   Miami Herald

2. **If the name of the city is not part of the name of the newspaper, supply it in square brackets.** If you need to add the state for further identification, use the two-letter postal abbreviation. However, nationally published newspapers do not require that a city of publication be given.

EXAMPLES

Times-Picayune [New Orleans]

Monitor [Concord, NH]

Wall Street Journal

USA Today

3. **Noting the edition** (such as "Late," "Final," or "Blue Streak") **with the abbreviation "ed." facilitates locating the referenced article,** for the same stories are not in all editions or always in the same location. The unit ends with a colon.

4. **Sections of a newspaper, usually designated by letters, follow the edition and precede the page number(s).** However, a section designated by a number is preceded by the abbreviation "sec." with the number.

5. **Articles that are continued, but not on successive pages, are signified by a "+" after the beginning page number.**

    E X A M P L E

    An article begins on the front page and continues on page 12 of the first section of the paper.

    You write: **A1+.**

D. Electronically Transmitted Publication Information

There are so many possibilities here that you need to sort out both the "history" of the source and the way you accessed it. For instance, an article that originated in a magazine but that you found on a CD-ROM requires two kinds of publication information (one for each medium), while that originating from an online chat group requires another sort of citation. Therefore, you will be better served by checking the various kinds of sources detailed in the examples in Chapter 9 as you require them for preliminary citation cards.

E. Nonprint Publication Information

Nonprint sources vary so greatly that the "publication" information you must include about them will also vary. However, in general, assume that the distributor or location of a work should appear, as should such relevant information as the medium (CD-ROM, videotape, and so on), timing, whether it's in color or not (if the material is visual), and anything else that will tell someone reading the information details of the source. For more details, see pages 97–98 and "Finding and Citing Nonprint Resources" later in this chapter.

CITING SPECIFIC SOURCES

Having identified print-on-paper, electronic, and nonprint resources for information you can examine for use, you now need to start consulting the individual items you discover. Therefore, the rest of this chapter will follow the order of the Research Paper Search Strategy Record, and note the contents of various sources and what you can expect to find in them. It will also show how to "read" entries and then "translate" the information in them into the forms already described for writing preliminary citation cards. (As you already read, you may have to provide capitals for titles or quotation marks and omit the sizes of pages or notes of illustrations that appear in the listings.)

One of the most important ways you can help your own research at this point is to **use the top left corner of a preliminary citation card to note the location of materials.** That is, if you find books, write the call numbers at the top left on the appropriate cards; if you determine certain material is available in microfiche, write on the card the drawer designation where it's stored; if a recording is in the music department library, note that on the citation card. In other words, note everything you can on the preliminary citation cards to simplify your next step—recording useful information from selected sources.

FINDING AND CITING PRINT-ON-PAPER RESOURCES

Encyclopedias

An encyclopedia—whether in bound volumes on book shelves or on a CD-ROM to be read on a computer monitor—is not a source from which to get a whole paper (although, unfortunately, some people believe it is). But it *is* a source of material that will usually give you a general view of a subject from which to start your research and initiate your understanding of the subject you selected. There are two different kinds of encyclopedias: a general encyclopedia and a subject encyclopedia. (If you decide to consult an encyclopedia on a CD-ROM, find out whether it's complete—that is, whether it's the same as a print-on-paper version or an abridgment.)

A **general encyclopedia** gives a broad picture of many subjects that students usually work with. To find out if a particular encyclopedia covers the subject you're looking for, consult the index (which is usually in the last volume of a set). However, the contents of most encyclopedias are arranged alphabetically, so you can also check directly to find if material you're looking for is available.

The *Encyclopedia Americana* and the *World Book Encyclopedia* are familiar to most students and are good for background information; most entries also include a bibliography. The *Academic American Encyclopedia* is known for the fine graphics that supplement its print entries.

The *Encyclopaedia Britannica,* though a general encyclopedia, has always been considered strong in the humanities. It is arranged differently from other encyclopedias, for it comes in three units. The *Micropaedia* is ten volumes, indicated by roman numerals, containing ready reference material and an index. Consult it first when you look for information, because it will either contain what you are looking for or tell you where to find more information in the *Macropedia.* The nineteen volumes of the *Macropaedia,* each designated by an arabic numeral, give knowledge in depth and will probably be the one you use most. The one-volume *Propaedia* offers a general outline of knowledge; its entries are probably too broad for you to consult for the kind of research paper this book is about, but they provide a good overview and direction for more specific sources. Should you employ this encyclopedia as a resource, note that the specific unit used is considered part of the book title, in this way:

`Encyclopaedia Britannica: Micropaedia. 1997 ed.`

A **subject encyclopedia** probably exists for whatever field you're working on. Consult it for more detailed and restrictive discussions of a subject. The content of most subject encyclopedias is arranged alphabetically. Some examples of the kind and range of subject encyclopedias available are *The Encyclopedia of Crime and Justice, The Encyclopedia of World Art, The McGraw-Hill Encyclopedia of Science* *and Technology,* and the *New Grove Dictionary of Music and Musicians* (which, despite its title, is actually a twenty-volume encyclopedia). Some of the many other subject encyclopedias are listed in Appendix A.

To write a preliminary citation from an encyclopedia, be sure you **find the author of an entry** so you can record that information on your citation card. Many encyclopedia articles are signed; if only the author's initials appear at the end of an entry, the person's full name can usually be found listed within the volume (or another volume of the set).

As in any **work that is organized alphabetically, do not write volume or page numbers as part of the citation.** Figure 15 is a sample of a preliminary citation card for an encyclopedia, with the spacing marked for you.

Bibliographies and Reference Books

A **bibliography** will help you find additional source listings to consult in your search for information. Many are newly issued or updated so that recent publications on a specific subject or in a particular publication are readily available. For instance, the *Bibliographical Index: A Cumulative Bibliography of Bibliographies* lists, by subject, all books and journal articles containing at least fifty bibliographic citations of works that have been published separately or that have

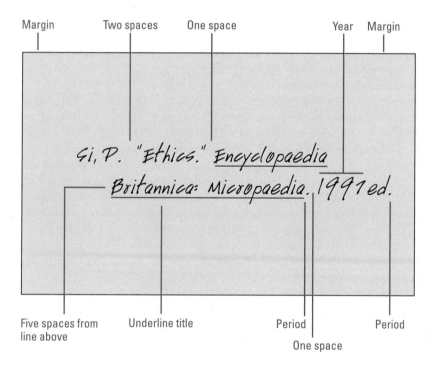

Fig. 15. Example of a preliminary bibliography card for an encyclopedia entry. Source: Peter Singer. "Ethics." *Encyclopaedia Britannica.* 1997 ed.

appeared as parts of books, pamphlets, or periodicals. "See" and "See also" listings, in addition to other entries, can lead you to other pages in the index for further sources of information to include in your preliminary citations.

A **reference guide,** such as *Guide to Reference Books,* identifies all sorts of reference books by field, so if you decide to check that book, you can expect to find other sources quickly in it. Figure 16 shows a portion of a page from this book as an example of the kind of sources it indicates.

A **directory** that, despite its name, may be helpful is the *Encyclopedia of Associations.* It tells which reference books identify organizations and institutions in a field. Its particular use for students preparing research papers is that in it you can find names and addresses to write to—or fax or phone—for special kinds of information.

Bibliography

Gebauer, Dorothea. Bibliography of national filmographies / comp. by Dorothea Gebauer with the assistance of the members of the Cataloguing Commission of the International Federation of Film Archives ; ed. by Harriet W. Harrison. Bruxelles : FIAF, c1985, 80 p.   **BH164**

Compiled as an aid to film catalogers, a country-by-country listing of national lists, reference works, serial publications, monographs, etc., that provide film and credit information on the country's output. Annotations for most items, describing organization and types of data included. Some unpublished sources are noted.   Z5784.M9G42

Gray, John. Blacks in film and television : a Pan-African bibliography of films, filmmakers, and performers. N.Y. : Greenwood, 1990. 496 p. (Bibliographies and indexes in Afro-American and African studies, no. 27).   **BH165**

Lists about 6,000 sources, more than half concerned with individual American filmmakers, actors, and actresses. Includes books, dissertations, periodical and newspaper articles, films, videotapes, audiotapes, and archival material relating to Africa, Europe, the Caribbean, and Latin America, in addition to the U.S. For Africa, identifies material on "colonial and ethnographic film activity as well as works on indigenous African films and filmmaking" (*Introd*), but excludes television. U.S. section also cites references on the image of African Americans in film and television. Appendix for film resources (archives and research centers, societies and associations, production companies, distributors, and festivals). Artist, film/series title, subject, and author indexes. Based largely on research collections of the New York Public Library.   Z5784.M9G72

Hecht, Hermann. Pre-cinema history : an encyclopaedia and annotated bibliography of the moving image before 1896 / Hermann Hecht ; ed. by Ann Hecht. London : Bowker Saur, c1993. 476 p. : ill.   **BH166**

A scholarly survey of the literature on precursors of modern film projection. Cites more than 1,000 books, scientific monographs, journal articles, manuscripts, etc., arranged by date from the 14th century to 1986. Covers camera obscura, magic lanterns, stereoscopic projection, and other forms of optical entertainment. Detailed bibliographic data for each item, with exceptionally full critical abstracts for most. Name and subject indexes.   TR848.H38

Manchel, Frank. Film study : an analytical bibliography. Rutherford, [N.J.] : Fairleigh Dickinson Univ. Pr. ; London : Associated Univ. Pr., c1990. 4 v.   **BH167**

A revision and reworking of the author's *Film study : a resource guide* (Rutherford, N.J. : Fairleigh Dickinson Univ. Pr., 1973).

A complex set, combining elements of a research guide, textbook, and bibliographic handbook. Organized around broad concepts (e.g., film technique and criticism, genre study, stereotyping in film, themes, film history), with many subsections, the first three volumes consist of extensively footnoted essays accompanied by annotated lists of English-language books and representative films. In all, provides critical analyses of about 2,000 books, often at review length. Vol. 4 contains: glossary; appendixes of periodicals, distributors, production codes, archives and libraries, bookstores, publishers, etc.; and indexes of authors, titles, personalities, subjects, and films. Despite the intricate arrangement and a small, poorly registered typeface, a useful survey of film literature in English.   Z5784.M9M34

Fig. 16. A page from *Guide to Reference Books.* Source: Robert Balay, ed. *Guide to Reference Books,* 11th ed. Chicago: American Library Association, 1996.

A **biographical reference book** will be helpful in finding out about persons mentioned in your research or about the author of material on your subject. *Who's Who in America, American Men and Women of Science, Contemporary Authors, Dictionary of National Biography* (usually referred to as DNB), and other volumes will give you dates of birth and death, nationality, and information about occupations. *The New York Times Bibliographical Service* is also helpful. The *Biography and Genealogy Master Index* lists 350 current and retrospective indexes and is much used for biographical research.

To write a preliminary citation from a reference book or a bibliography, identify the entry in which you expect to find information helpful to your research paper. You will then have to look at that source to be sure there really is information in it that you can use in your paper. If you suspect there is, even on the basis of the title, write a preliminary bibliography card with the standard three units on it: author name, item title, and publication information.

Handbooks

A book of concisely stated information and usually small enough to be held in a person's hand is called, unsurprisingly, a "handbook." It contains common information and usually provides a quick reference to more detailed sources. For instance, the subtitle of *The Whole Library Handbook* (compiled by George M. Eberhart [Chicago: American Library Association, 1991]) gives a good idea of the scope of this book: "Current Data, Professional Advice, and Curiosa about Libraries and Library Services."

Many students enrolled in composition courses are familiar with writing handbooks, one of which is often assigned as a text. *A Handbook and Charting Manual for Student Nurses, A Handbook for Citizens Living Abroad, Handbook for Electronic Circuit Design, Handbook for Parents of Children with Learning Disabilities,* and the *Handbook for Space Travelers* are just a few of the many subjects of handbooks. They are cataloged and shelved by subject.

Indexes

Some indexes are limited to a **specific subject so you can locate titles of works you want to read;** others detail the **contents of a medium, such as magazines, journals, or newspapers.** With a little practice, you will probably be able to figure out the information an index gives you. However, each index will have in it a sample entry explication or illustration to show how to "decipher" its contents.

Subject Indexes

Subject indexes focus on specific kinds of information. For example, if you are doing research about essays and other writings within longer works, you could consult the *Essay and General Literature Index.* It lists, by subject and author, and occasionally by title under catchwords or significant phrases, material you can't find in book titles alone. In addition to a person's works, it lists secondary sources about a person's life or work and published criticism of an individual work. At the end of that index is a list of publishers and dates of the books shown in the many entries, providing an additional aid in locating what you want to consult.

People writing about literature often use *Poetry Explication* as a resource. It is an index containing explications of individual poems and criticism of them that appeared in books and periodicals. *Granger's Index to Poetry and Recitations* is another source you might consult if you are working with poetry. *20th Century Short Story Explication* and the *Short Story Index* are addtional sources; their titles make the contents evident.

If your subject falls within the area of the social sciences, you could look at the *Social Sciences Index*. (See Figure 17; Figure 18 shows a preliminary bibliography card created from an entry.) In addition to the article titles shown under subject headings, additional headings are suggested in the "See also" listings.

For the titles of other indexes that yield helpful information and are available in many libraries, see Appendix A. Such standards as *Business Periodicals Index*, *Biological Abstracts (Biosis)*, and *Applied Science and Technology* are among the many indexes available in print volumes as well as in computer databases.

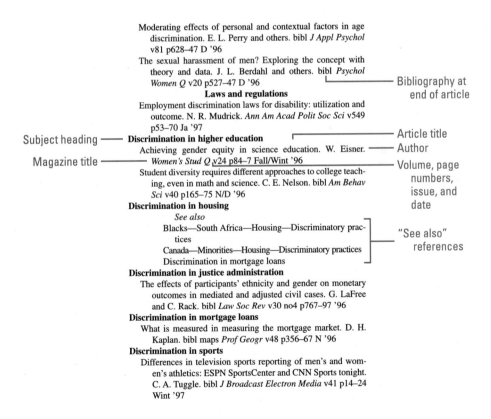

Fig. 17. Part of a page from the *Social Sciences Index*, and explanation of how to read an entry. Source: *Social Sciences Index*, v. 24 #1. June 1997: 170.

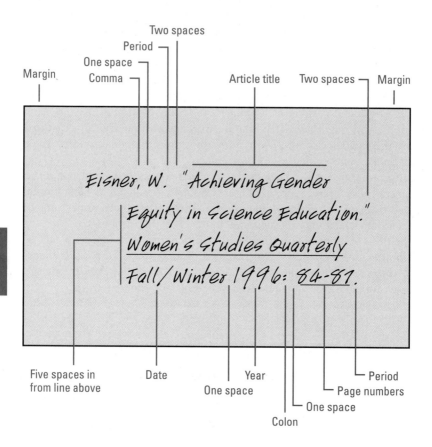

Fig. 18. Preliminary citation card for one item listed in the *Social Sciences Index* excerpt in Fig. 17.

Periodical Indexes

Any publication that appears at regular intervals (daily, weekly, monthly, semiannually) is called a *periodical*. General-interest magazines, trade papers, academic journals, newspapers, and special-interest magazines (such as *AOPA Pilot, Advertising Age,* and *American Indian Art Magazine*) are periodicals, and thus articles published in them will be listed in one or more periodical indexes.

Printed lists of the thousands of articles published each month are still available in bound volumes of such familiar publications as *Readers' Guide to Periodical Literature, Education Index,* and *The New York Times Index.* However, such information is increasingly becoming available through electronic delivery systems such as the convenient-to-use *InfoTrac,* a constantly updated CD-ROM system that most libraries subscribe to.

Because periodicals are published at least several times a year, you will find more current information in them than you will in books, which are often years in the writing and which usually take a year from manuscript completion to publication. Also, you will find a wider variety of information in periodicals, because each issue includes the thinking of several authors.

The entries in periodical indexes may vary from one another, but in the front of each issue of such an index you will find a list of periodicals represented in it, a key to the abbreviations used for titles and other information, and other details about the entries. Despite some differences, most follow similar conventions that are listed next, together with what they mean to you in preparing your preliminary citation cards.

Galston, William A., and David Wasserman
"Gambling Away Our Moral Capital." The Public Interest Spring 1996: 58-72.

Fig. 19. A preliminary citation card for one item.

Conventions Usually Followed in Periodical Indexes

- **Subjects are divided and titled in as many categories as the compilers of that index believe will be helpful in locating information easily.** Look under several headings to find all the material you can use on your chosen subject.

- **The names of authors are usually recorded by surname and initials.** Record them that way on a preliminary citation card, but be sure to change the names on the card to reflect the way the individuals actually use their names; you will want *complete names* should you need this card for a Works Cited listing.

- **Titles are not enclosed within quotation marks, nor is each word capitalized.** Remember, however, that when *you* write the title of an article on a preliminary citation card (and in a Works Cited list) *it must be enclosed within quotation marks* and *the first letter of each word is capitalized* (except for articles, prepositions, and conjunctions).

- **Abbreviations in the entry will show whether the piece is abridged, condensed, or illustrated or includes maps or diagrams.** Since such information is *not* entered in a Works Cited list, there is no need to put it on a preliminary citation card.

- **The title of the periodical in which a piece appears is usually abbreviated and isn't underlined, though it may be italicized.** Remember, however, to *underline the complete title of the periodical* on your preliminary citation card. If you're not sure of the actual name of the publication, check the abbreviation listing, usually at the beginning of the index you are using.

- **The volume number of each periodical precedes a colon in its entry.** Record the volume number in the preliminary citation entry only if the publication has continuous pagination, as explained on page 69. (However, you may want to note the volume number in the lower right corner of the preliminary citation card, because in some microfilm collections the drawers holding the film rolls are labeled by volume number.)

- **All page numbers on which an article appears will be shown in an entry.** However, record them according to the convention shown on pages 70–71: two sets of numbers separated by a hyphen if the article is on successive pages or one number and a plus sign if the article is not on successive pages.

- **Publication dates** are often shown in one- or two-letter abbreviations. You must record them on the preliminary citation card with the conventional abbreviations (three letters, except for Sept.) but spelled out for May, June, and July.

Magazine Indexes

Magazine indexes still appear in familiar volume formats, but increasingly are seen in libraries as computer databases, which are detailed in the next major section, "Finding and Citing Electronic Resources."

Probably the most familiar of all magazine indexes is the *Readers' Guide to Periodical Literature*, in publication since 1900. (See Figure 20.) It indexes, by subject and author, articles appearing in more than one hundred general magazines, some of them on scientific subjects, and has a separate author listing for book reviews. Twenty-one issues of the *Readers' Guide* are published every year, monthly in February, July, and August, but semimonthly the rest of the year. These issues are put into cumulative form quarterly and annually.

Be aware that many academicians consider the *Readers' Guide* inappropriate for any but the most superficial and general research material. Consult it if you think information on your selected subject is available in it and may be useful. But instead of depending entirely on it, consider it just one of many indexes in which you can find sources of information for your research paper.

Journal Indexes

Journals are usually published less frequently than mass audience magazines and are directed to narrow interests, often particular professions or academic disciplines. Their circulations are thus smaller than those of magazines, but people read them for more specific information and often for reports of research in that discipline. *The Negro Educational Review, Foreign Affairs,* and *Signs (The Journal*

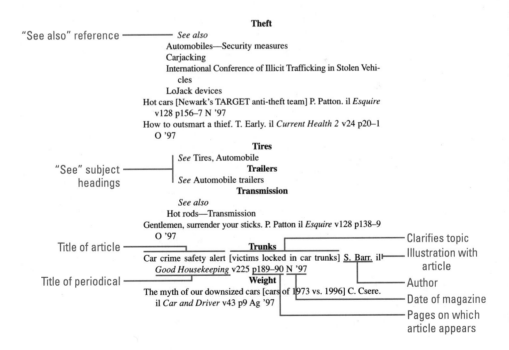

Fig. 20. Part of a page from the *Readers' Guide to Periodical Literature*, and explanation of how to read an entry. Source: Feb. 1998: 69.

of Women in Culture and Society) are examples of journals. Many journals are the publications of organizations in special subject areas, as are *College Composition and Communication* (the journal of the Conference on College Composition and Communication) and *The Journal of Southern History* (the publication of the Southern Historical Association).

The contents of specialized and technical periodicals, including scholarly journals, appear in many indexes. The variety of their titles will give you some idea: *Education Index, Business Periodicals Index, Cumulative Index to Nursing and Allied Health Literature, Applied Science and Technology Index,* and *Book Review Digest.*

The *Social Sciences Index* and the *Humanities Index* (formerly published together and at one time called the *International Guide to Periodicals* and later by the cumbersome title *A Guide to Periodical Literature in the Social Sciences and the Humanities)*—which you may have to consult in your information search—are good sources for articles in foreign magazines and in a variety of specific and scholarly publications.

The *General Sciences Index* is one of the newest indexes, containing articles published only since 1978. However, since it indexes about one hundred journals in the basic sciences (physics, biology, paleontology, and more), you should consider consulting it if your research subject is in the natural sciences.

To find the titles of periodicals related to your research subject, you will be interested in looking at *Magazines for Libraries* (3rd ed., edited by Bill Katz and Barry C. Richards). There, labeled by subject, you will find an annotated list of 6,500 periodicals selected from 65,000 titles! To find out where the contents of each periodical is listed, consult *Ulrich's International Periodicals Directory.* Also, see the titles of other periodical indexes listed under the subject headings in Appendix A.

Newspaper Indexes

Newspaper indexes (both print-on-paper and electronic delivery) are your richest source for current events and other newsworthy information that never appears in other kinds of periodicals. Chief among newspaper indexes is *The New York Times Index.* It differs from most other indexes in that it contains abstracts of news articles, editorials, and features. It also gives an indication of article lengths, as well as the date, section, page, and column of an article in addition to cross-references to related articles. Figure 21 shows how to understand this index, and Figure 22 illustrates how to write a preliminary citation card for an article. So many libraries have copies of this newspaper on microfilm that if you get a preliminary citation from this index, chances are you will be able to find the precise reference when you're ready to read it and take notes.

Many other well-known newspapers in this country are indexed, especially for issues since the 1970s, and copies of the papers are often available on microfilm in libraries. Among them are the *Index to the Chicago Tribune, Index to the Los Angeles Times, Index to the San Francisco Chronicle, Index to the Washington Post,* and (since 1949) *Index to the Christian Science Monitor.* Indexes to foreign

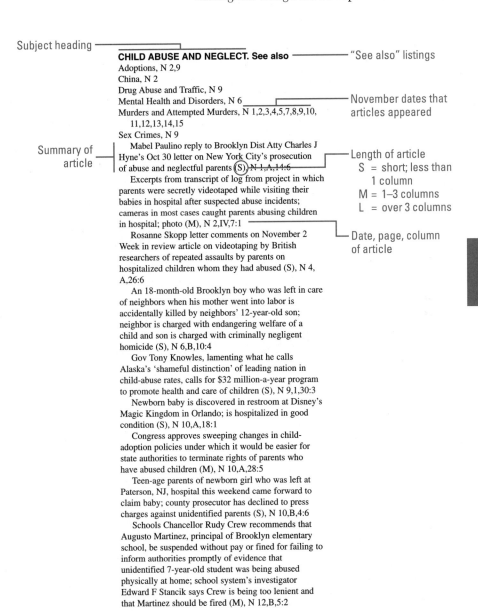

Subject heading

CHILD ABUSE AND NEGLECT. See also — "See also" listings
Adoptions, N 2,9
China, N 2
Drug Abuse and Traffic, N 9
Mental Health and Disorders, N 6 — November dates that
Murders and Attempted Murders, N 1,2,3,4,5,7,8,9,10,   articles appeared
    11,12,13,14,15
Sex Crimes, N 9

Summary of
article
    Mabel Paulino reply to Brooklyn Dist Atty Charles J
Hyne's Oct 30 letter on New York City's prosecution — Length of article
of abuse and neglectful parents (S), N 1,A,14:6   S = short; less than
                                                          1 column
    Excerpts from transcript of log from project in which   M = 1–3 columns
parents were secretly videotaped while visiting their   L = over 3 columns
babies in hospital after suspected abuse incidents;
cameras in most cases caught parents abusing children
in hospital; photo (M), N 2,IV,7:1 — Date, page, column
    Rosanne Skopp letter comments on November 2   of article
Week in review article on videotaping by British
researchers of repeated assaults by parents on
hospitalized children whom they had abused (S), N 4,
A,26:6
    An 18-month-old Brooklyn boy who was left in care
of neighbors when his mother went into labor is
accidentally killed by neighbors' 12-year-old son;
neighbor is charged with endangering welfare of a
child and son is charged with criminally negligent
homicide (S), N 6,B,10:4
    Gov Tony Knowles, lamenting what he calls
Alaska's 'shameful distinction' of leading nation in
child-abuse rates, calls for $32 million-a-year program
to promote health and care of children (S), N 9,1,30:3
    Newborn baby is discovered in restroom at Disney's
Magic Kingdom in Orlando; is hospitalized in good
condition (S), N 10,A,18:1
    Congress approves sweeping changes in child-
adoption policies under which it would be easier for
state authorities to terminate rights of parents who
have abused children (M), N 10,A,28:5
    Teen-age parents of newborn girl who was left at
Paterson, NJ, hospital this weekend came forward to
claim baby; county prosecutor has declined to press
charges against unidentified parents (S), N 10,B,4:6
    Schools Chancellor Rudy Crew recommends that
Augusto Martinez, principal of Brooklyn elementary
school, be suspended without pay or fined for failing to
inform authorities promptly of evidence that
unidentified 7-year-old student was being abused
physically at home; school system's investigator
Edward F Stancik says Crew is being too lenient and
that Martinez should be fired (M), N 12,B,5:2

Fig. 21. Part of a page from *The New York Times Index,* and an explanation of how to read
an entry. Source: *New York Times Index.* 1–15 Nov., 1997: 21.

papers, such as *The Times* [of London] *Official Index,* are also available in many
libraries, and you may have occasion to consult them. And if your research subject
has anything to do with business, you ought to look at the *Index to the Wall Street
Journal.*

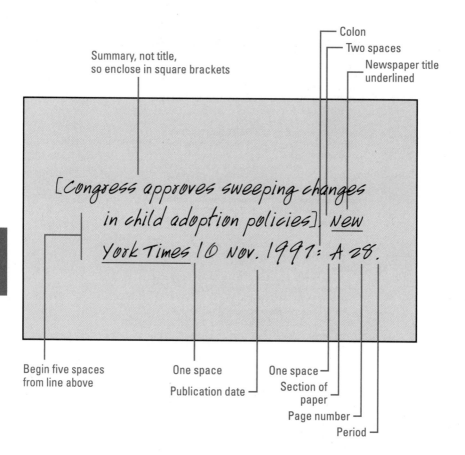

Summary, not title,
so enclose in square brackets

Colon

Two spaces

Newspaper title
underlined

[Congress approves sweeping changes in child adoption policies]. New York Times 10 Nov. 1997: A 28.

Begin five spaces
from line above

One space

Publication date

One space

Section of
paper

Page number

Period

Fig. 22. Example of a preliminary citation card written from a *New York Times Index* listing. Note that neither an author nor an article title is possible; they must be added later if the source is used.

Facts on File, published weekly, is a world news digest that will give more information; it also has a cumulative index.

If you're looking for local coverage of a news event, you may want to use *The Gale Directory of Publications* (formerly *Ayer's*) to locate a newspaper you might not otherwise know exists. This index is geographically organized and gives information about daily and weekly newspapers as well as about consumer, business, technical, trade, professional, and farm magazines.

When you write a **preliminary citation card for a newspaper article,** look for clues about the edition and section of the paper in which it appeared. Although you may not be able to find such information until you search out the article itself, do record it at that time on your card, for it should be included in the final Works Cited entry for a newspaper article.

To write a preliminary citation card from a periodical index entry, use the appropriate form as described on pages 80–81 (for magazines), pages 81–82 (for journals), or pages 82–84 (for newspapers).

Government Publications

These are a rich source of information, because the government is the country's leading publisher. Besides all sorts of free pamphlets you can send for (and which are often advertised on radio or television), many libraries regularly receive copies of the *Congressional Record,* the official daily report of proceedings of open sessions of Congress. The *Congressional Quarterly,* issued weekly and as an almanac, is a reliable news source for a summary of congressional activities. That publication also prints weekly *Editorial Research Reports,* a publication helpful if you are looking for sources of information on an issue of current national significance.

What you want to look for among the millions of government publications depends on your research subject. For some, you may seek documents that originated one or a hundred years ago. Other subjects on which you want information may be ongoing or very recent. If you have access to a home or library computer, you would do well to get an overview of what's available from the Government Printing Office (GPO), publisher for the U.S. government. Its Web site is <*www.access.gpo.gov*> (see Figure 23). For example, one student looking for specific information about the supposed alien landing at Roswell, NM, began by getting a copy of the Freedom of Information Act, conveniently printed out for him on his computer as a result of asking for it at the GPO site; from it he also learned the most likely source to ask for material on his specific interest.

The National Archives and Records Administration may also have something useful for you. Inquire by mail to Washington, DC. If you live in or near Boston, New York, Philadelphia, Atlanta, Chicago, Kansas City, Fort Worth, Denver, Los Angeles, San Francisco, or Seattle, you can visit one of the National Archives field branches. Lists of publications and ordering information are readily available, and some public libraries hold microfilmed copies of records from the National Archives. There are now also many presidential libraries that hold documents from that person's time in public office; one may be accessible to you.

Identify one of the approximately 1,400 libraries (many at universities) designated as a "depository library" for government documents by getting an address of one near you through the GPO home page. Congressional Information Services publishes indexes of bills, reports, documents, treaties, executive reports, publications, and public laws. So many items are available that documenting them can be difficult. But don't give up! There is help about how to document these riches in the *MLA Handbook, MLA Style Manual,* and in the *Publication Manual of the APA.*

In addition to what is available on the GPO Web site, the *Monthly Catalog of United States Government Publications* gives titles and prices of all publications available from government agencies. Since you are only looking for sources of information at this point in the process, you will find in it subject, title, and author information or indexes that are potentially useful. Many items listed in the catalog

Keeping America Informed
UNITED STATES GOVERNMENT PRINTING OFFICE

About the Government Printing Office

What's New Page

Access to Government Information Products

Services Available to Federal Agencies

Business and Contracting Opportunities

Employment Opportunities

Establishing Links to Documents in GPO WAIS Databases

Navigation Aids and FAQ's

Access to Government Information Products
    Superintendent of Documents
            What Is GPO Access?
            Search Databases
            New/Noteworthy Products from GPO
            Find Government Information
            Browse Federal Bulletin Board Files
            Find Products for Sale by GPO
            Government Information at a Library Near You
    Agency for Health Care Policy and Research
    Commission on the Roles and Capabilities of the United States Intelligence Community
    Bureau of Land Management (Colorado Office)
    Congress of the United States
    Department of Interior Office of Inspector General
    Executive Office of the President
            Council of Economic Advisers
            Office of Management and Budget
    Federal Labor Relations Authority
    Food and Drug Administration

Fig. 23. Example of what is available at the GPO (Government Printing Office) Web site.

may already be in the library you are using for research; others may be available via an electronic source, or, if you have time, you can send for them.

Other Sources of Print Information

Because there are such varied sources included in this category, different formats are required, especially for the "publication information" unit of a preliminary citation card. Look at the examples in Chapter 9 for models to follow.

1. **Reports, pamphlets, booklets, charts, maps, and other materials published by corporations, agencies, and professional organizations** may be

good sources of information for your particular research that many libraries either don't know about or couldn't catalog and store if they obtained it. For example, you might write to auto manufacturerers if you are researching auto safety or to an organization such as Habitat for Humanity if you are looking for information on low-cost housing. Annual reports of various companies are usually sent free on request, and it's instructive to "read between the lines" of this material, which obviously seeks to present only positives about its source. Be on the lookout for free offers of information, and send for what seems relevant. You may not be able to write a preliminary citation card for this sort of resource unless you know a title you seek or until the material arrives.

2. **Specialized library collections in museums, historical societies, legal or medical or engineering groups, and others** are available in many cities. Find out if any are located near you; if your subject is one that lends itself to those available, take advantage of them. Create your preliminary citation cards based on indexes and catalogs (whether cards in drawers or online in that library) that you find when you visit such collections.

3. **Letters from an individual or an organization** that are not otherwise cataloged can give you certain information you want for your research paper—provided you initiate such correspondence early enough to receive a reply. Send a brief letter containing specific questions. (Sending your request by e-mail may help, if you direct it to the proper person or job description.) You won't always receive a quick reply, but you may be pleasantly surprised at how many busy or well-known people are willing to take time to write to a student working on a well-defined school project. Also, you stand a better chance of a response if you address a particular person within an organization by name or, at least, by title. A librarian can help you locate the name and address of the person you should write to.

   Work on the assumption that you will hear from whomever you have written to, and make a preliminary citation card containing any information you have to start with.

4. ***Public Affairs Information Service*** (PAIS) ***International in Print*** (a result of the 1990 merger of the *PAIS Bulletin* and its *Foreign Language* arm) gives a brief summary of articles it lists from 1,400 periodicals as well as from government documents. The service is also available on CD-ROM in many libraries. Thus, PAIS is obviously a good source to search for preliminary citations you can later follow up on to see if the contents may be helpful to you.

Microforms

Once the photographed miniaturization of bulky or extensive collections of library materials became possible, storage capacities were instantly expanded and thus research students gained access to more documents than ever before. Known by the general designation of "microforms," they include microfilm and microfiche, each of which requires a different kind of hardware to enlarge the contents sufficiently to read. (Many of these machines can also provide you with photocopies of the materials.)

Microforms are usually cataloged with print-on-paper resources, for they are actually a variation of the print medium. Some newspapers, for instance, have for many years regularly been preserved on microfilm, and such ephemeral materials as individual studies and reports accessed into the ERIC (Educational Resources Information Center) system are immediately put onto microfiche, which libraries purchase if they so desire.

Write a ***preliminary citation card for microform material*** by using the appropriate information for the medium followed by the title (underlined) of the source in which the microform material is listed, the year of publication in parentheses, and the item's accession number. See Figure 24.

FINDING AND CITING ELECTRONIC RESOURCES

The Internet, Web sites, search engines, e-mail, newsgroups, bulletin boards—the terminology is probably familiar to anyone who owns or often uses a computer. Increasingly, also, you will probably find references to such computer sources in textbooks, such as the one in Figure 8 of Chapter 2.

Because books are already available detailing the research use of many of these sources, particularly the Internet and Web sites, no attempt is made here to give detailed information on accessing all of them. Besides, the number of such sources is increasing so fast that no sooner might a paragraph be written about one than it would be obsolete—or need to be expanded to several paragraphs. Rather, here is a brief overview of some of these research sources, along with mention of how to write preliminary citation cards from what you find on them.

Freud, Robert. "Community Colleges
and the Virtual Community."
ERIC, June 1996. 1 Fiche;
16. ED391871.

Fig. 24. Preliminary citation card for microform material.

Computer Connections

Some electronically transmitted sources of information are accessible only through a library, and some of them are not free. However, many of those noted in this section are readily available via most computers and a sufficiently fast modem. The capacity and speed of most up-to-date hardware change often, as does much of the content of sources described here.

Because changes are easier to make in many electronic sources than in print-on-paper resources, and because they are often unannounced, consider treating these electronic resources somewhat differently from those in other media. In addition to preparing preliminary citation cards for your research, get hard-copy printouts of these resource listings as you search through them. Increasingly, full texts are available on the computer, rather than annotations and summaries, so it's advisable to download copies of likely-looking sources to ensure that you will have them readily available should you need them later in writing your paper. (Also, items you can find on the computer are likely to change frequently, and it would be a shame to locate something you think will be useful, only to find after a lapse of time that it is no longer available where you thought it was.

Research for the sample research paper at the end of Chapter 10 was done partly through a specialized CD-ROM database ("Aquatic Biology, Aquaculture and Fisheries" because its very specific scientific article titles identified print re-sources that the library might have in full) and partly through a home computer (using search engines that identified and then downloaded selected files).

Author names and titles are in the same positions as on other preliminary bibliography cards. However, what is generally called "publication information" is variable, depending on the resource: online database, CD-ROM, bulletin board, among others. Include in a citation all relevant information you can find; consult the sample citations in Chapter 9 for models to use for preliminary citation cards.

Online Catalogs for Books

Increasingly, libraries have transferred their lists of holdings to online (that is, computer) catalogs, though some still maintain all or part of their catalogs on cards in banks of long drawers (occasionally also with the warning that these files haven't been updated since a certain date). Audiovisual or government document holdings in a library may be shown in online catalogs or by actual cards. Printed catalogs are also sometimes in use; they are bound volumes in which pages show reproductions of cards that would otherwise be in the more traditional drawers.

One of the wonders of an online catalog is that you can get information from places you cannot readily visit. For instance, a person using any community college library in Florida can also access the holdings of the other community colleges as well as the university system libraries in the state. And using the online catalog of one city or county library enables you to find out about holdings in other public libraries in the community or even beyond. Links will access information from a surprising number of additional sources.

Instructions about how to search for information in an online catalog are usually either near the library computer through which you access the information or, in printed form, very close to it. If in doubt about any aspect of making an online search, ask a librarian for assistance.

On a home (or other nonlibrary-located) computer, you can access a variety of search engines to browse the online catalogs of a number of university libraries around the country. If you have enough time then, a school or community interlibrary loan may allow you to have important books sent to your local library for your own use, though probably just knowing whether certain titles exist is about the best use you can make of this service.

Each book in a library collection is listed in its catalog, so you should search it and make preliminary citation cards on the basis of titles you find there. An online catalog lets you search for information by author, title, or subject. Fiction books have only title and author entries. Story titles within a book of collected stories may be recorded separately as well as in the book listing. Nonfiction books may have additional listings by alternate subjects, that is, "See" or "See also" subjects or links.

The Internet

The amount of information floating around in cyberspace is beyond belief, both as digitized text and as visual image. This information is brought into your computer by means of a modem and a "provider" to capture them. Schools and libraries usually have a provider available to their users. There are also many, many commercial providers, ranging from such nationally known ones as America Online and CompuServe to locally owned and operated ones. Users are charged by providers, but competition and accessibility have led to relatively low costs and to flat, monthly rates rather than hourly charges. Still, many rates are on the rise.

In order to find research information on the Internet, you also need a program called a "browser" that must be installed on the computer you are using for the research. Then, seemingly unlimited sources are available, either through the World Wide Web or by contacting an Internet "search engine" and requesting that it locate the desired information.

Web sites have an enormous number of "addresses" you can call up by typing in an appropriate URL (uniform resource locator); these combinations of letters, numbers, and symbols are announced on television programs; printed in many places, such as books, articles, and ads; and listed in directories available for purchase or for reference in libraries. Many such sites are managed by individuals in pursuit of special interests, but others are outright commercials. Some Web sites, such as <*www.NewYorkTimes.com*>, send material to your computer that has been previously printed; others, such as <*4adventure.com/Seaworld/frame.html*>, are designed solely for computer users. The quality of Web sites, from the personal to the commercial and professional, varies greatly, so always take into account what you are working with.

A particularly useful characteristic of many Web sites is their built-in links, which are similar to "See also" locations in many reference books. Therefore, in finding one reference location, you may actually be finding many more!

The OCLC (Online Computer Library Center), which offers services to libraries around the world, is often the first place called up on a computer by a librarian helping a student to locate information. First Search is also a popular first stop.

In lieu of starting with a single Web address to find information, you could ask a **search engine** to look for information on the specific subject you are researching. Some of the well-known search engines you may have access to are Lycos, Infoseek, Alta Vista, Gopher, and Yahoo. Especially important in using them is to make your information request as specific as possible and to try different entries to elicit the most helpful information. When Melissa Fernandez began the sample research paper in Chapter 10 by asking for information on "Dolphins," the computer gave her an impossibly long list of articles, some of which were about the football team of that name. Limiting the request to "dolphin intelligence" and then to "dolphin and Gulf War" and "dolphin and therapy" made the lists more workable and helped her to decide on a focus for the paper.

Material you find on the Internet should be handled differently from what is in print on paper and can be looked at again, for constant updating may mean changes in the resource that later results in the loss of what you want to look at. Therefore, when a search gives you a screen of bibliographic references, write out a listing of likely resources; if there are too many to make that feasible, print out a selective list. (Figure 25 shows a partial listing from the Electric Library.) Then try to pull up on-screen each likely resource, skim it to determine probable usefulness, and, if it contains anything you think you may need, make yourself a preliminary citation card and a hard copy of the material while you have it before you.

A *preliminary citation card* for articles you identify or obtain through the Internet follows the same format as other electronically accessed information. (See Figure 26.) After the author, title, and publication information, as appropriate, underline the title of the database you used, note that you obtained the material online, and show the name of the resource or computer service you used (such as Alta Vista or Electric Library) and the date on which you discovered the information.

Computer Databases

A *database* is a collection of records about a particular subject that is brought together and organized for easy access. Some have never been recorded in a print location, but most are electronic organizations of printed materials that can be searched infinitely faster and more effectively than any human could manage. Many are organized for researching specific subjects. The *Gale Directory of Databases* is helpful in locating those that might be fruitful in your search for specific kinds of information

Typically, a vendor collects, reports, and organizes information from thousands of journals, ranging from agriculture to zoology. Once the information is identified for your needs, either by title or by annotation (occasionally by the complete article), printouts are then available. Some vendors, such as Dialog (which carries

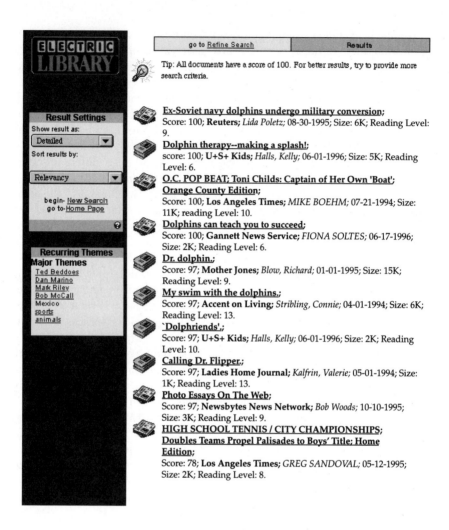

Fig. 25. Part of a listing from the Electric Library.

information from more than 450 databases), are fee-based and thus are most effectively used with the aid of a librarian, who can help you focus the search.

Not only libraries subscribe to databases, so do student clubs and dormitory groups, as well as business and professional people and some individuals who want to access the databases directly from home or office. For example, Knowledge Index is a service of Dialog that offers low-cost access to more than 17 million summaries during evenings and weekends, when most Dialog subscribers are not calling on its facilities and when telephone rates (for transmission) are lower.

Besides the author and title of the material, a ***preliminary citation card*** should include the title of the database (underlined), the date of publication, the name of the vendor (if available), and the date of electronic publication. If the title

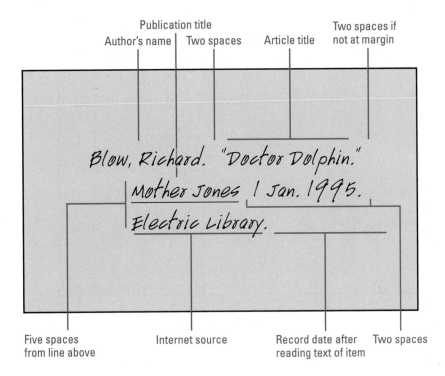

Fig. 26. Preliminary citation card for material accessed through the Internet.

and original publication date are available, show them also. Figure 26 shows a preliminary citation card written on the basis of a database search for the sample research paper in Chapter 10.

CD-ROMs

Because a CD (such as the familiar-looking ones for music) can hold enormous amounts of information on small-diameter discs, inevitably they began to be used to store research information. (ROM means "read-only memory," so changes to individual discs can't be made by their users.) See Figure 27.

Two kinds of CD-ROMs are available in many libraries. One is the full text of a single title that you might otherwise consult in print-on-paper form. Among these titles are *Academic American Encyclopedia* (all twenty-one volumes, including bibliographies and more than a thousand illutrations) and the *Oxford English Dictionary*. The second kind of CD-ROM contains information that also (or otherwise) is available on the Internet.

Although most CD-ROMs are set up at permanent stations in a library and are usually 12 inches in diameter, many current home computers include a drive to play the 4½-inch disc size, and people often purchase these single-topic discs; some libraries also make them available to users and include information about

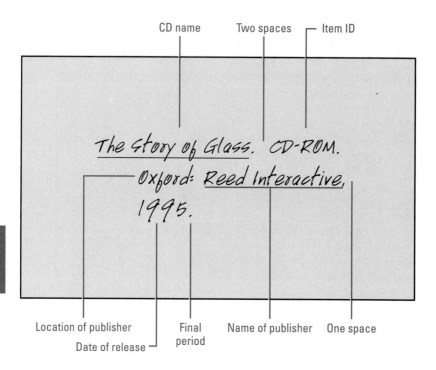

Fig. 27. Preliminary citation card for material found on a CD-ROM.

them in their regular catalogs (just as they do for audiotapes and videotapes). Be on the lookout for them, provided you have the hardware to use them.

InfoTrac® is a popular library-use CD-ROM, a database of materials subscribed to by many libraries and available without charge to its users; an updated disk is sent monthly to subscribers. Several versions of this database are available, and the subscriber can choose what is most applicable to its purposes, whether a large or a small academic or public library, including, in some cases, selected information in Spanish as well as English. As an example of the range of this library product, the library in which you are working may include "Academic ASAP" in its subscription, and that alone indexes 500 academic and general-interest journals ranging from *ABA* to *Zygor,* as well as the full texts of 250 titles plus a portion of the *New York Times Index.*

Another popular CD-ROM that librarians consult and that is usually available for direct student use is SIRS Researcher, which covers 1,200 domestic and international newspapers, magazines, journals, and government documents from 1988 forward.

Wilsondisc, from the well-known library supplier Wilson Company, a reference organization, makes available on CD-ROM many of its reference works formerly available only in bound volumes of print. Thus, the library at which you do research may have CD-ROM of the *Humanities Index,* the *Social Sciences Index,* the *Business Periodicals Index,* and *Readers' Guide Abstracts.* In addition to bibliographic citations, many CD-ROMs of familiar print-based reference works contain everything from abstracts to full texts. Examples are *Granger's Poetry Index* (more than 90,000 poetry citations and 8,000 full poems) and *Medline* (with abstracts as well as citations from major medical journals).

Clearly, you should never be satisfied with an abstract alone and should always try to find the complete text it is taken from. Under most circumstances, discard any preliminary citation card for which you can't find the original text, no matter how promising the abstract sounds.

Preliminary citation cards for material accessed from a CD-ROM begin, as usual, with author and title. If the material comes from a print source, give the usual publication information, but then give the title of the database, underlined, and note that you used a CD-ROM; follow that by the name of the vendor and the publication date of the item you used. (See Figure 28.) If the material doesn't also come in printed form, give the title in quotation marks and its date. Follow that by the database title, medium (CD-ROM), vendor's name, and electronic publication date. Use the examples in Chapter 9 as guides, and include whatever information is available.

Electronic Journals and Newsletters

As the costs of publishing and mailing materials rise, especially those on which the academic research community depends, many organizations and publishers have been exploring and then moving to "electronic publishing." When sent out

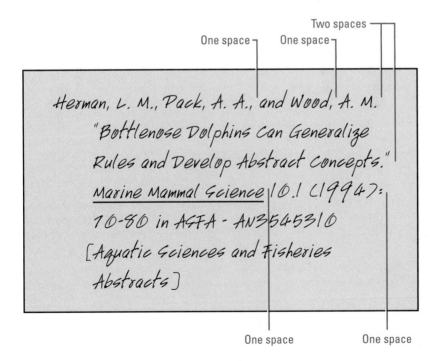

Two spaces
One space   One space

Herman, L. M., Pack, A. A., and Wood, A. M.
    "Bottlenose Dolphins Can Generalize
    Rules and Develop Abstract Concepts."
    Marine Mammal Science 10.1 (1994):
    10-80 in ASFA - AN3545310
    [Aquatic Sciences and Fisheries
    Abstracts]

One space   One space

Fig. 28. Preliminary citation card written on the basis of a database search for the sample research paper in Chapter 10.

over existing electronic pathways, this becomes an increasingly popular and necessary alternative to more traditional modes—faster to disseminate, too. Find out what is available in this electronic form by consulting the latest edition of *Directory of Electronic Journals, Newsletters, and Academic Discussion Lists* (available only in hard cover and thus not at all libraries) or by inquiring of librarians, especially those in specific discipline library collections. The Committee on Institutional Cooperation of the Association of Research Librarians has many computer-based products for member university libraries, including an Electronic Journals Collection list.

A ***preliminary citation card*** for resources thus obtained uses the author and title in usual form, the title of the journal or newsletter (underlined), and then other traditional information, plus the publication medium, the name of the computer network, and the date you accessed the information. See the model in Figure 29 below.

On that preliminary citation card, in addition to the more usual print periodical information, it is prudent to add a fourth unit acknowledging where you obtained this information, in case you should have to check back on it. As Figure 29 shows, allow two spaces after the end of the publication unit, then record the name of the database service where you found the citation, the file number you consulted, and the item number (ending with a period, of course). This final information will be needed only if the source is ultimately used in the Works Cited list of the research paper.

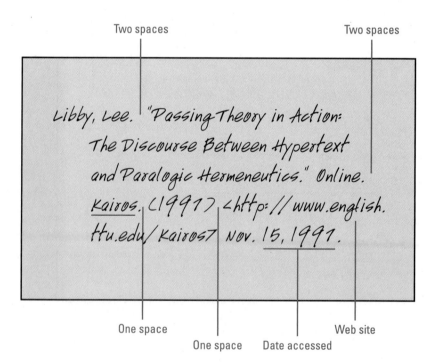

Fig. 29. Preliminary citation card for material obtained through an online journal.

Discussion Groups, Chat Lines, and Bulletin Boards

To look at the lists of discussion groups (or chat lines) and bulletin boards available on the Internet is to be completely overwhelmed by how many interests people have! Basically, all such groups allow anybody who so wishes to read a series of messages on a single subject—sometimes also following "strands" or subsubjects—and to respond at will by sending a message from one computer to those in the group. The more popular of these groups receive a great deal of use, with messages flying back and forth as postings to all or from individual to individual as friends are made on the basis of shared interests. The high level of expertise among these discussion group participants can sometimes be astonishing.

Some groups are a kind of free-for-all, and you may find such sites clogged with messages from many months ago. Others are monitored by an individual who assumes responsibility for keeping messages from piling up or who otherwise exercises some mild form of control.

These are probably some of the more interesting sources of electronically transmitted information that you can find on your research subject. However, be aware that what you find is likely to be of uneven quality and may not be accepted by a research paper reader with rigorous standards for content.

FINDING AND CITING NONPRINT RESOURCES

So much of your learning is through what you hear and see (apart from words) that you should certainly seek information from those sources we take for granted every day: television, radio, films, person-to-person speaking, and more. Besides, if you ever have occasion to do research in your vocation, you will quickly discover that using print or even electronically disseminated sources may not be enough. You may have to interview people, watch a traffic flow, or otherwise rely on information that isn't written out or even stored somewhere.

Public and academic libraries increasingly have videotapes and audiotapes available for loan. Schools invariably have media collections or media centers where such materials are housed and perhaps cataloged. Or they may be cataloged together with a library's print holdings. Often, library or media specialists can order special materials for your use from other collections or even from outside sources.

The extent to which such information sources are useful to you depends on the subject you're researching. In this section you will be reminded of many such sources—including such prosaic ones as your own radio and television—and read about how to make preliminary citation cards for the various nonprint media. Models for citing media not detailed here are presented in Chapter 9.

Three Units of Information in a Nonprint Preliminary Citation

Preliminary citation cards for nonprint sources carry the same three units of information as do other resources and in the same order: author, title, and publication information. However, there are likely to be many differences, due to the variety of mediums accessed.

Begin an entry with what is most important about that source for your research purposes. It may be an author (or composer), but it may be another element. For example, a preliminary citation for a television program is likely to begin with the title of the program or with the title of a performance. Some recordings will begin with the name of the performer, some with the name of a composer. Interviews begin with the name of the interviewee, and you must then note whether the interview was in person or over the telephone.

Publication information will be variable, depending on the medium. Pictures, if they are printed, may have the publication information of a book, pamphlet, or periodical. Yet if you refer to a painting or sculpture you saw in a museum, that location becomes part of its "publication information." Details about running time or distribution are considered "publication information" for films. Here are some other elements that are included in publication information:

- The *producer,* either a company or an individual, of a video or other nonprint resource is considered its "publisher."
- The *distributor* of a nonprint source is also noted as publication information.
- The *copyright date* may be known and recorded. If none is shown, the year of production or release is regarded as copyright date.
- *Technical information* is recorded as if it were publication details. Indicate whether the source is on video- or audiotape, is a CD or a 16-mm film, appears in black and white or color, and so on.
- *Running time,* especially for a film, is considered part of the technical information.

In the following example, for which no author is available in a film catalog and which thus can't appear on a preliminary citation card, all but the title comprise the publication information. Note that periods separate the producer and distributor (and copyright date) from the technical information.

EXAMPLE

Fastest Plane in the Sky. Nova. WGBH Collection.

   Films for the Humanities & Sciences, 1991.

   VHS 60 min. color.

There are almost as many variations in citations of nonprint sources as there are kinds of nonprint resources. Although the remainder of this chapter tells something about where to find such research sources and many mention some kinds of information to include on preliminary bibliography cards, for specific models see Chapter 9.

Radio and TV Programs

Although advance warning to tune in on a program may not be much more than a notice in that morning's newspaper, students often discover that radio and television carry a wealth of good material broadcast during a search for research paper sources. So be alert to every such possibility. And if you happen to tune into a broadcast that's useful to your study but that you didn't know about in advance, you can always write out a card that, instead of being a preliminary citation, turns out to be a Works Cited card.

A **preliminary citation card** for a radio or television program will include the title of the program, the name of the person or persons featured, and whatever production or broadcast information you can get.

If you audiotape or videotape a program, you can use a playback to get the names of people involved in production and broadcast, as well as other facets of preparation that you will need to record on the card. If you don't tape the program, be alert for the names of people whose function you know will be needed in a citation. See Chapter 9, page 232 for an example.

Sometimes videotapes are available for purchase. Less expensive, and usually just as useful for your research purposes, are transcripts (that is, the written scripts), including those of news (or "magazine") shows.

If needed information slips by you, call the broadcast radio or televison station (if it's a local one) and ask for the names of people involved or other information to help you to complete a preliminary citation card. (Letting the station know why you want the information will undoubtedly be helpful.)

Interviews

In periodical indexes you can sometimes find published interviews given by people of consequence about the subject you are researching. Occasionally, in media catalogs you can find a recorded audio or video interview. You may even happen on a useful interview on radio or TV. Try to record it for personal use if you have enough advance warning; otherwise, make a Works Cited card that contains the same information as other interview cards, but with the interviewer's and interviewee's name and call letters of the station, plus the date heard or seen as identification.

Other resources depend on your own creativity. One enterprising student knew the subject she was working on was in the news at the time, so she followed a hunch and called the White House. She was rewarded by receiving the transcript of a presidential press conference—an interview—that included questions and answers about the subject she was working on.

Usually, though, the most useful kind of interview for your own research is likely to be the one you set up yourself and conduct either in person or over the telephone. The person to interview may be an expert in the field you are researching. Or you may simply need some kind of personal response from individuals. You can set up either kind of interview easily, for most people are willing to help students get their homework finished. If you don't know the people (or others who know them), you might find those to interview merely by looking in the phone book for people in specific jobs or businesses. At schools you will find faculty members who are bound to be specialists and who you can interview.

One big advantage of an interview is that you can, to some degree, control the conversation. That is, you can ask the person you interview to repeat or clarify. Or you can move the conversation in a different direction by the questions you ask and the responses of the interviewee during the conversation. Remember, too, that an interview will often give you a primary source to work with.

Make an interview worthwhile for your research by adhering to the following guidelines.

Interview Guidelines

1. *Have good reasons for asking for an interview.* And know, at least in a general way, what kind of information you want to get from the interview.

2. *Call or write in advance for an appointment specifically for the interview.*

3. *Be well prepared for the interview.* Take a cue here from radio and television personalities who do a great deal of serious inverviewing, such as Larry King and Barbara Walters. Know the subject you will talk about sufficiently well to ask intelligent and useful questions. Know the interviewee well enough (though not necessarily personally) to be aware of what kinds of questions that person will be able to respond to.

4. *Prepare at least the key questions in advance,* and avoid asking questions that can be answered merely by "yes" or "no."

5. *Control the interview in such a way that you get responses to the questions that are most important to your research needs.* Often, to do so will be a matter of pursuing an idea the interviewee broaches or following up on questions.

6. *Record both questions and answers accurately.* A tape recording that is later transcribed is excellent, if the person you interview agrees to allow you to tape. (*Always* ask permission to tape record a person!) Experienced interviewers use both their written notes and a tape recording for maximum accuracy—especially for any quotations that might be used.

7. *After the interview, be courteous enough to send an additional "thank you" by note or phone call.* Also, be *sure* to let the interviewee know what you decide actually to use in your paper, particularly any quotations you want to include. (Good manners dictate that you invite the interviewee to check them for accuracy.)

A **preliminary citation card** for a published or recorded interview will follow the format for the appropriate medium; if it is untitled, just use the designation "Interview" after the name of the interviewee. The preliminary citation for a personal interview should be written at the time you set the appointment. (If, for any reason, the day of an interview is changed, be sure to make the change on your card. And, of course, if the interview is canceled, discard the card.) See the example in Figure 30 for a card on a personal interview. Record the date, and use the word "telephone" or "personal" in order to state accurately your method of conducting the interview.

Lectures and Speeches

You may have occasion to attend a lecture or speech (or hear one broadcast or listen to a recording of one) that relates to the subject you are researching. Class lectures are also categorized this way for purposes of research. Recording during a live presentation is usually prohibited (except in a class where a teacher gives permission), but you should listen especially closely for points the speaker makes that are most relevant to your research concerns. Also, take complete and careful notes.

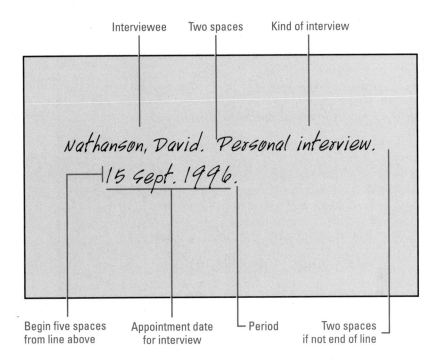

Interviewee   Two spaces   Kind of interview

Nathanson, David. Personal interview.
15 Sept. 1996.

Begin five spaces   Appointment date   Period   Two spaces
from line above   for interview   if not end of line

Fig. 30. Preliminary citation card for a personal interview.

If you have the opportunity to ask questions of the speaker, either as part of an open forum or informally after the presentation, you will have an even better chance of gathering information from this source.

A ***preliminary citation card*** is possible if you know in advance that you will be hearing a speaker on material related to your research. Write on your card the name of the speaker and the title of the presentation, if it has one; otherwise, use a descriptive label indicating a lecture, a keynote address, or a closing address. The more details you can give (such as the sponsor of the presentation, the location, and the date), the more useful the citation will be to you in writing information you garner from it and in developing the subsequent Works Cited listing. Figure 31 is an example of such a card.

Questionnaires, Surveys, and Polls

One kind of primary and original resource you may wish to use is a questionnaire, a survey, or a poll that you prepare, administer, and evaluate for your research paper. Like an interview, the only source available to get such information is your own creativity. Rarely do you have time to develop extensive statistical studies or write a computer program to handle the data from the results of any such studies, even though that may be your object or inclination. At any rate, you should consider using these methods as sources of information if you think one or more will

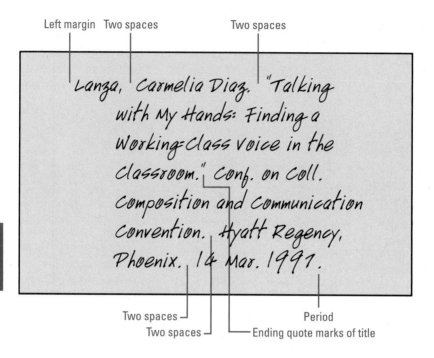

Left margin   Two spaces   Two spaces

Lanza, Carmelia Diaz. "Talking with My Hands: Finding a Working-Class Voice in the classroom." Conf. on Coll. Composition and Communication Convention. Hyatt Regency, Phoenix. 14 Mar. 1991.

Two spaces ⌐   Period
Two spaces ⌐   └── Ending quote marks of title

Fig. 31. Preliminary citation card for a speech.

be helpful to your research and to the paper you will write. Know, too, that if you elect to use any of these sources, the effectiveness of each depends on carefully framed questions and the people you select to respond to them.

If you seek written response to a questionnaire, technically you are probably using a written source for which you are the author. But for purposes of your research paper (and of this book), consider them among the sources of nonprint information. The category into which you put it is certainly less important than the material you can develop.

Write a ***preliminary citation card*** when you decide to develop a questionnaire, survey, or poll and give it a title for acknowledgment convenience. Use slightly different forms, depending on whether it was answered anonymously or by people who signed their names. Let people know which way you will cite their responses, and, if you have asked them to sign names, get permission to acknowledge the respondents, either as a group or as individuals. A model to follow is on page 232 in Chapter 9.

Films, Filmstrips, and Slides

New films that libraries order are invariably on videotape, and that has been standardized into a VHS-format cassette, so old worries about tape size and kind are eliminated. However, large academic collections of 16-mm films still exist, as do many filmstrips, slide collections, and even other formats of videotape programs that may yield helpful information for research papers. One problem, however, is that the equipment or hardware on which to view them may no longer be available.

As with other nonprint materials, these materials are cataloged either with the general collection holdings or in a separate group of audiovisual or media holdings. You will find out what may be useful by checking through subjects in either or both categories and most usually by subject. If you are looking for information about a specific title or a person, however, check those listings. For example, you might find information about the film *An American in Paris* under that title or with a listing of works by Vincente Minnelli (the director) or Gene Kelly (the lead actor and choreographer).

A *preliminary citation card* should begin with whatever aspect of the information you are emphasizing in your paper. Thus, the first unit on the card might be the film title, the director's name, the choreographer, or the principal actor. If you were researching and writing about movie musicals or Academy Award–winning films, the title would come first.

Neither preliminary nor final citation cards distinguish among fiction, live action, cartoon, or documentary films, though the content of the citation will be a good indication. Publication information on your card will include when a filmstrip or slide set is used, running time or number of frames, motion picture film size, plus whatever production or distribution information you can get from the source listing. Use the examples on pages 232–33 in Chapter 9 as models for your preliminary citation cards. Do not be concerned about every bit of information you know you will need for the final Works Cited listing, because you can get that from the source itself during your research.

Videocassettes, Laser Discs, and DVDs

New technology makes new demands on the researcher, both in finding appropriate material and in citing its use. As already mentioned, newly purchased films for educational institutions and for libraries are invariably on videotape cassette (as are many other titles in collections), and are so recorded on preliminary citation cards and Works Cited lists. Laser videodiscs are popular in homes, though they were once considered exotic and forward-looking in media centers. The DVD, or digital video disc, is now on the market, but libraries (and, at this writing, the general public) seem to be slow in acquiring players on which to run them. You will find these visual resources in the general catalog of a library's holdings and/or in those of an academic media center or in a departmental library. Depending on the subject you are researching, you may also find useful videocassettes, laser discs, or DVDs in your own or another person's private collection or at a local video rental shop as well as through a library.

The *preliminary citation card* for any of these visual media will include the usual three units of author, title, and production (publication) information. Because so many of these tapes and discs are performances that lend themselves particularly to this medium, you may also have to treat such citations partly as films, showing the names of performers as well as of authors and directors. Figure 32 presents an example of a card for a film on videocassette.

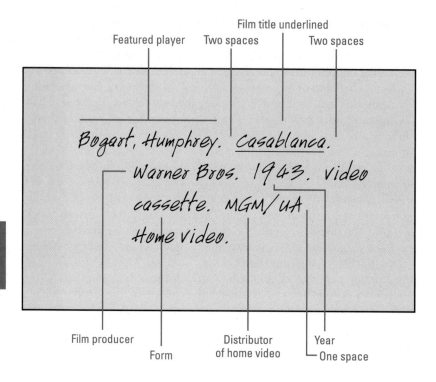

Fig. 32. Preliminary citation card for a film on videocassette.

CDs, Audiotapes, and Other Audio Recordings

Both music and the spoken word are easily and inexpensively recorded now, particularly on audiotape cassettes. Home-recorded CDs, the industry tells us at this writing, are imminent, though the digital quality of studio recordings, especially of music, will not be easy to emulate. The enormous growth and changing nature of the audio recording industry means that you have increased sources of information for particular kinds of research work. Music surely comes most immediately to mind. And there is an ever-expanding catalog of other kinds of tape cassettes, including lectures, instructions, and, especially, books on tape. A productive place to look for these materials, depending on the subject you are researching, may well be a local rather than an academic library.

The general catalog of a library may contain entries of these audio materials. Individual departments in larger academic institutions may have their own specialized libraries too. For example, if you were looking for information about anything connected with music, probably the best place to look would be the music department library at a college or university where the subject is taught.

A *preliminary citation card* for any audio recording—play, poetry reading, music, book, or so on—are handled as follows. (Should you happen on a vinyl record, and a machine to play it on, you can follow this format also. However, many such 78 or 33⅓ rpm LP recordings have been transferred to CD or remastered for them.) Feature as "author" the most outstanding quality of the work, in terms of your research paper, whether that be the title of an opera or a music album or the name of the performer. The performers must be noted, and often the producer is important enough to be featured. Always give the identifying number of the album or tape and, if possible, the date of recording or performance, whichever is more important for your purposes. (See other examples of audio recordings on pages 231, 232, and 234.)

Recording Information

WRITING NOTES

At last you're ready to look through all the potential sources you identified by searching out materials and then take down information you can actually use in your paper! Most students find the convenience of handwritten notes on cards that can readily be shuffled around for use is best for the purpose, so this chapter refers often to "note cards." (See pages 231; 232; 234 for additional information about such cards.) But if you have ready access to a computer and are comfortable with it, you may want to set up a note template to use in lieu of actual cards for your notes. At a later point in the process, however, you may find it expedient to print out all the notes and then separate them into the equivalent of cards for ease of manipulation when you start to organize ideas.

Organize your preliminary bibliography cards in groups according to where you will have to look for the actual books, periodicals, videos, CD-ROMs, and so on; then head for the sources. The order in which you actually take notes for your research paper depends on your own convenience and preferences.

A good idea is usually to begin with an overview, often obtained by reading relevant entries in encyclopedias and other general reference works. If you are very comfortable working with a computer, you may want to move to electronic sources next. However, students generally work initially with print sources. Because most people find it easier to take notes from print rather than from nonprint sources, you may want to leave the nonprint sources to last in your note taking. Nonetheless, if you are able to use nonprint items as primary sources, you may want to deal with them near the beginning of your search.

PLAGIARISM—AND HOW NOT TO COMMIT IT

If a source you work from has stated an idea so well that you can't imagine saying the same thing in any other way, it's tempting to record those exact words on a note card. But if you do, **remember the quotation marks and keep an accurate record of the source,** including the page number the quote came from, so you can give proper credit in your research paper. Otherwise you will be guilty of plagiarism!

A caution: never get so involved in writing note cards that you forget to indicate whether wording on a note card is a paraphrase, a quotation, or a combination of other kinds of notes, as defined later in the chapter in the section "Kinds of Notes." If you fail to credit a source accurately and fully while writing a note card, you probably won't be able to give proper credit in your paper—and therefore will commit plagiarism. There are no such things as slips and oversights; they're still plagiarism!

Of Words and Ideas—and Plagiarism

Plagiarism is using the words or ideas of another person without giving proper credit to the one who devised them. It is wrong to plagiarize, whether you do it deliberately or thoughtlessly. Print materials (including maps, charts, and graphs) and nonprint materials (including films, sculpture, and still photos) are protected by national and international copyright laws. As this is being written, internationally agreed-upon changes in those laws to include Internet and other digitally transmitted information are about to be considered by Congress, so surely such resources will soon be covered, also. Therefore, to present almost any of your researched materials as your own when they are not is to break the law as well as to act unethically!

The most blatant kind of plagiarism is submitting another person's paper as your own. Whether a friend lets you borrow a paper, or even part of one, to help you out or you buy one from a term paper ("research") service, letting a reader think that you did work you really didn't do is cheating yourself and others.

A more subtle kind of plagiarism is to let a reader think that particular words, phrases, or ideas are your own when they are, in fact, the property of other people who you failed to acknowledge. Paraphrases and summaries, as well as individual groups of words—facts, opinions, ideas—may be plagiarized. Varying a word here and there or changing singulars to plurals won't protect you from the label of "plagiarist." Even presenting common knowledge (see this chapter's later section entitled "Common Knowledge") in somebody else's words without credit is plagiarism.

Plagiarism is most likely to occur at two stages during the research paper process:

1. When you take notes and fail to credit each source fully and carefully on each note card.

2. When you write the paper and fail to observe the conventions of documentation in acknowledging the sources of words, ideas, or illustrations. (Chapter 8 will show you how to acknowledge sources in the text.)

Examples of how to make proper acknowledgments on note cards—and what *not* to do—appear in this chapter's later section on "Kinds of Notes" (pages 121–27).

How *Not* to Plagiarize

Preventing plagiarism, like many other aspects of the research paper process, depends on attention to detail. Follow the next four simple rules, and you will never need to worry about plagiarism.

1. **Use quotation marks around all words and phrases from any research source, *and also* cite the source, both on note cards and in the text of your paper.** Quotations require *both* kinds of acknowledgment; one alone won't do.

2. **Credit the source of any ideas,** including summaries and paraphrases, by documenting them when you take notes and when you write your paper. For the latter, the style shown in this book, which is recommended by the MLA [Modern Language Association] suggests that you dispense with superscripts and footnotes in favor of parenthetical documentation in the text. Thus, you credit each source immediately within the paper, and won't overlook one because you were busy writing out a thought. Two other widely used styles in writing research papers, those by the American Psychological Association [APA] and by the University of Chicago Press, also recommend parenthetical documentation; so, once learned, you can apply this method to varied disciplines.

3. **Be sure every source you document in your paper is also in the Works Cited at the end of the text.** That is, acknowledging something that is not original must appear *both* in the written part, the text, of your research paper and in the Works Cited list at the end of it.

4. **Give an adequate introduction or otherwise clearly delineate borrowed words and ideas.** Always give enough information for your audience to tell clearly what is your original work and what isn't. Examples of how to do so when you write your paper are on pages 175–78.

To see the documentation forms by which you credit materials that you don't originate, see pages 199–214 of Chapter 8. Examples of how to give adequate introductions to quotations, paraphrases, and borrowed ideas as you write are in Chapter 7, pages 175–78, and in the Sample Research Papers at the end of both Chapter 10 and Chapter 11.

Notes That Plagiarize

It's easy to plagiarize when you see something that is well written, and most resources you use—whether a book, a journal article, or a speech—are written well. Here, for example, is a paragraph from page 158 of *Marriages and Families: Making Choices in a Diverse Society*, 6th ed., by Mary Ann Lamanna and Agnes Riedman (Belmont: Wadsworth, 1997):

> There is evidence that occupation and income are related to marital status. As you can see in Table 6.3, married couples earn considerably more than singles, and this is true if both spouses are not in the paid labor force. Singles who are not living with any other relatives earn significantly less, with single

women earning the least. Married people are more likely to have white-collar jobs and higher incomes than are singles, regardless of age and education.

PLAGIARIZED NOTE CARD 1

> *Evidence says that occupation and income are related to marital status because married couples earn more than singles, even if only one spouse works for pay. Singles living by themselves earn less and single women the least. Married people, whatever their age and education, are more likely to have white-collar jobs and therefore higher income than singles.*

COMMENT 1

Even though the note omits the first two words of the original paragraph and joins the first two sentences, this note is already well on its way to being plagiarism. "Singles living by themselves" is dangerously like "Singles who are not living with any other relatives" in the original passage. Moving "age and education" from the ending of the paragraph to the first part of the last sentence is still too close to the original.

PLAGIARIZED NOTE CARD 2

> *Married couples earn more money than do singles, even if only one of the spouses works for pay. Furthermore, they probably have white-collar jobs and therefore higher incomes than singles. This is true regardless of age, education, and whether or not a single person lives alone or with any relative.*

COMMENT 2

Beginning with the final sentence and then moving to the second one in the paragraph doesn't rescue this passage from showing plagiarism. The last paragraph again attempts to combine ideas, but still the wording is too similar to the original to avoid being labeled as plagiarism.

As you may already have inferred, it is harder to keep from plagiarizing a short passage than a longer one, from plagiarizing a few sentences than many. There is always the danger, if you work with a limited number of words in the original source, that you will be tempted to make your note adhere too closely to what another person has written, because you don't have the range and flexibility to put more information into your own words.

Notes That *Don't* Plagiarize

Consider the same paragraph just used as illustration, but this time followed by acceptable wording on a note card:

> There is evidence that occupation and income are related to marital status. As you can see in Table 6.3, married couples earn considerably more than singles, and this is true if both spouses are not in the paid labor force. Singles who are not living with any other relatives earn significantly less, with single women earning the least. Married people are more likely to have white-collar jobs and higher incomes than are singles, regardless of age and education.

ACCEPTABLE NOTE CARD 1

> Unmarried people, especially women, earn less than married couples, even if only one spouse recieves a salary. Furthermore, age and education appear to have little effect on the higher earning power of married couples.

COMMENT 1

This time the sentence about who a single lives with is omitted from the note card, because it is of subordinate importance. However, the wording of this note catches the essential elements of the paragraph on which it is based, so it is acceptable.

Here is another passage to show how you can write note cards without plagiarizing; it is from page 128 of *Sociology: Discovering Society* by Jean Stockard (Belmont: Wadsworth, 1997) and is under the heading "Defining Deviance."

> Because norms apply to all areas of our lives, the concept of deviance is one of the broadest sociological ideas. Recall that norms include folkways, mores, and laws. Accordingly deviance may involve rude or unusual behavior, such as wearing formal evening clothes to class or talking loudly during a movie. It may involve choices that are inconsistent with cultural practices, such as wearing grass skirts and skimpy thongs to work. Or it may involve behavior that is proscribed by law, such as drug use, assault, burglary, rape, and murder.
>
> Most important, deviance is *socially defined*. Whether a given act is deviant can vary from one social situation to another and from one culture to another. For instance, cannibalism is unknown in most societies but is practiced in certain circumstances in a few societies. Similarly the ritual sacrifice of animals in mainstream religious services is unheard of in our society but has been common in many cultures. Even within societies definitions of deviance may vary from one subculture to another. For example, peyote may be an integral part of the religious ceremonies of some Native American groups in the southwestern United States, but its use is seen as deviant by other Native American groups.

ACCEPTABLE   NOTE   CARD   2

"Deviance" is a broad idea that describes a variance from normative behavior, customs, and laws of a society. Whether or not something is deviant depends on its context, for what is unacceptable in one society might be perfectly acceptable in another.

COMMENT   2

This succinct statement of the two paragraphs that define deviance is made relatively easy because a considerable portion of the original consists of examples (which are hardly ever included in notes from a source).

ACCEPTABLE   NOTE   CARD   3

> Stockard points out (128) that although deviance may be as innocuous as wearing inappropriate clothing, it may also describe behaviors that are "proscribed by law, such as drug use, assault, burglary, rape, and murder." Also, deviance has meaning only within a particular society or culture; what is acceptable to one group may be anathema to another.

COMMENT   3

Reference to the author and location of the information on this card is probably superfluous because it will be noted elsewhere. However, this card illustrates how summary can be coordinated with quotation, for the author of the note card probably decided that the wording of the author of the passage is best for his or her purposes.

COMMON KNOWLEDGE

Information that is well known or basic to a study is called "common knowledge" and does not require documentation. You identify the common knowledge for your own research paper either because you already knew such information or you find it repeated in a number of sources, therefore leading you to conclude that "everybody who knows anything about the subject already knows *that*."

You may want to write a note card about this information, but you don't need to cite a source, because it could have come from any number of them.

EXAMPLES

- Dates of a well-known person's life
- Chemical formula of a familiar substance
- Location of a famous battle

Even if the information is new to you, finding it in several sources means it's probably common knowledge.

Certain *value judgments* may also be considered common knowledge. For instance, so many critics have said that Shakespeare's *Henry IV, Part I* is a better play than his *Henry VI, Part II* that you may consider the judgment to be common knowledge.

However, if you want to quote a particular person's statement of common knowledge, you must give credit to that individual.

If you're not sure whether particular information is common knowledge, a safe rule to follow is "When in doubt, give credit."

READING TO TAKE NOTES

Effective readers use different methods for their varied purposes of reading. You might read a light fiction book very quickly, but you probably read new material for a course quite slowly in order to learn it. Similarly, you should acquire the habit of reading resources in different ways, depending on your purpose.

Previewing

When you *look for an overview and want to get a feel for a subject,* you are previewing. Don't try to take notes as soon as you get a book or turn to a magazine article. Instead, begin by becoming familiar with the subject you are going to read about—that is, by previewing a selection. Then you will have some idea about what to focus on so you can take notes effectively.

- **Discover the organization of what you are about to read.** You will be able to anticipate information by understanding the structure an author has used in a work.

- **Read over the table of contents of each book before you start to work with it.** If you know you are going to work with just part of a book, identify the section by checking the table of contents or the index to find the precise pages you will need.

- **Pay attention to chapter titles, headings, and subheadings before reading selections, so you will know what is coming.** These units are one way to see organization in a long work. In a shorter one, look for subheadings that will help you follow a train of thought or a line of reasoning.

- **Look at prefaces, forewords, glossaries, indexes, and appendices** before turning to the content of a book.

- **If you are working with an article, read all the subheads before you read the entire text.**

- **Look at beginnings and endings, at introductions and conclusions of whole works and units within them.**

Taking time to preview your source material will save you time and effort when it comes to writing notes. You will be better able to define your subject field and be developing the skill of effective reading. You will also spot what is most essential to your note-taking needs and, thus, be able to spend time efficiently.

Skimming

In previewing, you are looking ahead and determining content mainly through overview and structure. In skimming, you are looking quickly through a work to identify what will probably be valuable for you to read more slowly and carefully, and to spot what you might want to include in your research paper. Skimming is a quick way of reading that serves two purposes:

1. To get at the main idea of a selection and see it as a whole without undue attention to its details, which may distract

2. To tell if there is enough relevant information in the source to read it closely; if there isn't, you've saved yourself time

Skimming is particularly important when you have an entire book to go through and need to find the specific information from it that will be useful. Use the table of contents and/or the index to locate the information by pages; then skim them to decide whether or not the contents warrant additional or closer reading.

Journal and magazine articles should also be skimmed to locate what, if any, part of a piece you need to read more closely. Longer newspaper articles usually have subheadings to guide your skim reading.

Scanning

Scanning is a more focused way of looking for material, but still without reading in specific detail. In scanning, you *look for specific information quickly.* Therefore, in order to scan effectively, you should know in advance what you are looking for. Be alert for *key words, dates, or other specifics* that indicate you have found information to take notes on. Rather than stopping to read everything on a page slowly and carefully, scan until you come to information that you should pay close attention to. You will already have an idea—from skimming—whether what you're looking for is in that particular source.

EVALUATING SOURCE MATERIALS

Most of the materials you assemble for note taking have already been evaluated before you see them—except for the contents of newsgroups, chat lines, some Web pages, and bulletin boards. Print-on-paper sources are editorially evaluated before publication, and the cost of making films and many other nonprint resources available makes pre-evaluation necessary. Materials you find in a library may well have been evaluated by librarians before purchase, usually on the basis of published reviews. If you find materials in a school library, they have likely been recommended additionally for acquisition by faculty or other qualified persons.

Despite all that prior sifting, not all information you find will be equally useful or relevant to you. Therefore, you yourself will need to make evaluations at two stages of recording information for your research paper:

1.   Before you read, look at, or listen to something

2.   While you are reading, looking, or listening

The more closely you evaluate material, you more refined you make your judgment, and thus the more you hone your independent thinking abilities.

In the next sections are six questions you can use as aids to evaluating materials for note taking.

Before You Read, Look, or Listen

1. Which authors or sources seem outstanding in the field?

It's a safe assumption that if some names recur as you read, look, and listen, those people are probably experts in the field and thus are reliable sources of information. A person's credentials or his or her standing in the field are also guides. For instance, an article on retail merchandising by a department store executive will undoubtedly be authoritative. So will one on airline safety by a member of the National Transportation and Safety Board. The name of Donald Keene keeps showing up in material about Japanese literature in translation, so you may infer that he must be an expert in the field (and you'd be right).

Where can you find out about an author? Journals usually identify authors by stating an academic affiliation and previous publications. Material from a refereed journal (which means an editor or board decides what it will print) is probably going to be more authoritative than that from one that accepts anything sent its way. You can also learn about the work of some authors from a biographical reference book such as *Who's Who in America, Contemporary Authors,* or *Biography and Genealogy Master Index.*

Many electronic sources lack such background resources, so you may have to rely on your own intuition. If you have been lurking at a chat or discussion group, you will soon get a sense of which participants contribute frequently and seem authoritative, the more so if you have some familiarity with the subject matter or if the participants give indication of a vocational title or academic affiliation worth noting. (See also the upcoming section entitled "Source's personal qualifications.")

2. What is the date of publication?

While all that is new is not necessarily better, more recent materials are likely to summarize or be based on earlier works. Some will also lead you to works previously published, much as links on the Internet do. You might read materials in the order of their publication to help see a development of ideas. On the other hand, if you are dealing with a historical subject, a publication dated close to the time of an event will probably give a view different from one published much later—and may turn out to be a primary source of information.

Some scientific and technical fields, such as computer technology, change so quickly that finding recent materials may be a prime consideration for your research study. Or a research subject may depend on reaction to a book or an idea at the time it was first published in a learned journal or to an event when it took place.

Remember, too, that the time lag between writing and publication is often a matter of years, especially for books and journal articles. Even a documentary film being shot today may not be released for a year or more, so its release date (which is what you record) may be a reflection only of how things *were,* not how they *are.*

3. How credible does a source seem?

Five elements ought to be considered here, depending on whether your resource is print, electronic, or nonprint.

a.   Publisher's reputation

Ask your instructor or a librarian about the publisher, if the name is unfamiliar to you. Authors sometimes contract with book publishers to bring out their own works, and teachers and librarians can usually identify for you the names of some of these "vanity presses." Such books are not necessarily unreliable. But the quality of work is often better if a reputable company has spent the time and money needed to publish the book; there is a difference between paying to have one's own work put into print and having somebody else think enough of it to lay out the money.

Also, some publishers have known biases that might be reflected in the work they put out, so it's helpful to be aware of such leanings. For instance, an article in a magazine published by a particular religious group will probably reflect the theological attitudes of that denomination.

Magazines for Libraries and the *Classified List of Periodicals for the College Library* are two reference sources that librarians use to determine the bias, authority, and credibility for specific periodicals; you could consult them for the same kind of information.

b.   A book or film's critical reception

Most published books are reviewed somewhere by people concerned with their particular subjects. Professional, academic, and special-interest publications, as well as those for the general public, either review or note the appearance of books. *Book Review Digest* is a publication often consulted to find reviews. Film critics such as Gene Shallit, Gene Siskel, and Roger Ebert are regularly seen on television, and their evaluations are given enormous weight by the public.

c.   Author's documentation

When you are looking for accurate and authoritative information, as you are for a research paper, the author who documents work has more credibility than one who doesn't. Moreover, if at least some of that documentation is from primary sources, it is likely to have higher standing than if most of it had passed through many hands (or sources).

d.   Completeness of material

If you are working with a book, examine the introduction, preface, index, and bibliography. Journal articles usually have bibliographies, too. All show further evidence of an author's scholarship and, therefore, of credibility of a source.

e. Source's personal qualifications

Nonprint information, especially that from interviews and questionnaires, ought to be particularly scrutinized. So should that from many electronic sources. Make sure the person or persons you consult are qualified to give the information you are looking for. On the other hand, don't necessarily reject out of hand information you get from someone without formal or academic credentials. For instance, a knowledgeable collector of opera records and videos may know as much (or more) about the music as one with formal academic training in the field. And though you may get opinions about the need for more police patrols on the street in your city from interviewing shoppers at a mall, you are more likely to get informed opinions, and therefore gain credibility, from the local police chief or mayor.

When You Read, Look, or Listen

1. What does the language of a source tell you?

Language reveals something of the beliefs and attitudes of the writer; if you are properly attuned to it you may be able to learn more from your source than is immediately apparent. Even in the postings of an Internet chat group, a perceptive reader can detect the supercilious attitude of one participant, the helpful tone of another, the condescending voice of still another. Understanding how words are used will, thus, give you valuable clues about both the speaker/writer and the audience being addressed.

Language that is obviously slanted might affect your use of material—or the use you want to make of it. Discovering bias in a work doesn't mean that you should distrust the source or not rely on it, only that you should *be aware* of the bias when using the source or making judgments about it. Here, for instance is the opening of a newspaper article ("Dr. Benjamin Spock, America's Baby Doctor, Dies in California at 94" by James Barry [*Miami Herald,* 17 March, 1998: C1]):

> Benjamin Spock, the kindly "baby doctor" who helped America's postwar parents survive the raising of 76 million restive baby boomers by reassuring them that "you know more than you think you do"—then went on to help boomers raise *their* 72 million kids—is dead.
>
> . . .
> Celebrated as the Sigmund Freud of baby care, Spock revolutionized child-rearing during his 64-year career by helping parents understand in clear, sympathetic and sometimes poetic language how children thrive.
>
> . . .
> But at the same time, Spock bolstered parents' confidence by urging them to rely on their own instincts to love and nurture.

Look at the words this author chose: "kindly," "helped postwar parents survive," "reassuring," "celebrated," revolutionized," "helping parents understand," "clear, sympathetic and sometimes poetic language," "bolstered parents' confidence," "rely on their own instincts." How could anyone not immediately recognize the bias of this author as one of *admiration* for the man he was writing about?

2. Which sources seem to give you the most information for your purposes?

Some reference materials will tell you more than others about the subject you're researching. Also, some are especially provocative and lead you to think about issues and ideas you might otherwise not have considered. Others are valuable because they suggest additional sources you might decide to consult. The linkages provided by the Internet are also particularly helpful in this regard.

3. What facts or statements keep reappearing in your reading?

If you come across the same (or very similar) information in several places, it is probably important in your study. It may also be "common knowledge" and thus not need documentation, as explained earlier in the chapter. Once you have a sense of recurring facts from your preview reading of several sources, you can also tell if something that seems standard is omitted, which would indicate that the source is untrustworthy or biased in a way you need to keep in mind.

QUALITIES OF GOOD NOTES

A research paper is only as good as the notes it is based on. Several weeks or even months may elapse between the time you write notes and the time you consult them to write your research paper. Social events, other studies, family problems, all sorts of distractions will intervene. Therefore, you should be especially careful to take notes you can later read and work from easily. Deciphering garbled notes or redoing them will waste your time and effort.

Perhaps the most important quality of a good note is that it is a single idea limited to a single note card. Just this once, forget about saving trees, and use a little more paper. Don't try to cram lots of words onto a single note card. Don't put sequential ideas from a book or article or lecture on a single note card, because then you are bound to that one order. Also, the sequence in which one source presents information may not be the order in which you want to use the information. The whole point of putting notes on cards is to have them in a format you can use, and that usually means switching around order to make whatever points you wish in your own writing. You can do so most easily if your notes are legible, accurate, and complete.

Legibility

1. Take notes on 4- × 6-inch cards.

Unless you are taking notes on a computer, using this card size will give you enough space to write most notes on. Also, the cards are easy to arrange and rearrange as you begin to plan and then work out the content of your paper. Even if you've never before taken notes on cards, do so now; it will pay off.

2. Take notes that will last.

Write in ink, unless you are typing or using a computer. Pencil writing may easily smudge or become difficult to read after much handling.

3. Write on only one side of each card—and try to limit a note to just one card.

Better to see everything on a card at one glance than to flip back and forth looking for wording. Use the reverse side only to finish a statement or complete a quotation. Should you need to take a particularly long note, use additional cards and identify each in the series by number and author; then staple them together.

4. Use whatever abbreviations you find convenient.

Be sure abbreviations or symbols you use are those you are accustomed to for classroom or lecture notes and that they make sense to you. Also, be consistent so that they will continue to be understandable.

Accuracy

1. Read, look at, or listen to your research materials carefully.

That may sound like elementary advice, but distortions and misrepresentations result when material is misread. One word mistakenly substituted for another can change the whole meaning of a passage—and possibly of an entire portion of your paper.

2. Record precisely.

Emphasize only what the source of information emphasized; don't *ever* second-guess or misrepresent an author's or speaker's words. Be particularly careful to *check wording and spelling*, especially when you work with materials that are unfamiliar or highly technical.

One kind of error made by viewers and, more particularly, by listeners is to anticipate—erroneously—what will come next, thus skewing your understanding as well as your notes. This is one more reason that precise notes are imperative to your work.

3. Distinguish among fact, inference, and opinion.

- A *fact* is a statement that can be verified by evidence from the senses: something a person can see, hear, taste, touch, or smell.

- An *inference* is an educated guess based on at least one fact, but usually on several of them.

- An *opinion* expresses a belief held by an individual, but is not observable or verifiable.

Distinguishing among these three is crucial to critical thinking and judgment. You should distinguish among them when you take notes, in case you need to call on that information when you write your paper. For example, certainly you wouldn't want to be so lax as to present mistakenly an author's inference as a fact. The surest way to make these differentiations—unless the content of a note card makes the differences obvious—is to write out at the lower left corner of a note card whether what is recorded on it is a fact, an inference, or an opinion. (Some people find it convenient to use merely the letters *F, I,* or *O* in the lower left corner.)

Be sure to indicate if statements on note cards are *your own* opinion, belief, or inference rather than that of a source you consulted. Naturally, you wouldn't want to mislead readers by allowing them to confuse your thoughts with those of another person. Writing "personal comment" at the bottom of a note card (as explained on page 126) is one way of preventing this.

4. Use conventional mechanics of spelling, capitalization, and punctuation.

You are duty bound to copy the mechanics of your source when you record a quotation on a note card. Otherwise, use conventional spelling, capitalization, and punctuation on all your note cards. Doing so will make writing your research paper easier.

Be sure you record in notes all quotations, titles, and foreign words as you see them so you can do the same in writing the text. Use ellipses to omit portions of quotations, and use square brackets to enclose comments on the material. These and other customs are explained in the later section entitled "Conventions for Writing Notes."

Completeness

Think how frustrating it would be to discover, late at night while you are writing your paper, that you neglected to note down some important information. Or consider the wasted time if you need to hurry off to look at a source again or try to track down an interviewee to clarify some point you didn't handle fully or bother with initially.

Therefore, write down everything you think you might need (later, you can discard any excess note cards), to avoid having to backtrack. Consider the trauma you might face if a periodical or book you need to find again is in use by somebody else and not available to you. (If you do need to find something again, the call number or library location on a preliminary citation card will be invaluable.) The following three characteristics of complete notes are shown in the five sample cards in this chapter's upcoming section entitled "Kinds of Notes."

1. Identify the source of what appears on each card.

The **top right-hand corner** is a convenient place to note source information, because you can see it easily there. Write the **author's last name** alone if you consulted only one work by that person; otherwise, use both the author and the title (or a key word in it).

Identify other materials by the **title or a shortened form of it.** For instance, Deborah Tannen's book titled *You Just Don't Understand: Women and Men in Conversation* can be identified as <u>Understand</u> on a note card (with the underlining showing that it is a book title). **Dates of periodicals** will also be helpful for quick identification.

2. Note down page numbers, tape footage, CD or laser disc band number.

The **top right-hand corner** is also the most convenient place for recording this information. Then you can easily write documentation from that note in the text of your research paper. Be sure to record all page numbers from which you got specific information, even if you are summarizing a long passage. Remember that both words *and* ideas need to be acknowledged in your paper in order to avoid plagiarism!

3. Identify as specifically as possible the subject of each note card in the top left-hand corner.

The purpose of writing a single idea on each note card is so you can order them in any way you choose. Writing the *subject or key idea* on that card (often called a "slug," after the printing term that identifies content of a story) simplifies the later work of organizing these note cards. Instead of having to read through each one for contents, you will be able to tell at a glance what each card contains and thus arrange them more readily. *Never* use the entire subject of your research as a slug; all the cards you write will be on that subject, so such wording is useless because no separation of ideas will be possible.

KINDS OF NOTES

You can take any of the four basic kinds of notes: **summary, paraphrase, direct quotation,** or **personal comment.** A **combination** of two of more of these is another possibility. The choice of which kind of note to take is a matter of personal preference and of what you think you might need to use for your research paper.

You have already read that **each single note card should be limited to just one idea.** You also know that you should use corners of the card for several identifying kinds of information. Three have already been given; one more needs to be added: an indication of the kind of note you've written. When you always know what kind of note you've taken, you can write the text of the paper with the assurance that you can later document whatever is necessary. To recapitulate, put the following notations on all your note cards:

- *Top left corner:* slug line identifying specific subject on the card
- *Top right corner:* author and/or title and page number(s) or CD or laser disc band of material on the card
- *Bottom left corner:* whether the note or quotation is fact, inference, or opinion
- *Bottom right corner:* kind of note on that card (Though punctuation identifies a quotation, you can't hurt yourself by repeating that fact.)

The following passage will serve as the basis for illustrations in this section of the various kinds of notes you can take for your own work. Note that in the original the full passage runs onto two pages; where the page break occurs is indicated here by a slash mark.

ORIGINAL PASSAGE

Child abuse has by no means been decriminalized (all states have criminal laws against child abuse). Meanwhile, the approach to child protection has gradually shifted from punitive to therapeutic (Stewart 1984). Not all who work with abused children are happy with this shift, however. These critics prefer to hold one or both parents clearly responsible. They reject the family system approach to therapy because it implies distribution of responsibility for change to all family members, including the child. Nevertheless, social workers and clinicians—rather than the police and the court system—increasingly investigate and treat abusive or neglectful parents.

The therapeutic approach involves two interrelated strategies: (1) increasing parents' self-esteem and their knowledge about children and (2) involving the community in child rearing (Goldstein, Keller, and Erne 1985). One voluntary program, Parents Anonymous (PA), holds regular meetings to enhance self-esteem and educate abusive parents. Another voluntary asso / ciation, CALM, attempts to reach stressed parents before they hurt their children. Among other things, CALM advocates obligatory high school classes on family life, child development, and parenting, and it operates a 24-hour hotline for parents in stress.

Involving the community involves getting people other than parents to help with child rearing. One form of relief for abused or neglected children is to remove them from their parents' homes and place them in foster care. More and more, however, people are choosing alternatives, such as *supplemental mothers,* who are available to babysit regularly with potentially abused children. Another community resource is the *crisis nursery* where parents can take their children when they need to get away for a few hours. Ideally, crisis nurseries are open 24 hours a day and accept children at any hour without prearrangement.

Mary Ann Lamanna and Agnes Riedmann. *Marriages and Families: Making Choices in a Diverse Society,* 6th ed. Belmont: Wadsworth: 298–99.

Summary Notes

A summary is a statement in your own words of the main ideas of a passage. It *tells only what the author has said and may not include your own interpretation or comment* on the meaning. (Save those for the personal comment note cards.) Because a summary is limited to main ideas, it will be shorter than the original. However, follow the organization or order of the original source when you write a summary.

Summary notes are particularly useful, and widely used, because they pack lots of content into a little space. A page in the original may become a paragraph in your notes; a paragraph may become a sentence or a few words. Use summary notes to record

- An overall idea

  or

- A large amount of information succinctly

Begin to write a summary note by separating what is most important in a passage from what is less important. Being able to make that distinction is a reading skill, but it's also one closely related to writing, for every time you compose a main idea (or thesis) and develop it, you are using the same skills.

Writing a summary note in complete sentences is a good idea because of the practice that doing so affords. Also, when you write the text of your paper, you shouldn't feel held to using the exact wording of a summary you've put onto a note card; in a draft or any revision of your research paper you can always change any wording that isn't a direct quotation.

SAMPLE OF A SUMMARY NOTE CARD

New approaches to　　　　　　　*Lamanna &*
child abuse　　　　　　　　　　*Riedmann 298-99*

　The new approach is to treat child abuse
therapeutically by helping parents to greater self-
esteem and knowledge of children and by setting
up community programs to give support to
parents.

F　　　　　　　　　　　　　　　　*summary*

Paraphrase Notes

A paraphrase is a phrase-by-phrase statement in your own words of the original passage. Because it follows the original so closely, it has the same organization and is also approximately the same length as the original. *Do not interpret* material in paraphrasing; just restate it.

When you prepare to paraphrase, you examine each phrase and thought carefully, then write each in your own words. Be aware that one pitfall of paraphrasing is the temptation to use wording from the original. However, a paraphrase is a *complete rewriting*, not just a game of rearranging words.

Paraphrase note cards are particularly useful for any of the following:

- Restating technical passages or other specialized information into lay language or other language that is appropriate to a particular audience and helpful to your own understanding

- Exploring the meaning of poetry by "expanding" poetic expression into prose

- Making sure you understand exactly what an author said by putting it into your own words

Paraphrased notes are often preferable to summaries because of their detail and specificity. They are often preferable to quotations because the text is in your own words rather than in someone else's, thus ensuring that the wording of your paper will be original and in your own writing style. Paraphrases can also be turned into summaries, should you need to do that.

SAMPLE OF A PARAPHRASE NOTE CARD

New approaches   Lamanna & Riedmann
to child abuse   298-99

New approaches to protecting children from abuse are now mostly therapeutic rather than punitive. Not everyone is happy with the shift from focus on parental responsibility alone because it suggests change for all family members, even the child under consideration. It does seem to make sense, though, because increasingly social workers and clinicians, rather than only police and courts, are involved in dealing with abused or neglected children.

One strategy used is to help parents develop their self-esteem and knowledge of children. A second strategy involves community support. Organizations with such acronyms as PA and CALM are primarily for parents.

Community involvement may also include moving abused or neglected children to foster homes. Increasingly people are also choosing to allow "supplemental mothers" to babysit regularly or to place at-risk children in "crisis nurseries" to relieve stressed-out parents briefly any time of the day or night.

F   paraphrase

Direct Quotation Notes

A direct quotation copies exactly what your source said or wrote and is therefore the easiest kind of note card to write. If you create this kind of note card, be as accurate as you can with punctuation of the spoken word and copy the written words accurately, down to every comma or possible misspelling.

Resist using direct quotation notes unless there is good reason to write them out, because the more note cards you have with quotations, the more tempting it is to overuse quotations in your research paper. Then, instead of being an original piece of writing reflecting your own sense of person, the paper easily becomes a cut-and-paste collection of other people's words (and their styles of writing).

There is, of course, some advantage to having note cards containing quotations, for you can use the wording for either a summary or a paraphrase if you wish.

Take direct quotation notes for any of the following reasons:

- The material is so significant or controversial that wording must be exact.
- The style is so perfect, so suitable, or so vivid that it seems beyond changing.
- The source is so authoritative that you want to be sure not to violate the precision of the wording.
- The wording of the source needs to be transmitted with absolute accuracy.

When you write a quotation on a note card, be sure to follow carefully the conventions that will ensure you give proper attribution should you include the quotation (or a summary or paraphrase of it) in your research paper. Here is what a quotation note card based on the original passage presented earlier might look like.

SAMPLE OF A QUOTATION NOTE CARD

New approaches to   Lamanna &
child abuse   Riedmann 298-99

    Various community supports are available. "One voluntary program, Parents Anonymous (PA), holds regular meetings to enhance self-esteem and educate abusive parents. Another voluntary asso / ciation, CALM, attempts to reach stressed parents before they hurt their children."

                                    quotation

Personal Comment Notes

Your own comments on your research subject are important to the research paper. Writing them on note cards while you are taking notes from other sources is best because:

- They catch your own insights quickly and preserve them in writing for future use.

- They help you make the synthesis between what you discover about your subject and your own ideas—the basis of a research paper.

Record all these thoughts, opinions, and even fleeting notions rather than leaving them to memory or to random scraps of paper. You obviously can't note down a source in the top right corner, but the "personal comment" at the lower right accounts for that lack on your card when you go back to work with it. This next example is a comment on the same passage used for other illustrations in this chapter.

SAMPLE OF A PERSONAL COMMENT NOTE CARD

Effectiveness of new approach

Despite the ever-increasing media coverage of abused children, I wonder how many parents actually see themselves as abusers and will voluntarily seek help available in their communities to stop the cycle of violence.

0   *personal comment*

Combination Notes

You can **combine summary, paraphrase, quotation,** and **personal comment notes in any way that is workable for you.** Just be sure you note the source at the top right so you can give accurate attribution in the text of the research paper and record in the lower right *what form of note is on the card* so you can maintain accuracy.

SAMPLE OF A COMBINATION QUOTATION
AND SUMMARY NOTE CARD

New approaches   Lamanna & Riedmann
to child abuse   298

Now "social workers and clinicians—rather
than the police and the court system—
increasingly investigate and treat abusive or
neglectful parents." Therefore the development of
programs that enable parents to feel better
about themselves and know more about their
children fits in with the approaches of these
workers who represent community involvement.

quotation and summary

NUMBER OF NOTE CARDS

Nobody can tell you how many note cards you will need for a particular research paper. If you already know something about the subject (and depending on how much), you will need fewer cards than if everything you discover is brand new to you. If you take effective notes, you will need fewer cards than if you don't. Some students find that thirty cards are enough for a 2,500-word research paper; others need three times that number. The quantity of note cards isn't really important; the *quality* of each one is what counts.

If you are in doubt about whether or not to record information or commentary, better write it down. If you discover later that you have more information than you need, set aside some note cards and don't use them, but don't discard them until you've received a grade on your research paper. No rule says you have to use every note card you write! But it's better to have too much information than not to have enough and be forced to track down additional materials at the last minute.

CONVENTIONS FOR WRITING NOTES

Readers expect to see certain customs followed when they see quotations, punctuation, italics, and spelling in a research paper. The easiest way to be sure your audience isn't disappointed or surprised is to follow those customs or conventions on the notes you take. Pay particular attention to the usual conventions for spelling (and give special care to unfamiliar words) and punctuation. This section gives you the conventions that apply to some special problems, and their solutions, that you may encounter in taking notes.

1. Quotations

All wording taken completely from a written or spoken source *must be acknowledged in two ways:*

- by enclosing the words in quotation marks
  and
- by crediting the source

The only way to prevent plagiarism, either deliberate or inadvertent (see the discussion at the opening of this chapter) is by making the proper acknowledgment on your note card when you write it.

Use conventional punctuation for quotations, both within your notes and in the written text of your paper. (In the final text, quotations within a sentence are separated from your own words by a comma, unless the quotation is the main portion of the sentence.)

a. Quotations at page breaks

If you *use a quotation that goes from one page to another,* note on your card where one page ends and another begins so you can document the passage accurately. A slash, or diagonal line (/), is conventional for the purpose.

EXAMPLE OF NOTE CARD

learning   "Reinforcement" 255-56

   Pryor's friend told her that the dolphin "made a long series of completely wrong responses. The animal was being reinforced by fish dispensed from a feeding machine; examination revealed that the fish in the machine had dried out and become unpalatable. When the fish were replaced, the / dolphin resumed making correct responses."

EXAMPLE IN PAPER

   Pryor tells a true story communicated to her by another
researcher, who said that after making many correct
responses, one day the dolphin being studied "made a long
series of completely wrong responses. The animal was being
reinforced by fish dispensed from a feeding machine;
examination revealed that the fish in the machine had dried
out and become unpalatable. When the fish were replaced,
the / dolphin resumed making correct responses"
("Reinforcement" 255-56).

b. Quotations within quotations

A quotation within the source you are quoting will be signaled by double quote marks. However, you need to show that fact in your notes (and in the text of your research paper) by using single quote marks within the double ones.

EXAMPLE OF NOTE CARD

sonar   *Blow 28*

   "A dolphin's sonar can cause a phenomenon
called cavitation, a ripping apart of molecules. (You
see it in everyday life when, for example, you throw
the throttle of a speedboat all the way down, but the
boat doesn't move; for that second the propeller is
cavitating the water.)
   "'It's very possible that dolphins are causing
cavitation inside soft tissue in the body,' Cole says.
'And if they did that with cellular membranes, which
are the boundaries between cells, they could
completely change cell molecules.' That could mean
stimulating the production of T cells or the release
of endorphins, hormones that prompt deep relaxation."

                                                  Quotation

EXAMPLE   IN   PAPER

The theory is that the dolphins' echolation energy causes "cavitation, a ripping apart of molecules. . . . inside soft tissue in the body." Cole says if that same process happens with cellular membranes and that if these are boundaries between cells, they could change cell molecules and thus assist the production of T cells (Blow).

c. Poetry quotations

If the passage you want to quote is two or three lines, use a slash (diagonal line that appears on typewriter and computer keyboards) with a space on either side to indicate the end of one poetic line and the beginning of another. The whole passage will be within quotation marks on your note card, and you should retain the capitalization and punctuation of the original poem, of course.

EXAMPLE   IN   PAPER

"In the room the women come and go / Talking of Michelangelo."

If the line you are quoting begins at a point other than the left margin of the poem, copy the spacing as you see it on the printed source or use ellipses (see upcoming section about "Words omitted from a quotation").

Poetry that has unusual spacing must be reproduced as accurately as possible from the original so that you can copy that spacing in the research paper itself.

EXAMPLE   IN   PAPER

King David was a sorrowful man:
  No cause for his sorrow had he;
And he called for the music of a hundred harps,
  To ease his melancholy.

If the poetry you want to quote will take *four or more lines when you write it in the final text of your research paper,* you must follow the typography of the poem you are quoting. Therefore, copy the poetry onto your note card *exactly* as it appears on the printed page that is your source. Long or "overflow" lines across a page should be treated the same way on both your note card and in the text of your paper: continue the line by indenting it an additional three spaces from the left margin you establish.

d. Italics within quotations

Any word or words italicized within a quotation should be underlined in your notes. This custom stems from the fact that printers seeing underlined words will automatically set them in italic typeface. In the text of your research paper, use the underlining if you are typing; but you may use italics if they are available on the word processing program you write with.

2. Words Omitted from a Quotation

You may decide to omit a word, a phrase, a sentence, or even a paragraph from a passage you are quoting, as long as doing so doesn't violate the sense of the original wording or idea *and* you maintain scholarly accuracy by showing that something is left out. Do so by substituting **an ellipsis: three periods with a space before and after each one.** If the omitted wording is at the end of the quotation, use four periods: three for the ellipsis and one to mark the end of the sentence, but don't leave any space before the first period or after the last one. (In the text of your paper, put the parenthetical reference after the last period.)

Four spaced periods are used on both note cards and texts to show omission of one or more lines or paragraphs from the original source. However, you must compose gramatically complete sentences both before and after the indicated omission.

Should you want to omit one or more lines of poetry within a passage you are quoting, signify that by a line of spaced periods approximately the length of the lines before and after it.

3. Interpolations or Commentaries

An *interpolation* is an interrupter that you supply as commentary to the text of a quotation or to your own wording as you write. **Enclose an interpolation in square brackets** both in notes and in the text of your research paper. Most computer and some typewriter keyboards have square brackets on them. If yours doesn't, draw in the brackets by hand both on the notes and on the paper itself. Three reasons you may want to make an interpolation are as follows:

a. To relate a pronoun to its antecedent noun.

Your interpolation following the pronoun supplies the antecedent noun that doesn't appear in the passage but without which the wording doesn't make much sense.

EXAMPLE OF NOTE CARD

therapy   Blow

　　In 1971 the researcher's young, mentally retarded
brother waded into the water with two dolphins normally
called "pretty rough" but they didnut act that way with him.
"'The dolphins were around him [the brother], still, gentle,
rubbing on him.' Somehow they knew he was different."

F   combination

But she reported that in this circumstance, "'The dolphins were around him [the brother], still, gentle, rubbing on him.' Somehow they knew he was different" (quoted in . . .).

b. To show that something is copied accurately, even though you recognize that it's wrong

The word *sic,* meaning "so" or "thus," in square brackets is evidence that you are aware something in a quotation is wrong, such as spelling or punctuation, but that you have, indeed, copied it down accurately. If you fail to make this interpolation at the time you write out the note card, you may mistakenly believe you've made a mistake when, in fact, the error is that of the source you are working from. Sometimes printing errors do occur, but you must not correct them, just copy down what you see and indicate to your own audience that you recognize the error.

EXAMPLE   OF   NOTE   CARD

Bacteria change   Morris 2

"The presents [sic] of modified bacteria are readily observable within 15 minutes of treatment."

c. To express a personal comment

Your comment can clarify an idea or wording drawn from some other source, or it can merely be a brief remark that comes to mind when you are writing the notes. Include your comment by putting it in square brackets within notes. (A longer comment will, of course, rate a note card of its own.) You can then either use or choose to omit that comment when writing the paper.

4. Foreign Words and Phrases

Non-English words or phrases are sometimes printed in italics, but often with no change in font. However, they are customarily underlined in your notes and in your paper, for underlining regular typefaces is the equivalent of italics in printing. If your computer program and printer support italics, use them in the research paper, provided your instructor does not object to your doing so.

5. Titles Within Quotations and Sources

Follow the writing conventions for handling titles when you write note cards, even though the source you are working from uses a different method. For example, if book titles are in quotation marks or boldface type in your source material, show them as underlined or italicized, unless they are part of a quotation. If they are, you are bound to reproduce them exactly as in the original source, but you can follow with an explanation in square brackets.

Put **quotation marks** around the titles of short stories, poems, essays, chapters in books, newspaper or magazine articles, songs, lectures or speeches, and individual episodes of radio and television series shows. Exceptions are sections of sacred writings, such as the names of books of the Bible.

Underline titles of books, plays, pamphlets, long poems, periodicals, films, laser discs, computer software, CDs or record sets, radio or television programs or series, paintings or sculptures, and even spacecraft. Exceptions are the titles of sacred writings, such as the Bible, the Koran, and the Talmud. You may italicize such titles in the text of your research paper, if your word processing program can do so. Internet and Web site addresses may be enclosed within "greater than" and "lesser than" symbols (< and >) found on computer keyboards.

A NOTE ABOUT PHOTOCOPIES AND PRINTOUTS

Take advantage of the convenience of photocopying relevant materials from books, periodicals, or microforms that you would otherwise have to work from only in a library. And once you start printing out what you find on the Internet or Web sites, you will quickly have a bundle of papers that form the bases of your research work. It would seem that there's no need for tediously writing out note cards when you can spread in front of you on a desk or table all you will need for your research paper.

But no matter how much you underline or highlight or otherwise mark up your photocopies and hard copy, they are still less effective to work from than note cards! *Only with cards do you have*

- easy-to-see slug lines that help you organize information
- information in flexible and movable form that can be readily organized, switched around, and reorganized as you plan and write a paper
- summaries, paraphrases, and key quotations that eliminate the need for continual textual searching

- easy integration of information from print, electronic, and nonprint resources—together with the personal observations you make that are elementary to what a research paper really is

IF YOU USE A COMPUTER

If you are familiar with personal computers, if you have one readily available, or if you are accustomed to working on one, you will probably use one for preparing your research paper. Most students who use computers seem to rely on word processing for writing and revising the paper. There are spell checkers, of course, to help with that aspect of writing. There are grammar checking programs and outlining capabilities for many word processing programs.

Battery-powered notebook computers are more readily available than ever before; their compact size and light weight make them convenient to carry with you to take notes from reference materials in a library or during interviews.

A computer can also be set up as a database for taking notes. Instead of using a note card, you can store the same information on a database program. Use the same categories of information (called "fields" in a database) that you would put on a note card:

Slug line or key word

Author

Title

Call number of book or location of periodical

Page numbers

Text of note

Type of note (that is, paraphrase, summary, or so on)

The difference between where to put this basic information on a database program entry and on a note card is dictated by the difference in the ways we write for each of them.

Leave plenty of room for your text. And remember to **limit yourself to just one idea per screen or citation,** just as you would if you were taking notes on 4- × 6-inch file cards.

If you don't know how to set up a database—or prefer not to—you can achieve the same effect by setting up a "template" on the computer through a word processing program. That is, use the categories shown for the database suggested, but write them out on a word processing program and repeat the format a number of times. Save them all to the data disc and then simply fill in the spaces when you take notes. A complete printout will give you these notes, and you can cut them apart to organize your information.

In all other aspects, adhere to the same customs and recommendations about writing note cards that you have been reading about in this chapter, including the conventions for writing notes, being complete and accurate, taking various kinds of notes, and, certainly, avoiding plagiarism.

Organizing Ideas

RECONSIDERATION TIME

If you've ever seen an iceberg—or a picture of one—what is visible above the water is only 10 percent of that amazing chunk of ice. If it's a big iceberg, you may find it hard to envision or even appreciate how much bulk and weight remain hidden from view. A research paper is very much like an iceberg, because what you can see is only a small part of the story. Only somebody who is familiar with the entire process of selecting a topic, locating and assembling and recording information, selecting what is most useful, and organizing the whole into a coherent work can best appreciate the research paper. What takes only fifteen minutes to read in its final form is the result of innumerable hours of painstaking work.

The part of the process you are now about to start is probably one of the most challenging:

- Looking hard at material you've gathered
- Evaluating the notes you've taken
- Organizing the notes you select

At this stage you show your critical judgment when you are willing to discard anything you believe is irrelevant or repetitive. No matter how difficult it is to delete material you've spent time finding and recording, it's better to keep the flow and focus of your paper than to try cramming in the content of every single note card.

As you begin to organize ideas, think again about *the audience* for this research paper you're writing.

- Do you know, or can you assume, that the audience has particular background or basic information about this subject? (If so, there's no need to repeat it in the text.)
- What do you expect the readers are likely to want to know about this subject? (Use the answer to that question as a guide to the content of your paper.)

In order to organize ideas effectively, you have to consider again some *decisions you have already made:*

- Are you satisfied with the approach you selected? (If not, can you change it and still fulfill the assignment?)

- Will the materials you gathered and your thinking support the approach you selected (or were assigned)?

- Do you need/want to consult any other resources? (Do so now.)

PUTTING THE PARTS TOGETHER

Until now, you have been working with parts of your research paper—with individual sources and separate note cards. But now you are ready to organize the ideas you've collected and make a transition from working with the parts to seeing them as elements in the whole unit: the research paper.

1. Consider each note card on its own merits.

As you read through the note cards, begin thinking about the main point you want to make in your paper. See if what you've written on a particular card relates directly to that main point and what you think you want to put into the paper. If the card content doesn't fit well, put the card aside rather than try to cram in extraneous material. (Advice: don't throw away any note cards you set aside; you may decide as you are writing that you want some of the information on them.)

2. Group the note cards according to slug lines or key words in the top left corner.

If you've done a good job of choosing these identifying words, you have a ready-made way of grouping ideas, and one step of organization is done. If you have too many cards with the same key words or find that a particular key word doesn't really express the idea of a note as well as you thought when you wrote it, try "renaming" the note card. Look again at cards with matching or similar key words and consider putting some of them together in order to make groups.

If you've taken notes on a computer or database, now is the time to sort the notes by key words. You should also make a printout, or hard copy, of the information so you can see exactly what you have to work with.

3. Make personal comment note cards.

In learning about your subject initially, and in thinking about it now, you surely must have encountered ideas you want to question or to comment on. If you haven't already noted them, do so now.

Because you have become an informed source on your subject, your comments are worth considering; putting them on note cards at this point will ensure that you don't overlook them in the haste of writing. Besides, incorporating your own views is an importatnt part of the synthesis that separates a research paper from a simple report.

4. Look for a central idea in all that you've learned through research.

By this stage in the process you certainly know enough to be able to take a stand on your subject and support it. As you review your notes, decide what you want to emphasize about your subject and what you want to build your work around. That central idea will become the thesis statement for your paper.

5. Alphabetize the preliminary citation cards.

When you start writing the initial draft of your paper, you will need these cards in order to write in-text citations. Of course, you will also need them to write the Works Cited listing at the end of your paper. Therefore, putting these cards in alphabetical order now, according to authors' last names or according to first words in titles of anonymous works, will make it easy to consult them for both purposes.

Now is also a good time to be sure you've examined all the sources you may need. If you were instructed to use both primary and secondary sources, both books and periodicals, some nonprint works and articles from scholarly journals as well as from the popular press, make sure you have fulfilled all those requirements.

WHAT A THESIS STATEMENT *IS*

A thesis statement is a declarative sentence that summarizes the point of view you will take in your paper. It states what you consider most signif-icant about your subject and is the touchstone of your paper—the starting place that synthesizes your discoveries and your evaluation of them. It is usually a single sentence, though it may be several if you plan to write a particularly long paper or your subject is especially complex. The more succinct and specific you make your thesis statement, the easier it is to use as the basis for an outline, which is the next step in organizing ideas and which should be completed before you begin actually writing your paper.

People arrive at thesis statements in different ways, depending on how they think and work. For some, the statement comes first—an immediate, overall, total view of the paper. For others, the statement evolves after grouping individual ideas into units (according to the slug lines on note cards) and then looking at the units to see how they fit together in a general way. One helpful way of working is to list specifics you want to include in your research paper and then to find the unifying idea(s) underlying them. Whichever method you use, the goal is to develop a thesis statement that you can work from in organizing the ideas within your paper.

Here are the characteristics of a successful (that is, workable) thesis statement:

1. The thesis statement is limited so it can give direction to the paper.

Earlier you decided on an approach to your subject: to examine or analyze it, evaluate it, compare and contrast it to something, establish a relationship, or argue a point of view. If your research and study have led you to a slight change of ideas or to a somewhat different approach, now is the time to make that change, provided your work will still fulfill the assignment. The thesis statement sets limits on the scope of the paper, so it should reflect the contents accurately.

UNLIMITED

Modern medicine can extend human life.

LIMITED

Helping people live longer is not good if the patient's quality of life is severely impaired.

2. The thesis statement is specific.

Anyone reading the thesis statement should know what the paper is about. Vague words won't do.

VAGUE

Environmental issues are very important.

SPECIFIC

Destruction of fresh water, clean air, forests, and mineral resources will lead to necessary lifestyle changes in future generations.

3. The thesis statement is a way to unify ideas within the paper.

That's why it is written *first*, before you begin to draft the text. Ideally, it should also be written before you spell out the specifics of an outline, so looking at the wording you put down will keep you from straying to extraneous ideas when you outline and then write the paper, no matter how individually interesting those ideas may be to you.

4. The thesis statement is an aid to coherence for your paper.

A good thesis statement holds together diverse aspects of the paper. Check every element of the outline and text against it, and omit anything that doesn't relate directly to it.

WHAT A THESIS STATEMENT *IS NOT*

Sometimes it is easier to understand an idea when you can see what it isn't rather than only what it is. The following four statements illustrate what a thesis statement *is not.*

1. A promise or statement of purpose is not a thesis statement.

Instead of promising to say or do something in your paper, go ahead and say or do it. But phrase the thesis statement to show that you have fulfilled your expectations, not simply that you *have* expectations.

PROMISE (Not a Thesis Statement)

In this paper I am going to show that opening the international Olympics to both pro and amateur athletes was a good rule change.

THESIS STATEMENT

Because the international Olympic games are held only every few years and maintaining "pure" amateurism in sports is beyond the ability of most would-be competitors these days, changing the rules to enable professionals to compete was a needed revision.

2. **A topic or subject by itself cannot serve as a thesis statement.**

The topic or subject tells only what the paper is about rather than what you have to say about the matter. Also, it is too generalized to be a thesis statement.

SUBJECT (Not a Thesis Statement)

Gourmet cooking

Capitalizing the first letter of each word, or even adding a few words, does not make a thesis statement—although doing so might eventually make a title for a paper.

SUBJECT OR TITLE (Not a Thesis Statement)

The Growing Popularity of Gourmet Cooking

Adding a predicate to a subject, however, might yield a thesis statement.

THESIS STATEMENT

The growing popularity of gourmet cooking reflects an increasingly affluent society that has the time and expendable income to indulge in food preparation as a hobby.

3. **Words added to a title but *not* forming a complete sentence cannot be a thesis statement.**

Although the contents of the paper may be suggested, unless there is a full sentence that expresses the attitude to be embodied in the paper, it is unacceptable. Also, only a gramatically complete sentence can serve as a thesis statement.

RESEARCH PAPER SUBJECT (or Title)

TV Rating Systems

NOT A THESIS STATEMENT

Ways around TV rating systems

THESIS   STATEMENT

A TV rating system will not work, because letter codes alone do not give enough information for parents to make informed choices and because stations carrying the programs cannot enforce the system.

4. A question cannot serve as a thesis statement.

This is obvious, because a question isn't a statement at all! A question only suggests that an answer is forthcoming.

QUESTION   (Not a Thesis Statement)

What can be done to begin solving environmental problems?

THESIS   STATEMENT

Effective and lasting solutions to environmental problems come about when activists use legal and nonviolent tactics to gain their ends.

HOW A THESIS STATEMENT EVOLVES

You should be thinking about the central idea for your paper while you write note cards, while you sort through them, and when you look again at the contents carefully. If you haven't already decided on a main emphasis by the time you've done all that, you should make a decision soon in order to develop a thesis statement.

Write out a statement you think will serve as a controlling idea or thesis for your paper. Keeping it in your head won't serve the same purpose as putting it on paper; it's too elusive. You need to put this very basic element of your research paper in writing so you can keep it in front of you while you're working with it from this point on. You may then readily tinker with it, rephrase it, further limit it, or enlarge the scope.

However, don't try to keep stretching a prospective thesis statement to accommodate every phrase or idea that comes to you. Realize that it's impossible to incorporate every single piece of information you've learned about your subject; you have to be willing to discard ideas, just as you must be willing to eliminate note cards that don't fit a structure.

Remember, too, that you will want to keep the interest of whoever reads your paper. Both of the sample student papers in this book (that by Melissa Fernandez in Chapter 10 and the one by Flaubert Lau in Chapter 11) are on "local" subjects these people felt others in their classes could relate to and therefore would also interest them.

Melissa Fernandez, the student whose MLA format research paper appears as a sample for you in Chapter 10, was assigned to write a persuasive research paper, so she began by expressing a position she could defend. Here is her record of the various tries at forming a workable thesis statement and her evaluations of each form that led to changes.

FIRST TRY

Dolphins are so intelligent they can be trained to help people in many ways.

COMMENT

This is a little vague. Further, some of the "help" they give is not necessarily the result of training. Also, the paper ought to include findings from research.

SECOND TRY

Echolocation is a dolphin skill that ought to be explored further for how it can benefit humans.

COMMENT

Limiting the paper to echolocation is a little too narrow. Also, why leave out the entertainment function? Further, most readers know nothing about the costs of keeping dolphins, so something on that subject ought to be included.

THIRD TRY

The most important and promising use for captive dolphins is in therapy for humans.

COMMENT

This is only learned through research. Also, limiting the paper in this way would be an imbalance by not recognizing other ways the dolphins interact with people.

FOURTH TRY

Although keeping bottlenose dolphins in captivity is expensive, it is worth doing because they adapt readily to recreational interaction with people and have many natural skills and an intelligence that make them especially useful for research purposes.

COMMENT

This will probably work out O.K. because it overs a lot of territory and I can put in some background information. Also, it allows for writing about their skills as well as their natural intelligence.

HOW AN OUTLINE EVOLVES

A thesis statement leads the way to an outline or pattern to follow when you write the paper. If you've grouped the note cards according to slug lines at the top left corner of each card before composing the thesis statement, you have completed the first step toward writing an outline. However, if you've not yet done this grouping, you must do that now.

Putting the written thesis statement in front of you when you sit down to compose an outline is a good idea, for then you can keep glancing at it and know you are staying on track. If you've already decided on an order that will help lead your audience to the understanding of or belief about your material that you want them to have, arrange your note cards to fit that order. If you haven't yet made that decision, the next section suggests some ways of ordering your information.

Some subjects dictate their own organization; in others, the thesis statement points the way. Still another way to organize a paper is to think in terms of your sorted note cards and decide what should go into each section of your paper.

Here are some possibilities based on two sample thesis statements shown earlier in this chapter.

THESIS STATEMENT #1

The growing popularity of gourmet cooking reflects an increasingly affluent society that has the time and expendable income to indulge in food preparation as a hobby.

The subject of this research paper will be gourmet cooking. The operable part of the statement is in the predicate: "reflects an increasingly affluent society that has the time and expendable income." The thesis, therefore, suggests that it will *explain why this hobby requires an affluent society*—that is, why time and expendable income are needed for it. A listing to support that structure might look like this:

Qualities of an affluent society

1. **Leisure**
2. **Possible self-indulgence**
3. **Income beyond necessities**

Qualities of gourmet cooking

1. **Expensive ingredients**
2. **Variety of equipment needed**
3. **Time for preparation**
4. **Many "unusual" ingredients used**

These lists then become the basis for an outline to support the thesis statement.

THESIS STATEMENT #2

Effective and lasting solutions to environmental problems come about when activists use legal and nonviolent tactics to gain their ends.

Here there is a built-in *argument:* that legal and nonviolent tactics will produce lasting solutions to environmental problems. The research paper author might first have to decide which environmental problems to consider: acid rain, destruction of old-growth forest, ocean pollution, noise pollution, decimation of animal and plant species by human encroachment, global warming, or others. After choosing a limited number of such problems, depending on time available and thoroughness anticipated, a preliminary organizational listing might begin with the possible tactics that will solve those particular environmental problems; from them, the writer could select those that were legal and those that were nonviolent, and then narrow the selection to solutions that had both qualities.

```
Limited Environmental Problem: Destruction of old-growth
                           forest
Possible solutions: Picketing tree-cutting
                    Spiking trees
                    Getting preventive injunctions
                    Buying forest lands
                    Naming land as national forest with no
                    cutting rights
Effectiveness of each solution
Support for method(s) selected
```

This is the beginning structure for a paper that will work for argumentation.

WAYS OF ORGANIZING CONTENT

The few examples just presented show how a carefully written thesis statement may lead to ideas about organization, an intermediate step before starting to design a formal outline. Whether or not you feel a "necessity" for organizational form stemming from your thesis statement, consider the following six ways of organizing ideas:

- Time
- Known to unknown *or* simple to complex
- Comparison and contrast
- General to particular *or* particular to general
- Problem to solution *or* question to answer
- Cause to effect *or* effect to cause

If you have taken a composition course, then this list, and the information that follows, will look familiar. They are ways of organizing material for *any* kind of nonfiction writing, from answering an essay exam question to writing a magazine article. Choose the method that will most easily and clearly help you to convey to the audience your approach to your subject and the content of your thesis statement.

Time

Many subjects clearly lend themselves to presentation in chronological order. Some examples are a paper that examines the critical receptions of a novel over a period of time, one that shows background leading to a historical event, or a paper showing a manufacturer how to phase in new production methods to keep up with increasing orders.

Known to Unknown or Simple to Complex

One of these methods leads readers from what is familiar to what might not yet be known or understood. The other begins with what is simple or easy to comprehend and takes readers to more difficult content. For example, a paper on the relatively new field of gene splicing might begin with a quick survey of what is already familiar about the role of genes in heredity. Or a research paper on the ethics of assisted death might begin with the more traditional, and simple, notions of what have long stood as the criteria for human death.

Comparison and Contrast

Both comparison and contrast show relationships among things, ideas, or people. But *comparison focuses on similarity,* while *contrast concentrates on dissimilarity.* Differences will be more effective, however, if shared characteristics are first established. The methods may be used separately, but they are often combined in a research paper. Comparison-and-contrast organization lends itself readily, for example, to examining the relative merits of three sites for building a proposed new sports center or to an analysis of different publications addressed to the same audience.

One of two organizations is usually used in comparison and contrast: *point-by-point* or *item-by-item.* In the first, you deal with one aspect of the subject at a time, showing comparison and contrast of one element of similarity and difference before moving on to show another element and its similarity and difference.

EXAMPLE OF POINT-BY-POINT COMPARISON

You have four elements of relationship that you propose to present in comparing and contrasting Idea A to Idea B.

Compare Element 1 of Idea A to Element 1 of Idea B

Contrast Element 1 of Idea A to Element 1 of Idea B

Compare Element 2 of Idea A to Element 2 of Idea B

Contrast Element 2 of Idea A to Element 2 of Idea B

(and so on)

In *item-by-item* organization of a comparison-and-contrast paper, you present all the material about one aspect of the subject before moving on to all the material of another aspect.

EXAMPLE OF ITEM-BY-ITEM COMPARISON

You have four points to compare and contrast Idea A to Idea B, so you compare
and contrast all the material about one point before moving on to all the
material about another point.

Explain Points 1, 2, 3, 4 of Idea A

Show how Points 1, 2, 3, 4 are the same in Idea B

Show how Points 1, 2, 3, 4 are different in Idea B

One drawback some readers find with the item-by-item organization is that by
the time they finish reading extensive information about one point, they forget
what came at the beginning and so may have some difficulty following the comparison and contrast that the author is establishing.

General to Particular or Particular to General

When you begin by writing some fairly broad ideas or statements and then
arrange the remaining information as a series of specific points, you are following
the general-to-particular arrangement of the content for your research paper. Or
you might organize your paper on the opposite basis: first present a series of
specific pieces of information that you later put together into a general conclusion
or statement.

Every good piece of writing will contain both specific and supporting points
within it, but that isn't the same as the structural or organizational framework now
being described. For example, a research paper on the short stories of James
Baldwin (or any other writer) might begin with the broad issues he wrote about
and then move to the instances of how he treated those issues in particular short
stories. Or the entire organization of the paper could be reversed, with the examination of the stories being presented first.

Problem to Solution or Question to Answer

If your research has been about how a particular problem was solved—or
how to go about finding a solution to something—you might use the problem-to-
solution organization for your paper. That is, you would begin by stating the problem that exists (or existed) and then make suggestions for its solution (or show how
it was solved).

This kind of organization is often used for business and technical papers written either in school or outside of it. The familiar organization for scientific papers
that proceeds from formulating a hypothesis to evaluating proposals and then to
solving a problem is a variation of the problem-to-solution method.

Cause to Effect or Effect to Cause

When the content of your paper lends itself to matters of causality, you might
begin by writing about an event (cause) and then show its result (effect). Or you
could specify a stituation (effect) and then trace its causes. A subject that might

lend itself to either of these kinds of organization is how limiting the use of certain national park areas (cause) has led to a resurgence of particular plant and animal species within them (effect) or how county school overcrowding (effect) came about (causes).

RELATING ORGANIZATION TO OVERALL APPROACH

In Chapter 3 you read about five possible approaches to the subject you decide to research: examine or analyze, evaluate or criticize, compare and contrast, establish relationships, and argue or persuade. You were also urged to select one of these approaches before you began searching for information and recording it. Adopting an overall approach is not the same as finding a way to organize the presentation of content in your paper; and though an overall approach may suggest an organizing principle, you can still consider a variety of possible organizing methods.

EXAMPLES

Approach: Examine or Analyze

Possible Subjects	*Possible Organizing Methods*
living arrangements for elderly	problems to solutions
deep space probes	known to unknown
Title IX impact on women's sports	time

Approach: Establish Relationships

Possible Subjects	*Possible Organizing Methods*
movies and violence	cause to effect
applications of studies in space	known to unknown

Approach: Argue or Persuade

Possible Subjects	*Possible Organizing Methods*
same-sex marriages	question to answer
school library censorship	particular to general

Courses or books about composition will show how to go about presenting the content within each of the organizing methods. In general, the emphasis will be on supporting statements with details—and in a research paper, many of the details will come from the notes you have already taken and the sources you have consulted (and which will be documented according to the techniques you will read about in Chapter 8).

VISUAL ORDERING—CLUSTERING AND MAPPING

Writing is linear: you start at one place and proceed in order to another and another. Some people, either through habit or because of the way they think, find that working with something more visual—with diagrams, or "pictures," rather than only with words—is easier, more agreeable, or preferable. The result is an ordering of ideas, but arrived at in a slightly different way from either listing or outlining (information on both of which follows). Called **clustering** or **mapping** (although the terms have slightly different meanings, the words are often used interchangeably), these visual ways of ordering ideas depend on using key words in a way that shows their relationships to each other.

Clustering begins with one word in the center of a circle drawn at the approximate middle of a page, just as illustrated in Chapter 3 on finding a subject for research. However, here it is used to show relationships among ideas. As thoughts occur, words expressing them are added to the page, each enclosed in its own circle, and lines are drawn to connect one to others. Using clustering to organize information already found and thought about is likely to be more organized than if it's applied in earlier stages of the research paper. Figure 33 presents an example of clustering done by the author of the student sample research paper at the end of Chapter 10.

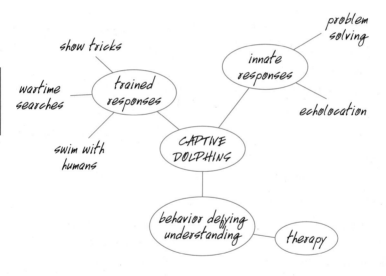

Fig. 33. Clustering preparatory to the writing of the sample research paper in Chapter 10.

Mapping is a bit less freewheeling and tends to have more order imposed on it from the start. It is a visual representation, or "map," of the author's way of leading the reader through the content of a research paper. For example, a map to show the order of ideas might be developed as a tree trunk and branches. Or the map may be a drawing of other recognizable things, such as the maze that one student thought represented environmental problems and that she drew as an organizational arrangement for her research paper. Figure 34 shows a map of the many ways the author of the sample research paper presented at the end of Chapter 10 believes a group of captive dolphins interact with humans within their enclosure.

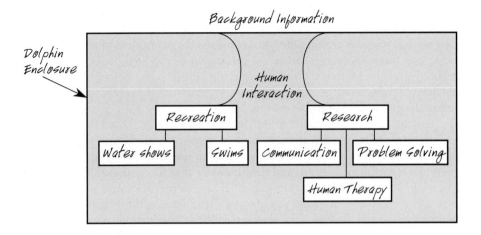

Fig. 34. Map (visualization) of the relationship of ideas for the sample research paper in Chapter 10.

Neither mapping nor clustering requires you to follow rules or conventions. Indeed, the result may be so idiosyncratic that only you, the author, can make sense of it and use it as the organizational basis for writing. Or you may decide to use the cluster or map as the basis for a formal outline, particularly if the latter is required as part of the research paper assignment.

OUTLINES

An outline is **an orderly plan, in writing, showing the division of ideas and their arrangement in relation to one another.** Its function is to show which ideas are of major importance and which are subordinate to the several major points your paper will make.

The outline is developed *after you have decided on the thesis statement*, because its purpose is to amplify the many ideas inherent in the thesis statement and to show how they relate to one another. It is usually written after you decide how to organize your material, because then you have a guide on how to proceed. You may find, however, that one organization doesn't work and you need to try another.

An *outline is always written before the text of a paper.* Making one afterward, just to fulfill an assignment, is foolish and useless!

Even though you have an order of presentation firmly in mind when you write the thesis statement, the outline is important because it:

- Keeps ideas firmly in mind, even if writing the paper takes a long time
- Lets you rearrange ideas and try out new arrangements without difficulty
- Shows visually how parts and transitions fit together
- Exposes strengths and weaknesses of the research paper in time to make adjustments before (or even during) writing

Don't be surprised if your outline isn't "perfect" the first time you put it down on paper. Few processes in writing are! Make changes as you go along. In fact, be free enough to make several different outlines as the many ideas of your research come into focus and you envision the proportion of the final paper. The whole point of an outline is to work out the structure of your paper before you sit down at computer or typewriter or desk. Then, when you write the paper, you need only follow the plan—the outline—you've made.

Perhaps your head is so full of the information you've gathered that you don't find the main ideas readily. If that's the case, prompt yourself with a bit of role-playing: pretend to be your audience, and ask questions based on the thesis statement. Jot down the questions, and then consider that the responses may well be the main ideas to develop in your paper. (If your actual audience, such as class-mates, is available, let them ask you questions based on the thesis statement.) The outline you develop becomes the sketch for your research paper. As with a paint-ing, subsequent details of the work emerge from that sketch. The outline shows key ideas and emphases and where various levels of development fit in.

There is no way of telling how long an outline should be in relation to the finished paper. Since it is only a guide, it shouldn't be so minutely detailed that it becomes a paper in itself. On the other hand, it shouldn't be so brief or vague that somebody reading it would have to guess about what you meant.

Content of Outlines

The most important part of an outline is what you put into it—the words that carry your ideas and help you organize what you plan to say in your research paper. Here are some guides for making the content of your outline meaningful and therefore helpful to you in writing.

1. Every word in the outline should say something about the content of your paper.

For this reason, "Introduction," "Body," and "Conclusion" are words that do not belong in an outline. They indicate the parts of every piece of writing—each of which must have a beginning, a middle, and an end—but give no information about the subject or what you plan to say about it. Instead of such "empty words," always use content-giving words in an outline.

Similarly, "who" or "why" statements (as in "Who responds to the ads" or "Why magazines are used") are not helpful in an outline. Rather than such vague state-ments, use language and information that tells exactly what your final paper will contain.

EXAMPLE

Thesis

Polygraph tests, as they are currently used by private
businesses, should be abolished as a condition of
employment because they are intrusive, demeaning, and often
inaccurate.

"Empty Wording"

  I. **Why use polygraphs**

      A. What they're good for

      B. What's wrong with them

Content-Giving Wording

  I. **Principles of the polygraph**

 II. **Current uses in business**

      A. Employment checks

          1. Time taken

          2. Costs to run

      B. Discourage thievery

      C. Screen characteristics of people

and so on

2. The information for each subheading must be directly related to, and subordinate to, the heading under which it appears.

Because an outline shows relationships among ideas, its entire content is a matter of showing visually how each thought relates to every other thought. That is, although some content will be of equal importance to other content, what is supportive and subordinate must be so designated.

Note, too, that because the entire content of the outline (and of the research paper) is related to and subordinate to both the title and the thesis statement, *neither one can appear as an individual item within the outline* itself.

If you have only one thing to say about any part of the outline (and, of course, you can't divide something into just one part), instead of trying to make artificial subdivisions, revise the wording or rethink the idea.

E X A M P L E

Thesis

Nonviolence movements in the 1960s eventually led to legal changes that advanced the cause of civil rights.

Wrong Outline

  I. **Economic**

      A. Boycotts

 II. **Physical**

      A. Sit-ins

      B. Bus rides

      C. Marches

Improved Outline

  I. **Economic action: boycotts**

```
II.  Physical action
     A.  Sit-ins
     B.  Bus rides
     C.  Marches
```

3. Make relationships clear by using the same kind of symbol (that is, roman numerals, capital letters, or so on) for ideas of equivalent importance.

Because the outline divides ideas, the symbols must show how the ideas or content of the research paper will be divided or subdivided into groups of thoughts related to one another.

EXAMPLE

Thesis

```
Somerset Maugham's experiences gave rise to many of his
most memorable literary works.
```

Wrong Outline Content

```
  I.  Sadie Thompson in "Rain"
 II.  From medical student to novelist
III.  Ashenden or the British Agent
      A.  Other successful early novels
      B.  Other genres
```

COMMENT

The phrases after each roman numeral are not equivalent, because they give three different kinds of information: a character, something autobiographical, a book title. And the two items under point III are not really subordinate to that roman numeral item.

Proper Outline Content

```
  I.  As medical student
      A.  Background for first novels
      B.  Insight into people in special circumstances
 II.  As World War I secret agent
III.  As world traveler
      A.  "Exotic" settings
      B.  Range of unusual people
 IV.  As prolific writer
      A.  Of fiction
      B.  Of nonfiction
```

COMMENT

All the roman numerals now show key periods in Maugham's life, and the capital letters indicate how each period had an impact on his literary output.

4. Only principal points appear in an outline.

Illustrations, amplifications, and development of the main points are added in the actual writing. To include everything in the outline would make an unwieldy, overly long document with little difference from the paper itself. You will be reminded of these details when you rearrange your note cards to coincide with the structure of the content you have decided on. Therefore, you should concentrate on putting principal ideas, rather than their support, in the outline.

Forms of Outlines

Outlines follow very specific forms and customs, and everyone reading an outline knows what to expect. The two principal forms are **topic outlines** and **sentence outlines.** Also used occasionally for particular purposes or disciplines are *paragraph outlines* and *decimal outlines.*

Topic Outline

In a topic outline, you write your ideas in *a word, a phrase, or a dependent clause* after one of the traditional symbols. There is no end punctuation after any words in a topic outline, because there are no complete sentences. However, do try to use a parallel and consistent grammatical structure throughout the topic outline.

EXAMPLE

I. Principles of polygraph

II. Uses by private businesses

    A. Discourage thievery

    B. Screen prospective employees

Sentence Outline

The sentence outline presents *statements as grammatically complete sentences,* with a period at the end of each. (Questions are *never* used in an outline.) Sentence outlines are widely used, because they force you to think through ideas completely in order to write them in full sentences.

EXAMPLE

I. The polygraph measures physiological changes in response to questions.

II. Private businesses use polygraph testing for at least two reasons.

    A. Employees are tested to thwart thievery.

    B. Potential employees are tested for characteristics that would make them undesirable employees.

. . .

Paragraph Outline

A paragraph outline has the same symbols as topic and sentence outlines, as shown in the next section (on conventions), but each symbol is followed by several sentences that make a paragraph. Such outlines are generally used for extended material (certainly more than 3,000 words) and for complex material. Otherwise, writing the outline would be tantamount to writing the whole paper.

Obviously, paragraph outlines are not as quick to make as topic or sentence outlines. Also, there is a danger that students who aren't careful in constructing a paragraph outline will end up writing a whole paper, merely putting outline symbols in front of each paragraph. The result is not a plan but an executed work, though not really a paper either.

Decimal Outline

The decimal outline uses a different symbol system from those just illustrated (and described in the following section). Each main item in this kind of outline is assigned an arabic numeral, and the support for it carries the same numeral followed by a decimal point and numerals to indicate further subdivisions. Thus, a decimal outline looks like this:

```
1.
   1.1
      1.1.1
      1.1.2
      1.1.3
   1.2
      1.2.1
      1.2.2
2.
   . . .
```

Either phrases or sentences follow each numerical designation throughout. This kind of outline is used more frequently in business and scientific writing than in other academic or professional work.

CONVENTIONS FOR OUTLINES

The most general convention for outlining is to use a **consistent form.** Decide in advance whether you will use a topic outline or a sentence outline, and then *stick to it throughout.* If you start with a topic outline, you may not write sentences within it. If you start with a sentence outline, you must write sentences all the way through.

1. Numbers and letters are used alternately.

These are the symbols you use to show relationships in all outlines except the decimal form. Basic to outlining is that *ideas of equivalent importance in the overall concept of the paper will have the same kind of symbol.*

- Roman numerals show the major divisions of the paper, so each major idea you propose to write about will be noted next to a roman numeral.
- Capital letters indicate the first subdivision.
- Arabic letters show divisions of the content indicated by the capital letters.
- Lowercase letters are used to subdivide information further.

Even narrower subdivision is possible, but it is seldom necessary for school research papers. However, should you want even more subdivision, follow the numeral–letter sequence, first using arabic numerals within parentheses, then small letters within parentheses.

2. Symbols in an outline must always appear in at least pairs.

That is, if you have a *I*, you must also have a *II*; if you have an *A*, you must have a *B*. The reason for this convention is obvious: an *outline shows the division of ideas* you will include in your paper, and *since you can't divide anything into just one part, you must have at least two parts of everything divided.* If you can't find two subdivisions for a unit, try combining the ideas of that single symbol with the one above it.

Two more notes about symbols in an outline:

- You may have *more* than two subdivisions for any item.
- There is no need to make an equal number of subdivisions, even under similar symbols. Your material and what you have to say about it should be your guides.

EXAMPLE

```
I.
    A.
        1.
        2.
        3.
            a.
            b.
    B.
    C.
```

II.

   A.

   B.

     1.

       a.

       b.

       c.

     2.

3. Every symbol in an outline is followed by a period.

The period acts as a separation between the symbols that establish the relationships and the wording itself. Put two spaces after a period and before the first word.

4. Capitalize the first letter of the first word after every symbol.

You would normally do that at the beginning of a sentence, and therefore in a sentence outline, but one outline convention is to capitalize the first word even in a topic outline. Thereafter, capital letters are used only in normal ways: for titles, names, places, and so on.

5. Grammatically complete sentences require normal sentence punctuation.

There may be commas, colons, and semicolons, as well as periods, in sentence outlines. Obviously, there will be no question marks, and exclamation marks should be avoided.

6. All symbols of the same kind should be in a vertical line down the page.

Doing so will emphasize the relationships among ideas and make reading the outline easier. Lining-up will take a little juggling on a typewriter or computer because the roman numerals will take one, two, or three spaces, but you should try to compensate and set up an easy-to-read format, as illustrated throughout this book.

One way to line up symbols is to type the first roman numeral two spaces (three columns) in from the left margin, which should be one inch from the edge of the paper. Roman numerals of two digits can then be indented one space and those with three digits begun at the left margin. To keep successive columns of symbols even, indent each five spaces, or a multiple of five spaces, from the left margins. Thus, all capital letters will occur in the same column, all arabic numerals in the same column (you probably won't be using more than a single digit), and so on.

7. Begin succeeding lines of writing under the start of the first word after a symbol.

That is, if a statement requires more than one line, begin the second and subsequent lines under the first word of the previous line. This format prevents interference with the vertical alignment of the symbols of the outline and thus keeps relationships among ideas visible, so adhere to this convention insofar as possible.

A. **This is an especially long statement and requires three lines, so the subsequent lines begin under the first word after the symbol.**

8. Type an outline in double spacing.

That is, keep the spacing in an outline the same as in the rest of your research paper.

REVISING OUTLINES

Even if you think your outline is pretty good, don't be satisfied with the first one you make. The next version will be even better! Test the outline constantly as you work, by thinking through each idea in relation to the others you want to express. Move ideas around and try them out in different relationships until you feel comfortable with the structure and content of what you will be writing. It's easy enough to make adjustments from one outline draft to another. When you think you've finally devised a satisfactory outline, put it away and forget about it for a few days (another good reason not to let writing a research paper go until the last minute!).

When you take the outline out again, test it by putting yourself in the position of the audience. Could whoever will read the paper follow your ideas and understand your viewpoint on the basis of the outline? If the audience will be someone from whom you expect no familiarity with the subject, try the outline on a friend or relative to whom the subject is new; if your "stand-in" audience can get a sense of what the final paper will be like, you can be satisfied with the outline.

Here is an example of two drafts of a topic outline developed by a student. On the left is an early version (though not the very first); on the right is her final version. Notice how the student cleared up problems of the division of ideas (as in point II.A.1), of focus (statistics and research studies are used to support ideas but are not principal points by themselves), and of emphasis (with the three elements cited in the thesis initially buried within the outline as divisions of section III). The final outline also shows that section II will be the emphasis of the paper.

EXAMPLE

Thesis

Animals can fulfill the social, physical, and emotional needs of elderly people whom society has neglected.

Early Version	*Final Version*
I. **Early man-animal relations**	I. **Precedents**
	II. **Benefits**

II.   Current statistics
    A. Elderly population
        1. Nursing home
           costs
    B. Animals as pets
III. Benefits of animal
    relationship
    A. Mental
    B. Social
    C. Physical
IV.   Research studies
V.   Support
    A. Organizations
    B. Government
        legislation

A. Companionship
    1. Physical
    2. Communication
B. Decreased isolation
C. Medical
    1. Blood pressure
    2. Heart disease
D. Reduced depression
E. Better self-
    perception
    1. Esteem
    2. Autonomy
III. Arguments for use
A. Individual
B. Professional
C. Governmental

COMPUTER AIDS TO OUTLINING

Because many people outside of academics need to organize information and thus need to work with outlines, there are many aids to outlining available for computers, and others will continue to be developed. Some are commercially available "idea processor" programs, and many are built into word processing programs. Find out what is available for the computer you usually use for writing. The advantage of using a computer for outlining is that it allows for easy changes and moving of words. On the other hand, many computer screens display only a limited number of text lines at one time, so if you work best by having everything visible simultaneously, you may be comfortable using the computer for an outline only if you can immediately print a hard copy after working on-screen.

A FINAL CHECK

As soon as you have a satisfactory outline, **put your note cards into working order by keying each with the outline symbol its content will be used to support.** The top left corner where you have written a slug line or key word is a good place to put this notation. That is, you might write *I.A.2.* on one card to indicate it contains information about the second item listed under roman numeral *I* and capital letter *A* of the outline, and write *I.A.3.* on another group of cards. Write these symbols in a different-color ink from what you wrote the note in (for instance, use red or green for them), and you'll be able to locate groups of symbols readily. Moreover, if the cards should become scrambled, having outline symbols on them will help you to put them back into working order quickly.

At this point, unless your instructor objects, show your outline to at least one other person. That "other" may be your instructor, especially if she or he has time for this preliminary look and is following along on the research process with you. Or the "other" may be a classmate. Ask whoever reads your outline to give it a really critical reading—which means that it is subjected to a serious, evaluative reading. The least helpful response you can get is "Yes, it's good." (If anybody tells you that, ask why and get some details.)

Begin by having your helper tell you on the basis of the thesis statement what she or he expects to find in your research paper. If that isn't what you plan to write, ascertain areas of disagreement and adjust either the outline or your proposed writing. Then ask your helper to assist by making sure that all of the following are true:

- The outline shows a progression of ideas that supports your thesis statement.
- Major and subordinate ideas are so designated by units and symbols.
- Subordinate units are reasonably balanced throughout the outline (such as not having eight units under one heading and only two under its parallel heading).

Overall, let your helper serve as your audience at this stage of the process.

Writing Your Paper

REPRISE OF WRITING PREPARATION

Consider how far you have come from thinking about and then deciding on a subject for your research, exploring numerous sources of information and selecting those to work with, taking notes, and then organizing your notes so you can demonstrate a flow of ideas as in your outline. The relationship between note cards and outline is readily apparent in these few excerpted note cards—taken from the sample research paper at the end of Chapter 11—and the beginning of the outline written for the paper. Note that the outline symbols have been added to other information on the note cards so the writer was able to follow her outline (as in Figure 35).

WHAT "DRAFTING" MEANS

People unfamiliar with this process are likely to call the next stage "writing" the paper, but those who are knowledgable will say they are "drafting" it. The latter term is preferred by many people because they know that a draft of a paper doesn't have the finality that a completed paper does; it's only a step in that direction. That is, all the time you are working at putting various versions of your research onto paper, you are actually drafting (or writing drafts) of it.

Drafting—or writing—doesn't come easily to most people, and you may be one for whom words don't flow readily onto paper, even when you have carefully thought your ideas through. Don't expect your writing habits to change suddenly and dramatically, even if you've done your preparatory work well. That's no guarantee that you can quickly write out a paper and then merely "fix up" spelling and punctuation before turning it in. Writing just doesn't work that way.

But *do* expect that all your serious and concentrated preparation *will* pay off when you take pen to paper or sit before the typewriter or computer keyboard. And *do* expect to produce a good piece of work because you have a plan to write from and the material with which to fill it in and see your research paper take shape.

Writing is a complex activity that involves constant thinking through of ideas and searching for the best wording and phrasing, all the while putting your ideas

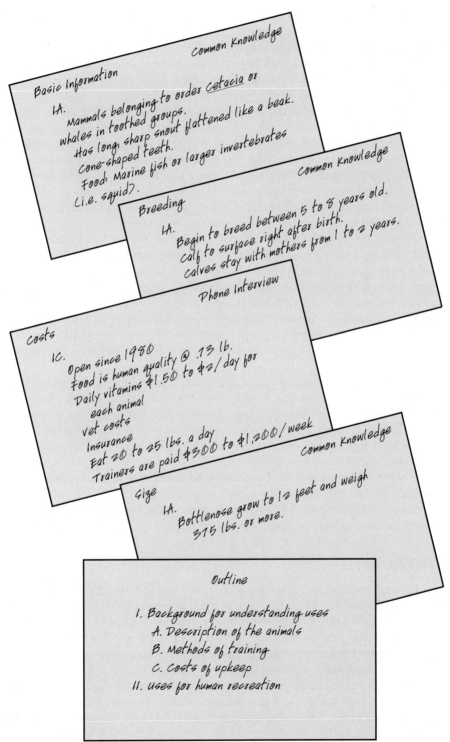

Fig. 35. Examples of note cards preliminary to outline and writing.

on paper. New thoughts will occur as you write, and as you proceed you should certainly fill in with common knowledge and with your own thinking rather than relying solely on notes you've taken.

People compose drafts in all sorts of ways. Some say they can only work on notebook paper when they sit in the library; others swear by late night sessions at the computer. Some prefer to write slowly and carefully from the beginning, making changes and corrections as they go along. Others find the best way to write, especially for a first or "zero" draft, is to put everything down on paper as quickly as possible and then later make extensive revisions. For many writers, drafting means moving ahead slowly, backing up to rephrase something, rushing ahead with ideas, then getting stalled. Drafting does take a long time, but it's certainly worth doing well. And it's definitely smart to hold off checking the mechanics of spelling and punctuation until you've finished what you think will be the last draft, because there's no need to stew over details that you may eventually discard.

Time is always a problem for busy students. So, better than frenzied, last-minute writing—which seldom shows the best work a student can do—a more useful method is to set aside chunks of time during which to draft your research paper. Work on it as much as you feel you can and in sessions as long as you can manage without interruption. For instance, aim at drafting the text of sections I.B. and I.C. of your outline at one sitting; then take a break before tackling section II. If you don't have time to work through certain passages as you go, write yourself a note or use some symbol to indicate you will pay special attention to that part in another draft.

Many people find that drafting on a computer is less inhibiting than composing in longhand or on a typewriter. It's also easier to make changes as you compose and to make subsequent changes when you revise. You will probably also want to follow the lead of many authors who compose on the computer keyboard but need to see a hard copy of the work in order to make final revisions and be completely satisfied with what they've produced!

If you're going to use word processing to write your paper, be completely familiar with the program *before* you begin writing with it. Trying to figure out how a computer program operates at the same time you're figuring out how best to present the materials you've found just doesn't work!

WRITING STYLE

Because your primary objective is to communicate clearly to your audience, work at clarity and keep your audience in mind as you draft. The way you write a research paper is not very different from the way you would write any other discourse. As in any good piece of writing, you should *vary sentence structures and sentence length*. Insofar as possible, *write in the active voice rather than the passive voice* to help readers keep moving along.

Especially in a research paper, you should write as specifically as possible, and certainly *avoid unsubstantiated generalizations*. Also, beware of catchall words. For instance, "young" may mean any age from six months to twenty (or more) years, depending on the age and orientation of the audience; but "eight years old" is precise.

Consistency in the way you write is particularly important in a research paper, because you are working from notes, including quotatations that may sound like a far different person from yourself. By and large, refer to a composition textbook or handbook for particulars about writing style and conventions.

However, despite its similarity to other kinds of writing, in a research paper you *are* expected to adhere to a number of stylistic conventions.

1. Usually, write in the third person.

That is, the words "I," "we," and "you" will not normally appear in the text, except as they occur in quoted material. A sense of distance between you and your material is customary in a research paper. Besides, the focus has to remain on what you have to say rather than on you, the person who is saying it. Writing in the first person (*I*) focuses attention on you, the author, and writing in the second person (*you*) draws the attention of the audience to itself. Therefore, third person directs the readers' entire attention to what you have to say.

2. Write straightforwardly.

The style of a research paper should be neither artificially formal nor as loose and relaxed as a personal letter. Some instructors feel that contractions have no place in this style of writing. For example, they may prefer "Writers do not usually..." to "Writers don't usually..." Check with your instructor if in doubt about her or his preferences.

3. Always refer to individuals by their full name (given name and surname) or by surname alone.

Never refer to a person by first (or given) name alone. Thus, "Alice Walker writes..." is the form to use—*not* "Alice writes..." Follow this custom even if you've interviewed a person with whom you are on a first-name basis or if you've read enough of (or about) a person to feel you know the individual well. Although such an ordinary title as "Ms" or "Mr." or "Mrs." is not generally used with a person's name, special titles usually are, as in Dr. Spock, President Truman, Dame Kiri Te Kanawa, Sir Paul McCartney.

4. Guard against wording that shows bias regarding a person's age, gender, race, political attitude, religious beliefs, sexual orientation, or national origin.

Unless such information—laudatory as well as derogatory—is necessary to what you are writing, strive for balance and nondiscriminatory language. If any such language appears in a passage you are quoting, you may want to acknowledge your awareness of such bias in the original by writing "[sic]," as appropriate.

Changes in job designations have helped eliminate some biases; for example, the terms "police officer" and "flight attendant" are a way of recognizing that both men and women hold those jobs. Writers and their readers are increasingly sensitive to the fact that "he" and "his" are masculine pronouns and thus inappropriate as pronouns referring to groups that include both sexes. Your own wording should certainly be gender fair.

Unless an individual's race or religion has some bearing on what you are writing, you may safely omit such a references even though a source you worked from might have mentioned the matter. The same is true for the other common biases just noted.

In sum, fairness should be evident in your writing, whatever the subject.

STARTING YOUR PAPER

As in all aspects of writing, people work in different ways: slowly, stop and start, straight through. Some are ready to start drafting a paper as soon as they sit down. Others are intimidated by the blank paper or screen and can't get out the first words, even though they are familiar with the subject matter. Even with a good outline, the actual act of writing is difficult for many.

You may like to start writing at the beginning of your paper. But if you have trouble getting started, *don't waste time worrying over it*. Instead, begin with another part of your outline, with a part that seems easier to write. Then *return* to the opening. Or you may even write the opening last. No rule says you have to write material in the same order your audience is going to read it!

Good Openings

As with so many other aspects of writing, you have many possible choices. One of them is how to open your research paper. Here are nine different kinds of beginnings you might use for your research paper, each illustrated by a sample paragraph. Consider these as idea starters rather than as what you should imitate slavishly. The best opening for your own research paper is the one that comes most naturally to you on the basis of what you've decided to say about your chosen subject.

1. Clarify the subject you are going to write about.

> Through the years, people have found various ways of
> communicating political thoughts and ideas to others.
> Speeches, books, letters, and articles are among the older
> ways. More recently, radio, TV, songs, and films have been
> the vehicles for political expression. Now there is the
> Internet. One other way that political messages have been
> conveyed is through a means often regarded, erroneously, as
> entertainment meant only for children rather than for the
> serious communication it often was: nursery rhymes.

(from "An Expose of Mother Goose" by Hilda Waldstein)

COMMENT

This opening points to the content of the student's research paper—nursery rhymes—by calling on readers to change from conventional belief in nursery rhymes as amusement for children to viewing them in a more serious light.

2. **State your position on the subject you have chosen.**

> The compulsion to gamble has often been the topic of psychological and sociological studies, especially as more states set up lotteries and gambling casinos as well as off-track betting. The psychology of the gambler has also spurred the imagination of creative writers. Two of Russia's foremost authors, Pushkin and Dostoevsky, each produced short works whose subject was gambling. The works are not only similar in subject matter, but also in the development of their major characters and in the approach both authors take in describing the workings of the mind of a gambler.

> (*from* "The Compulsion to Gamble in 'The Queen of Spades' and in *The Gambler*" by Richard Hildreth)

COMMENT

This paper will obviously be one of comparison and contrast regarding characters in two literary works. The author, however, will not take sides but seems to promise an even-handed approach.

3. **Relate your subject to something current or well known.**

> In the 1990s two of every three new workers are women. By the year 2000, experts project that 80% of women from twenty-five through fifty-four years of age will be employed and comprise nearly half (47%) of the paid labor force (Yalow 49). With such a large number of women in the workforce, many of them mothers, employers need to take into account some of these women's needs. Some employers have already done so. They have started by acknowledging that, besides having to work, many have family responsibilities. To ease the burden, especially that of child care, employers have started assisting their employees by offering a variety of benefits. They, in turn, have received tangible corporate payoffs.

> (*from* "Positive Impact of Employer-Sponsored Child Care" by Lissette Feijoo)

COMMENT

That a large part of the workforce in this country consists of women who also have child-care responsibilities is certainly well known. Statistics at the beginning of this passage serve to emphasize that familiar idea. However, because such information comprises proportionately less than half the passage, the paragraph amply illustrates a research paper beginning with what is current and well known.

4. Challenge some generally held assumption about your topic.

> If you worked hard until you were 65 years old, you could look forward to spending your last few years comfortably retired on a company pension plus government help from Social Security. No more getting up early and spending the day away from the home you worked hard to buy and maintain for your wife and family. Now there was time to fish or read or talk politics with cronies at the courthouse square. That was the "ideal," the picture sold to the public through the media and word of mouth: a dominantly male, small-town, imaginary kind of life. Today we know better. Retirees may be any age; they are as often female as male. Moreover, with companies increasingly cutting off or misusing pension funds--or even firing workers just before they are due to retire--many may not have incomes that were counted on; they often have ever-mounting and overwhelming medical bills; and many choose to lead active, involved lives--even to the point of starting new careers.

> *(from* "Redefining Retirement" by Gene Dana)

COMMENT

This paragraph starts by sketching a "traditional" view of retirement, especially as promulgated until relatively recently in various media and among large segments of the working public. It concludes, however, by pointing out present realities and shows how elements that will follow in the research paper are at odds with that view.

5. Show something paradoxical about your subject or about the material you will present.

> Television is certainly one of the most influential forces on society in this last half of the twentieth century. Yet although it is called "educational," it teaches little. Though it is called "real," it is fakery of the worst sort. Though it is said to embody American values, its programming choices have worked to destroy them. As so well illustrated in the novel *Being There*, what television

has actually encouraged is illiteracy, violence, passivity, and complacency.

> (*from "Being There* May Be The 'Great American Novel'"
> by Michael Davids)

COMMENT

The paradoxes of television are introduced here as a way of developing the paradoxes the reader will encounter in this research paper about the novel.

6. Use a brief quotation if you can find one that is applicable or provocative or that makes a general statement about your subject.

A look at the 1990 U.S. Census Bureau figures is enough to set the stage for an examination of the changing lifestyles of members of the 500 tribes and bands of Native Americans in this country. As Hodgkinson wrote:

> **Of the 1.9 million, about 637,000 are living on reservations or Trust Lands. However, 46,000 live in the New York/Long Island/New Jersey/Connecticut Combined Metro Area (CMA); 87,000 in the Los Angeles CMA; 15,000 in the Chicago CMA; and 40,000 in the San Francisco CMA; just to name the largest. A minimum of 252,000 Native Americans lived in cities in 1990. (1)**

> (*from* "Changing Lifestyles Among Native Americans" by Jason Robertson)

COMMENT

Given the still-widespread stereotypical views about Native Americans, this quotation of statistics sets the stage for the subject and thesis of this student's research paper.

7. State some striking facts or statistics you discovered about your topic.

A 1991 estimate (Yanowki 1231) is that at least 5% of young women in the United States between the ages of 15 and 25 are sufferers of bulimia, an eating disorder in which a person alternately binges and purges to lose or maintain weight in order to be thought slender enough to be "socially acceptable." It is a disorder sufficiently widespread to become the subject of television investigative reports and plays. There is also evidence that as the disorder becomes even more widely known and therefore more readily

identified, the percentage of women afflicted may prove to be greater than when this estimate was made.

(*from* "Bulimia and Society: Unrealized Expectations" by Christi West)

COMMENT

The student who opened her research paper with this paragraph tried unsuccessfully to find an approximate number of women believed bulimic at the time Yanowki wrote this information; she thought a number rather than a percentage would be more striking.

8. **Place your subject in time by giving some historical or chronological information.**

For as long as there have been liars, there have been attempts to find the truth. Those on trial in ancient China were made to chew rice powder while testifying. If the powder was dry when the suspect spat it out, he was judged guilty because it was assumed that nervousness over telling lies had dried the saliva in the suspect's mouth. Other ordeals were set up for suspected liars in other times, including being subjected to boiling water or red-hot stones ("Lie Detectors in Business" 69). Finally, with the invention of the modern polygraph (commonly called a lie detector) in 1921, it seemed that there was at last a foolproof way of finding out if people answering questions were lying or being truthful.

(*from* "Polygraph Tests and Employment Practices" by Ronnie B. Londner)

COMMENT

Instead of incorporating the thesis statement of this research paper into the opening paragraph, the writer puts it immediately in the next one. Ms. Londner used this method because she felt students reading her paper ought to know something about the strange history of lie detection.

9. **Give a brief description or background résumé of some person or event of significance to your topic.**

Seldom do we have the chance to watch a dramatic character develop throughout various works by the same author. It is, therefore, a fascinating glimpse into the mind of playwright Arthur Miller to follow the growth of Roslyn. She is first apparent in the thoughts of the three cowboys (Gay, Perce, and Guido) in "The Misfits," but doesn't appear in the story. Roslyn is unmistakable, however, in

another short story, "Please Don't Kill Anything," although
she is not named but is referred to as "the girl." Miller
finally combined the two characters for Roslyn in The
Misfits, which he called a cinema-novel because it used the
perspective of film and its images; it was also the basis
of the screenplay he wrote for the film of the same name.

    (from "Roslyn: Evolution of a Literary Character" by Judith Matz)

C O M M E N T

By setting out some background for the literary character that is the focus of this research paper, the author readily draws the audience into the approach she is taking.

Bad Openings

Just as there are good openings for your research paper and first paragraphs that draw the reader into your work, so are there also poor openings that detract from the quality of your paper. Six ways you should *not* begin a research paper follow.

1. Don't repeat the title.

It has already been read, usually just before beginning the text of the paper, so repeating it in the first paragraph is an obvious attempt to fill space and stall for time.

2. Don't tell what you propose to do in the paper.

Simply do it! A propositional statement may be customary in certain styles of business and technical reports, but it's unsuitable for research papers written for class. Any writing that says "In this paper I am going to . . ." is not only juvenile, but it also puts off readers and makes them impatient. Besides, it shows lack of imagination and subtlety.

3. Don't feel compelled to repeat the thesis statement completely in the opening of the paper.

Although you may certainly use the wording of the thesis statement—and, in fact, many teachers prefer that you include it by the end of the first paragraph—remember that you wrote it mainly *as a guide to yourself in your preparatory work* and as a way of focusing your paper. Besides, such a statement may disclose more than you want the audience to know at the outset of your paper.

You could, however, vary the wording of the thesis statement or begin by stating an idea inherent in it.

4. Don't ask a question.

You might get an unexpected answer.

5. Don't give a dictionary definition.

You may certainly refer to a dictionary, as you would to any other source of information. But beginning with a definition you didn't write, or one that is as poorly written as many definitions in dictionaries are, suggests that what follows the opening will be just as dull and lifeless as the definition. Instead, you can probably define any necessary terms more effectively in your own words. If you really feel you must quote from a dictionary, try holding off until later in your research paper.

6. Don't write a cute or folksy opening.

Such wording often falls flat and ruins the whole effect of your paper. Besides, a research paper, usually considered a serious work of scholarship, has no room in it for cuteness or excessive informality.

DRAFTING THE BODY OF YOUR PAPER

The body of your paper is where you explain and support your thesis. Obviously, you will acknowledge the sources you consulted as you write. As you do so, bear in mind that you are doing original writing about your subject, not just stringing together a series of quotations and paraphrases.

All the skills you have learned in writing courses through your many years of schooling should be applied to this task! Take time to put into practice all you know about explaining and supporting ideas fully. Clarify information that may be new to your audiences, and give needed background or illustrations to your readers. Names and terms that may now be familiar to you through your research might need to be defined or identified for your audience.

At this point in the research paper process you will need to recall what you've learned about the qualities of good writing. If you've forgotten some of what you once knew, take time to consult one or more books on composition and rhetoric—either those you use (or used) in classes or those available in any library.

The next four sections are reminders of some of those qualities that you should be particularly aware of in drafting your research paper. If they sound familiar, it's because you've probably read the same information in your composition textbooks.

Unity and Coherence

A **unified** research paper is one that deals with a single subject and has a central idea it sticks to about that subject. If you have chosen a subject carefully and prepared a good outline that you basically stick to as you write, you may be certain that your paper is unified. Resist any notion of getting carried away with an idea that strikes you while you are working, or of being tempted into a digression, for either will detract from the unity of your paper.

A **coherent** research paper is one that hangs together well, that not only holds the attention of readers but also helps them move from one point to another. A well-structured outline from which you write a carefully organized paper helps tie everything in it together.

The following are elements of writing that make for unity and coherence:

- **Transitional words** ("therefore," "however," "because," and others) and phrases ("in the second place," "at the same time," "as a result," and others) are signals to a reader that you are moving from one thought to another and that you are establishing a relationship between them. Use transitions between sentences to move from one idea to another and between paragraphs to tie them together.

- **Pronouns** (such as "he," "she," "they," "them," and "those") tie ideas together because they substitute for nouns, thus integrating the writing. Remember, however, that the noun that each pronoun replaces (that is, its *referent* or *antecedent*) must appear just before the pronoun, not several lines before it and certainly not after it. Clear and unequivocal pronouns help writing achieve coherence.

- **Repetition** of important words and phrases acts as an interlocking device. Repetition doesn't mean simply beginning a sentence with the words that ended the previous one. Besides being recognized as a padding device, doing so is boring and unnecessary. Although your repetition could involve the same wording, it's better to make it synonymous, but in varied language.

EXAMPLE OF BORING REPETITION

Gradually, more people are taking up the cause of **nonviolence to protect the environment.** *Protecting the* *environment by nonviolence* **has worked in several states.**

COMMENT

Note that the underlined wording and the italicized wording are so close it's almost like reading the same thing twice.

EXAMPLE OF REPETITION FOR COHERENCE

[Some dolphins] are kept in captivity. Keeping them in **artificial habitats such as cement tanks or fenced-in** **sections of free-flowing water . . .**

COMMENT

The "captivity" referred to in the first sentence is explained at the beginning of the following sentence as "artificial habitats such as cement tanks or fenced-in sections of free-flowing water."

- **Consistent point of view** means that the attitude or stance you take toward your subject remains the same throughout. Jumping from being one who figuratively sits back and contemplates the overall view of a situation to one who vigorously supports a course of action in relation to that situation is to be inconsistent in point of view. The writing that results tends to be fragmented rather than coherent.

- **Integration of information** is necessary so that quotations, summaries, and other information drawn from sources are joined within the text to make the writing flow. If these elements are simply plopped down, one after another, on a page, the result is choppy and disjointed. But if they are carefully introduced and integrated so that the whole reads smoothly, the entire research paper holds together and sounds as if one person—you—wrote it. A later section of this chapter, "Integrating Resource Information," tells about integrating sources into your own text; this is another element to work at when you draft your research paper.

Adequate Support

Writing that simply tosses out ideas has little believability, no matter how worthwhile or intriguing the thoughts may be. On the other hand, were those same ideas supported adequately, they would demand credence and even acceptance by readers.

Support for various statements in your research paper can take many forms, details of which are in most composition books. For instance, you might offer examples or statistics. Furthermore, using *authoritative sources* and *careful documentation* throughout your paper will be the major support for what you write. (See "Integrating Resource Information" in this chapter and the early sections of Chapter 8, about forms of documentation.)

How much support is "adequate" can't be described in any general terms, nor can it be pointed out before you begin drafting a paper. One thing you can do is to choose the most *specific words* possible. Another is to *assume the role of a detached observer* and, as you draft, keep asking yourself if you understand completely what is written; if you need further information at that point, then add it.

Emphasis

When you speak to somebody, you can emphasize what you believe is important by repeating words, by stressing particular ideas with your voice, or by pausing before making an important statement. You also get visual clues from an audience when you are speaking—both by facial expressions and by body language—that let you know whether to repeat ideas or to speak more slowly or more quickly. If your audience is just one person or a small group, you can be asked questions or receive verbal response. Lacking such clues, you can provide emphasis for readers on the written page by the following methods.

- **Use proportion.** That is, give proportionately more space to important ideas, and downplay less important or subordinate ideas by allotting them less space.

- **Use repetition.** Feel confident enough in writing to repeat words and ideas that are important and that you want the audience to be sure to notice. (This doesn't mean, however, that you should use unnecessary repetition.)

- *Use position* to put what you want to emphasize in "strong" sentence and paragraph locations. Beginnings and endings are two such places that readers pay particular attention to, because they are easy to spot in a text. These are also emphatic locations within entire pieces of writing.

- *Structure sentences to work for you.* *Parallel sentence structure* will draw attention to a series of ideas, particularly if you also use position within the sentence for even more emphasis. *Coordination and subordination* thoughtfully worked out for sentences will also give emphasis to what you are saying. *Sentence length* is still another way of controlling emphasis: short, easy-to-read sentences generally have more impact on readers than very complex ones that allow a reader to lose the train of thought within its convolutions.

- *Use visual devices,* such as underlinings, bullets (as in this list), boldface type, or italics, to give emphasis to particular thoughts within your research paper. Special layouts, such as vertical lists, can be used to set some information apart from regular margin-to-margin text. Subheads for units, provided the text is ample enough to support them, are still another visual device that gives emphasis.

Concreteness and Specificity

Good writing tells the audience exactly what you want to convey, leaving nothing to chance or guesswork. Therefore, wording ought to be concrete rather than abstract, and specific rather than general.

Concrete words name what you can ascertain through the senses: what you can see, hear, smell, touch, or taste. "A white, two-story Colonial-style house with green shutters" is concrete, because the words tell what you can see. **Abstract words,** on the other hand, name feelings, beliefs, or ideas. "Love," "sadness," "honor," "intellectual freedom," and "the American way" are examples of abstractions, because they may signify different concepts to those who read or hear the words. Although you can't do much advanced or sophisticated writing without using abstractions, concrete words are of great help in conveying your own thoughts (even abstractions) directly to your audience.

Specific words limit meaning in another way; they narrow the concept expressed by a **general word.** "Animal" is a general word, because it signifies a wide range of living creatures, from whales to amoebas. "Whale" is more specific than "animal," but even it can be made more specific: "baleen whales" describes a particular group, and "humpback whales" differentiates between that species and other kinds of baleen whales. In writing your research paper, the more specific the wording you use, the more accurately you convey your thoughts to readers.

INTEGRATING RESOURCE INFORMATION

The chief characteristic of research writing is that it not only acknowledges the sources of ideas used in the paper but also does so in specific forms. Such sources are the backup—the support and explanation—for what you have to say.

However, documenting them isn't an end in itself, and you must be careful not to let the resources become the dominant element in your research paper.

Examples of Well-Integrated Resource Information

Here are three examples of how a source, in the form of author and page number (which are adequate documentation for most purposes), can be used to acknowledge a quotation. In each example, information is sufficiently integrated with the text that it doesn't interfere with smooth reading or call attention to itself.

EXAMPLE 1

The novelty of the first air race exclusively for women pilots, denigratingly dubbed the "powder puff derby," in 1929 captured the imagination of great crowds who greeted them at every scheduled stop during the eight-day flight from Santa Monica, California, to Cleveland, Ohio. Many in the crowd were women. "They came to see what the powder puffers themselves looked like and after that what kind of airplanes they had. Some were so interested in these they poked umbrellas through the fabric on the wings to discover what was inside" (Earhart 153).

COMMENT

Documentation, consisting of both author and page location, is in parentheses and follows the quotation that must be acknowledged.

EXAMPLE 2

In writing about her 1929 participation in what was called the "powder puff derby," the first air race exclusively for women pilots, Earhart commented that many in the crowd who greeted them at every scheduled stop during the eight-day flight from Santa Monica, California, to Cleveland, Ohio, were women. "They came to see what the powder puffers themselves looked like and after that what kind of airplanes they had. Some were so interested in these they poked umbrellas through the fabric on the wings to discover what was inside" (153).

COMMENT

Here the author's name is part of a sentence leading into material that must be acknowledged, so only the page number is noted in the parentheses.

The same would be true if the author's name were in the text after the quotation.

EXAMPLE 3

On page 153, Earhart points out the novelty that women pilots were, especially to other women, in their scheduled stops during the 1929 air race exclusively for them. "They came to see what the powder puffers themselves looked like and after that what kind of airplanes they had. Some were so interested in these they poked umbrellas through the fabric on the wings to discover what was inside."

COMMENT

Because both author and page source are in the text, the acknowledgment is complete and no other documentation is required. Full information about the source will appear in the Works Cited at the end of the paper.

Acknowledging sources right in the text at the point where you use them is called **parenthetical documentation,** because the information is often given within parentheses. Use this form in the research paper you are preparing, because it is the standard for the MLA [Modern Language Association] that is customary in the humanities and is the basis of this book; it is also similar to that employed in several other academic disciplines. (See Chapter 11 for conventions of other documentation systems.) You will find the conventions of parenthetical documentation and some examples of how to use them explained at the beginning of Chapter 8. Each parenthetical documentation in your text must be supported by a complete citation, such as you have written on the preliminary citation cards and will write in the Works Cited at the end of your paper.

To keep the focus of your writing on your own ideas instead of on the documentation, you should integrate the two as smoothly as you can so as not to disrupt the flow of writing in your paper or call attention to differences in style and tone between what you write and what your reference sources wrote. Therefore, the mark of a well-integrated resource item is that it doesn't call attention to itself!

Six Ways to Integrate Documented Information into the Text of a Research Paper

1. Use wording that shows what follows is not your own.

That is, if you indicate at the beginning of a passage that you are about to present material that will be documented, you prevent misunderstanding or confusion on the part of the reader. Careful readers are often frustrated to come on a passage they ascribe to the author of the research paper, only to find later in the paragraph that it was actually a summary, a paraphrase, or an idea the author had carefully credited. (Quotations are evident by their punctuation, so the problem is less acute.)

HELPFUL LEAD-IN

For example, Dr. David E. Nathanson, whose Dolphin Therapy Research facility is next to Dolphins Plus, said in an interview that he contracts with that organization to use some of the dolphins it owns for his own work.

COMMENT

Merely saying that the Dolphin Therapy Research facility does not own all of the animals it uses would not have the weight of believability that does this informal summary of part of an interview. Readers can find the date of the interview in the Works Cited for this research paper.

2. Vary the wording of introductory phrases.

Easy as it is to write that a person "says" or "writes" something you use in your research paper, good writing style demands that you be more imaginative and less repetitive in introducing such material. A dictionary or thesaurus may be helpful in solving this problem.

POSSIBILITIES

Professor Joshua Ryan *states*

> *asserts*
>
> *believes*
>
> *thinks*
>
> *insists*
>
> *contends*
>
> *confirms*
>
> *declares*
>
> *emphasizes*
>
> *adds*
>
> *affirms*
>
> *points out*

Varied wording such as this may be used to introduce indirect as well as direct quotations or any other material you are documenting.

3. Document information anywhere in a sentence or in a paragraph.

Looking at a paper with documentation parentheses at the end of every paragraph gives most readers the impression that the author has done little more than paste together pieces of information, one after another, without much thought of the relationship of other peoples' ideas to the author's own. End-of-paragraph documentation is particularly disturbing to readers if the endings of paragraphs are quotations. Therefore, as you write, try to vary the location of documentation in both sentences and paragraphs. Your goal should be to prevent a cut-and-paste look!

EXAMPLES

Documentation at the beginning of a sentence and a paragraph

Herman, Pack, and Wood have reported their experiments in
having dolphins respond to signals in which the arm/hand
configuration represents a word or idea, much as American
Sign Language does. The dolphins are able . . .

Documentation within a sentence and in the middle of a paragraph

Because of the success with dolphin-assisted therapy with
the mentally and physically disabled so far, the method
holds out hope "for patients with head and spinal injuries,
cancer and other conditions" (Kalfrim). Obviously, in order
to provide such therapy, some dolphins need to be kept
captive in order to be available to help humans.

Documentation at the end of a sentence and/or the end of a paragraph

. . . also regularly made grants available to researchers,
as did the National Science Foundation; funding from such
sources is acknowledged in published journal articles (see
Herman, Pack, and Wood; Mackay).

4. **Make documented material fit grammatically into your own sentences.**

   Do this in any of three different ways:

   a. Delete words from a quotation and use an ellipsis to show you have done so.

      EXAMPLE

      Furthermore, as Blow summarized, ". . . there seems
      little doubt that dolphin swims can help humans with
      disabilities such as Down's syndrome, autism, depression,
      attention deficit disorder, muscular dystrophy, and
      spinal cord injuries."

   b. Use square brackets to clarify or provide information that would other-
      wise not fit in the context of you own writing.

      EXAMPLE

      Yesterday, before the break of dawn, Bebe, a 40-year-old
      AB [American Bottlenose] dolphin and mother of 6, had
      her 7th successful calf.

   c. Use only the most relevant part of a passage you document; no rule says
      you have to use in the final paper every single word you put on a note card.

EXAMPLE

NOTE CARD

feeding behavior   *Wursig 143*

*Dolphin schools spread out as far as 25 meters
apart, possibly accoustically scanning a large
area of water 15–35 meters deep to find the
most food, then begin to dive and mill around.
They were probably herding schools of anchovies
to the surface for feeding.*

F   *Summary*

USE IN RESEARCH PAPER

**This is necessary for them to find food, as they often do
cooperatively (as pointed out in Wursig 143), as well as
keeping track . . .**

5. Instead of documenting every line in a paragraph, group the citations for a single passage.

To document every line suggests you have little to say for yourself. Also, excessive documentation is unnecessary and awkward. Instead, combine ideas and use one citation for several sources.

EXAMPLE

**. . . even when given the choice of roaming free vs. being
in pens, most who are used to living in the latter
willingly return to them (Borguss; Pryor "Domestic" 346;
La Puzza; Cousteau 189).**

6. Use paraphrases and summaries, not just quotations, to support what you say.

Certainly you will want to use quotations in your research paper. But as you come to a note containing a quotation, consider whether you could convey the same idea by paraphrasing or summarizing it in the text of your research paper.

EXAMPLE

NOTE CARD

Pryor/Schusterman 253/54

"The training of behavior in terrestrial domestic animals is almost always accomplished by means of negative reinforcement, coercion, and restraint, and it is enforced with punishment. . . . The dolphin, however, is not easily trained by these negative methods. You cannot use a leash or a bridle or even your fist on an animals which just swims away. The dolphin thus has become one of the few large mammals with / 254 which we have had extensive experience in the shaping of behavior primarily, and indeed in most cases almost exclusively, by the use of positive reinforcement."

USE IN RESEARCH PAPER

No wonder, then, that dolphins are usually trained by the behavioral method we call "positive reinforcement." To do otherwise would be impractical because, as Pryor points out ("Reinforcement" 253), dolphins will just swim away from anyone who attempts to train them by coercion or restraint.

Inexperienced writers often ask, "How much documentation do I need to include in my paper?" The answer is, "Nobody can tell you." Certainly you need to give the sources of content in the paper that you didn't already know or that is not common knowledge. Therefore, the more information that was totally new to you, the more you will have to document.

Another concern in drafting the text of the research paper is how heavily to rely on quotations versus summaries and paraphrases. Again, there is no pat advice that anyone can give. As already stated in Chapter 5 on "Recording Information," you should record quotations if your source is well known or carries weight in the field you are writing about, if the quotation is your hedge for accuracy, or if the person's words seem so excellent that they bear repeating directly.

Your concern at this point, especially in initial drafts, is how to work into the body of your research paper the various elements needed, including your personal comments or observations, and how to do it all smoothly.

RECORDING AND PUNCTUATING QUOTATIONS

Note cards will show the spelling, punctuation, and capitalization of any quotations you decide to incorporate into your research paper—and, of course, you are duty bound to record them exactly as they appeared in the original source. When you blend such wording into the text of your paper, follow the usual rules of punctuation and a few conventions that are found in writing handbooks and textbooks (several of which are repeated here and illustrated for your convenience).

- If the end of a quotation is also the end of your own sentence, put one period for both inside the concluding quote marks.

  EXAMPLE

  He goes on to say that dolphins can therefore communicate with each other by what he calls mind-to-mind transmission, "directly transmitting imagery to another dolphin."

- Use a comma to signify the end of the quoted sentence that is not the end of a text sentence. Put a period at the end of the entire sentence you write that includes the quotation.

  EXAMPLE

  Au and Turl's findings (2448) that the dolphins could differentiate between "a hollow stainless steel cylinder . . . and a cylinder consisting of coral rock aggregates encapsulated in degassed epoxy with the same outer diameter and length," certainly indicates the sophistication of the animals' abilities of echolocation.

- A question mark or an exclamation mark that ends a quotation goes inside the concluding quote marks, even though your own sentence continues to its conclusion and may have a period at its end.

  EXAMPLE

  Free-swimming dolphins taught to find and report objects larger than a breadbox and manufactured "soon found engine blocks, a movie camera, quite a lot of fishing equipment,

`and a World War II airplane!" in the water around the pier`

`where they were trained.`

- Direct quotations are either part of a sentence or are separated from introductory wording by a comma, depending on the construction of the sentence. Only occasionally does a colon introduce a short quotation.

  EXAMPLE

  `Furthermore, ". . . there seems little doubt that dolphin`

  `swims can help humans with disabilities such as Down's`

  `syndrome, autism, depression, attention deficit disorder,`

  `muscular dystrophy, and spinal cord injuries" (Blow).`

- Use a capital letter to begin a fully quoted sentence, even if it does not also begin your own sentence of text.

  EXAMPLE

  `As Karen Pryor, herself a former trainer and later`

  `Commissioner of the Marine Mammal Commission, writes,`

  `"Techniques for the maintenance and training of dolphins`

  `were being developed during roughly the same decades in`

  `which experimental psychologists were reaching an`

  `understanding of the laws of operant conditioning, and the`

  `ways in which behavior could be modified by using positive`

  `reinforcement" (254 "Reinforcement").`

- Retain any special punctuation or other markings of the original passage when you reproduce it as a quotation in your paper.

  EXAMPLE

  `Merimee alludes to the earthiness of his main character in`

  `several ways. For example, "Carmen, who had a sharp tongue`

  `in her head, said, 'Isn't a broomstick good enough for you,`

  `then?' " (22).`

In addition to setting apart the words of another person from your own, **quotation marks are used to enclose familiar words that are used in a special sense.**

  EXAMPLE

  `. . . on or in the water, and "tail walking" across an`

  `enclosure.`

As in all writing, **a quotation within another quotation** (that is, when the source you quote contains a quotation) **is indicated by single, instead of double, quotation marks.** Any comma ending the quotation appears before either of those quote marks.

EXAMPLE

But, as Blow wrote in his article, in this circumstance,
" 'The dolphins were around him [the brother], still,
gentle, rubbing on him.' Somehow they knew he was
different."

Short Prose Passages

A "short" prose quotation of either fiction or nonfiction is one that occupies *four or fewer lines of text* in your research paper. Write it as part of the regular text of the paper, using the same spacing but observing the conventions just noted for punctuating quotations.

EXAMPLE

A similar phenomenon was described by Chris Connell of the
Dolphin Human Therapy and Research Program in Key Largo,
FL, who said, "I remember a boy whose leg had been badly
damaged by cancer. Almost as soon as he got into the water,
a group of dolphins began to softly rub against his wounded
leg" (Halls).

Parenthetical documentation is placed as close as possible to the passage, either in the lead-in wording or outside the ending quotation marks, as long as it doesn't interfere with the flow of the text.

Longer Prose Passages

Quotations of *five or more lines of text* in your research paper are considered "longer" and are signaled to the audience in a different way. There is usually introductory wording that often, but not always, ends with a colon. Then the entire quoted passage is *indented ten spaces from the left margin.* Do not use quotation marks (the block indentation marks it as a quotation), and do not change the double spacing of the rest of the text.

EXAMPLE

Strauch is intrigued by the possibility of dolphins
transmitting imagery among themselves:

> Think about a dolphin that has been the
> underwater equivalent of over the mountains and
> wishes to tell its peers about the experience. . . .
> By stereophonically reproducing the waveforms it
> received while it was echolocating, the dolphin
> can communicate the full acoustic image of what
> it 'saw,' placing it directly in the minds of

```
those it is communicating with. It could also

selectively filter and interpret that experience,

highlighting aspects that it wished to emphasize

and playing down aspects it wished to

deemphasize. (114)
```

Put any needed page reference or other identification for a long quotation *in parentheses two spaces after the period* that concludes the quotation.

If there is a *new paragraph within the quotation, indent it three spaces from the left margin of the quote* (that is, thirteen spaces from the left margin of the text).

Short Passages of Poetry

One line or part of a line of poetry may be quoted as part of a sentence. *Two to three lines* may be treated as part of a sentence or otherwise incorporated into the text, provided you retain the capitalization of the original and put a slash mark with a space on each side to show where lines are separated in the original typography.

E X A M P L E

```
In Sonnet 116, Shakespeare announces, "Let me not to the

marriage of true minds / Admit impediments. Love is not

love / Which alters when it alteration finds."
```

Longer Passages of Poetry

Quotations of *four or more lines of poetry* should appear in the text of your research paper the same way they do in the original poem, and each line should normally begin ten spaces in from the left margin of the text. Note, though, that the text of quoted poetry continues to be double spaced when it is included in a research paper.

Because the accurate quotation of poetry requires you to reproduce the original typography and formatting, you may need to ignore customary indentation if the poem you are reproducing has an unusual format. Then, copy the poem exactly it appears in the original source, as in this example of "Easter Wings" by George Herbert.

E X A M P L E

```
Lord, Who createdst man in wealth and store,

   Though foolishly he lost the same,

      Decaying more and more,

         Till he became

            more Poore:

            With thee

         O let me rise,
```

> As larks harmoniously,
>
> And sing this day Thy victories:
>
> Then shall the fall further the flight in me.

Identify the author and title of a long poetry quotation as part of the text, as shown in the introduction to the preceding example, or at the beginning of the poem, this way:

> **Easter Wings**
>
> **by George Herbert**

If you can't get a complete verse line on a single line of type that's indented ten spaces on your paper, or if doing so would make the quoted poetry look unbalanced, you may begin each line closer to the left margin. Lines of poetry that don't quite fit a line in your research paper should be continued on the next line with a three-space indentation following the ten spaces.

EXAMPLE

> Meanwhile Aeneas held his fleet on its course
>   through the deep sea
> Undeviating, and clove the waves that were gloomed
>   by a Northwind.
> He looked back at Carthage's walls; they were lit
>   up now by the death-fires of tragic
> Dido.   (Book V, Aenid)

If the source of a long passage of poetry is not acknowledged at its beginning, do so two spaces after the last period of the poetry, as in this last example.

Drama

Dramatic quotations will be in either prose or poetry, so follow the form recommended for the genre of drama you will be quoting from. That is, up to three lines of dialogue or stage direction may be incorporated into the text, but longer passages (four or more lines) should be indented ten spaces from the left. Be sure to include the name of the character speaking, either in the introduction to the dialogue or just as it appears in the source you use. If you quote a passage that represents more than one speaker, indicate the first line of each speaker by beginning with the character's name in capital letters ten spaces in from the left margin followed by a period; subsequent lines of that dialogue are indented an additional three spaces. Start a new line for the dialogue of each character.

EXAMPLES

Short Quotation

Romeo begins what is popularly called the balcony scene by saying, "He jests at scars that never felt a wound."

Longer Quotation

Here, in Act V is the beginning of the scene in *The Taming of the Shrew* in which Petruchio shows off his wife's obedience:

> BAPTISTA.   O, O, Petruchio! Tranio hits you now.
>
> LUCENTIO.   I thank thee for that gird, good Tranio.
>
> HORTENSIO.   Confess, confess! Hath he not hit you here?
>
> PETRUCHIO.   He has a little galled me, I confess.
> And as the jest did glance away from me,
> 'Tis ten to one it maimed you two outright.
>
> BAPTISTA.   Now, in good sadness, son Petruchio,
> I think thou has the veriest shrew of all.

Longer Quotation

The following exchange takes place in Olivia's garden, Act 2, Scene 5, in *Twelfth Night*:

> SIR TOBY.   Here comes the little villain. He now, my metal of India!
>
> MARIA.   Get you all three into the box-tree; Malvolio's coming down this walk. He has been yonder i' the sun practising behaviour to his own shadow this half hour.
>
>   . . .
>
> MALVOLIO.   'Tis but fortune. All is fortune. Maria once told me she did affect me; and I have heard herself come thus near, that, should she fancy, it should be one of my complexion. Besides, she uses me with a more exalted respect than any one else that follows her. What should I think on't?

COMMENT NOTES

Sometimes, while drafting the text of your research paper, you may find that you want to add to or qualify something that doesn't lend itself to simple parenthetical documentation and that can't be accomplished without distracting from the text. Rather than break into thoughts being expressed in the paper, make such comments—sparingly—in the **endnotes** that, in the MLA style, appear **at the conclusion of the research paper.** (In APA style these are called "footnotes," although they, too, are put on a separate page at the end of the text rather than at the bottom or foot of a page. See Chapter 11.)

Comment notes are used for any of the following:

* Brief elaboration, qualification, or addition to what is in the text
* A necessary evaluative comment on a source
* Identifying a series of sources that, if shown in parenthetical documentation, would interrupt the text of the paper

Signal comment notes by numbering them successively throughout the paper with superscript arabic numerals, such as this,[1] at the place where they are most relevant and after punctuation markings, except dashes. Use the same arabic numerals at the beginning of the note; then give the information.

EXAMPLE

[1] **No periods or other marks appear with the superscript numeral and no space is used before it. However, *one space always follows the numeral,* both in the text and on the note page.**

Start endnotes on a separate page headed "Notes" (centered one inch down from the top of the page) at the conclusion of the research paper and before the Works Cited page. Double-space after the heading and throughout the notes on the page. Begin each note by indenting the superscript numeral five spaces from the left margin; leave a space after it and then start the words of the note, writing as far as necessary toward the right. Second and succeeding lines of each note begin at the left margin of the page.

You can see endnotes used for comment on the text of the sample research paper on page 260.

ENDING THE PAPER

Stop writing when you finish what you have to say. When you come to the end of your outline and note cards, conclude gracefully but not abruptly. Don't pad at the end, and don't try to write a sudden one-sentence "summary" of the whole paper. In particular, *don't introduce or even suggest any new ideas in the last paragraph or so of your paper!*

Good Endings

The following are some suggestions about how to end a research paper. The ending you decide on may not fit into such specific categories, or it may be a combinition of these, but you should let the ending stem from your text rather than trying to change it to fit a formula.

1. **If you have written an argumentive or persuasive paper, remind the audience of what you want them to do or think in response to your presentation.**

    EXAMPLE

    ```
    Society continues to dictate that the ultra-thin body is
    the ideal for women. The intense pressures on young women
    to achieve this false, Madison Avenue image lead many into
    the desperate downward spiral of bulimia. For society to
    drastically change its ideals of the "proper" body
    appearance is unrealistic. However, to combat this,
    people should be encouraged to be more accepting of
    the differences in weight and physical appearance among
    individuals. Even more immediately attainable is the
    realistic and very desirable goal of providing affordable
    treatment for bulimia.
    ```

    (*from* "Bulimia and Society: Unrealized Expectations" by Christi West)

    COMMENT

    The two major points this author has made in her research paper—individual acceptance and affordable treatment—conclude the work as a reminder of the direction that this entire persuasive paper has taken. Because they are the last words readers read, they are the most likely to be remembered.

2. **Use a brief quotation that summarizes the ideas or attitudes you have expressed throughout the paper.**

    EXAMPLE

    ```
    Thucydides made mistakes, to be sure, but the historical
    significance of his work cannot be disputed. Like any great
    leader, he needed courage to break away from tradition and
    to introduce new ideas. His contributions are summed up
    this way by Finley:

                    For he, as clearly as any tragedian, indeed as
                    any Greek author, possessed the greatest of Greek
                    abilities, the ability to observe the actualities
                    of life with unflinching candor, yet at the same
                    time, without falsifying these actualities, to
                    reduce them to their generic and hence their
                    lasting patterns. To have performed this feat
                    both of record and of simplification on a plane
                    of strict reality, and at a time when the basic
    ```

> **political ideas of Western man were at issue is**
> **Thucydides' monumental triumph. (325)**
>
> (*from* "Thucydides as a Historian" by Gerald Douthit)

COMMENT

Use a quotation only if it bears out the points you've made within your research paper—as this one does—and if you think the style is particularly suitable to the subject.

3. **Make some statement about your thesis instead of merely repeating it.**

EXAMPLE

> **Both "The Queen of Spades" and The Gambler end on bitter**
> **notes, for it seems that fate deals bad hands to Hermann**
> **and to Alexey. Pushkin tells us that Hermann goes out of**
> **his mind. He is confined to room 17 of the Obkhov Hospital,**
> **where he never speaks, save to mutter, "Three, seven, ace.**
> **Three, seven, ace." Alexy learns by chance that Polina**
> **loves him and he vows to join her. But then he thinks about**
> **his unusual luck a few months before, when, almost broke,**
> **he won a hundred and seventy gulden. Dostoevsky tells us**
> **that he thinks on. "Tomorrow, tomorrow. . . ." Alexey might**
> **as well be in room number 17 with Hermann, for he is just**
> **as surely a prisoner chained to a hopeless dream of**
> **something that never was and never will be. Both these**
> **masterful works of literature show that gamblers are**
> **not victims of fate but of chance and of their own**
> **shortcomings.**
>
> (*from* "The Compulsion to Gamble, as Represented in 'The Queen of
> Spades' and The Gambler" by Marischa B. Cooke)

COMMENT

The thesis of this research paper was that there are similarities between the two literary characters because though both believed fate led to their compulsive gambling, it was actually due to their personal character flaws as well as simple circumstance.

4. **Return to some initial generalization and show how you have proved, disproved, or enlarged on it.**

EXAMPLE

> **Don Quixote, then, was not simply a mad old man. Rather,**
> **he was a person of deep humanity whose misadventures stemmed**
> **mainly from attempts to help the oppressed. Furthermore,**
> **what seemed to be his foolish dreams are really the hopes**

of the sanest and least foolish people everywhere; what
seemed to be his useless persistence is really idealism;
what seemed to be his inability to cope with his time is
really the doubt and tension that every human lives with.
Cervantes implies that if the character Don Quixote is mad,
so are we all. For he is a composite of us all--and each of
us has within the self a bit of Don Quixote.

(from "The Madman Who Was Most Sane" by Ida Kaufman)

COMMENT

    This concluding paragraph begins with a generalization that has pervaded the text of the research paper. The specifics that support the generalization are summaries of those characteristics that have been offered throughout the text as proof. So to end this paper, the author merely drew together the various strands already developed.

5.   **Link what you have written either to something known or to what seems a future possibility.**

EXAMPLE

    Diet and exercise, then, have been shown to affect the
longevity of various lower forms of animals. Increasingly,
researchers are showing the relationshp of these two
factors to human longevity. In addition, medical advances
are preventing or treating an assortment of diseases and
illnesses once thought impossible to battle. Even the
psychology of growing old is increasingly being understood,
so people are learning how to cope with attitudes and
outlooks. Every year we hear about more centenarians. In
short, there is a good chance that by the next century,
living to be 120 or even 130 years old will not only be
possible but will become a fact for many people.

(from "Growing Older Gracefully" by Norman Raimundo)

COMMENT

    The first four sentences summarize what has been examined in this research paper, so the conclusion does not come to the reader without preparation.

6.   **State a conclusion you have reached about your subject.**

EXAMPLE

    The Roslyn of Miller's original story, the girl that the
men wanted too much to please, evolved into the charming
but somewhat cloying girl of a later Miller story. When she

was transformed into a major character in **The Misfits**,
Roslyn grew in complexity and lost the simple definition of
innocence or sophistication that each of her "ancestors"
had. In these three works, Arthur Miller has provided us
with an excellent and unusual view of the development of a
dramatic character from first sketches to boldly colored
completeness.

(*from* "Roslyn: Evolution of a Literary Character" by Judith Matz)

C O M M E N T

By recapitulating the conclusion of each section of this research paper, the author is then able to note what an unusual view into the creative process Arthur Miller offers readers because he has used the same essential character in different stages of her development.

Bad Endings

The ending is the last of your paper that the audience reads, so it will leave a strong impression, despite anything else you may have written in your paper. To keep that impression good and maintain the impact of a well-written paper, avoid these bad endings.

1. **Don't bring up a new idea.** The end of a paper is the time to finish everything, not to make a fresh start.

2. **Don't stop abruptly or simply trail off.** Your paper needs a specific ending and deserves one that brings your ideas to completion.

3. **Don't ask a question.** You might get an answer you didn't count on!

4. **Don't make any statement or suggestion that needs extensive clarification.** The time to make explanations has passed.

5. **Don't fumble.** Stop when you have nothing more to say.

6. **Don't tell explicitly what you have done in the paper.** Give your audience credit for having understood what you did in the paper. Also, don't be so unimaginative as to write anything like "In this paper it has been shown that . . ." The audience realizes what you have shown.

7. **Don't make a change in your style.** Keep your writing style at the end the same as it was at the beginning.

REVISING AND EDITING YOUR PAPER

Good writers—students, businesspeople, journalists, attorneys, and everyone who writes often or makes a living by writing—make changes in wording and presentation of ideas as they write. That is one kind of revision, of tinkering with a piece of writing until it says exactly what you want it to say.

Another kind of revision comes after the first draft or first complete writing of the paper. Then you may add, delete, or rearrange words and ideas. Even if you are working from a satisfactory outline, you may find that when the whole research paper is written out, there are parts that would fit better in one place than in another.

Revision is another chance to look at what you've written and change it, to make it convey your intentions to your audience more precisely. Writing is actually a matter of multiple drafts and is often described as a "messy process" because of constant revision.

You don't have to be a professional writer to be dissatisfied with a first draft. In fact, such writers not only rewrite extensively themselves, they follow revision advice from their editors. You can emulate that working arrangement by conferring with classmates, either during class time set aside by the instructor or by getting together outside of class to exchange papers. If you do work with peers, be sure to give praise for writing that is good as well as to note portions that could be clarified, augmented, or otherwise improved. As you become an increasingly proficient writer, you will develop your own critical facilities so you know what parts of a piece of your own writing can profit from revision, especially in idea presentation, word choice, sentence structure, and accuracy.

Revising is easiest when you approach a work as if seeing it for the first time— admittedly a difficult job if you've been working for weeks on a research paper. However, you will find it helpful to put the first draft away for several days or even for a week, if you have time, before looking at it with an eye toward making changes.

When you are satisfied about content and structure of the overall research paper and when you are sure that citations and documentation are accurate, it is time to **edit** your work. That is, you finally attend to the niceties of mechanics: correcting spelling, punctuation, capitalization, and paragraphing. Save these tasks for the last reading before typing your paper or printing a hard copy from a computer disc. After all, there's no sense changing some of these mechanics if you decide, through revision, not to use the word or the passage. Use a dictionary, and refer to a composition handbook if you need to as a way of sticking to the conventions of Edited American English that your audience will surely expect to find in your research paper.

Editing for Word Choice and Sentence Structure

People engrossed in writing down their ideas sometimes can't find just the right word at the moment they need it. Instead of stopping and losing a train of thought, they use a second-best word. A better way of finding the right word is to mark the passage, as you write, with a symbol to show that you know you need to improve some wording or restate the passage. If you've gone along with a second-best word or marked some wording for revision, now is the time to check back and find wording you believe should be changed or improved. Take time in editing to select the best words for every idea in your paper!

Remember that when you read your own writing, *you* probably know what you mean, but your reader might not. Therefore, look for precision in wording when you revise. And don't let sentences get away from you; editing is the chance to tighten them.

DRAFT SENTENCE

The decision was not only about the right of the student in this particular case to artistic expression in the figure she chose to sculpt, but it was also about freedom for students to express themselves in schools without a principal's arbitrary imposition of personal whims and standards.

INTENTION

The decision was about one case, but it had far-reaching consequences.

REVISED SENTENCE

The decision went beyond the student's right to sculpt what she chose by bringing into focus a principal's responsibility to involve others in setting up guidelines that override personal whims and standards.

Remember, also, that wording in the text of your research paper must be accessible to the audience. During your research you may learn a considerable amount of jargon—words and terms characteristic of a particular field and used by people knowledgeable in it. However, unless you are absolutely sure that your audience understands this special "language," wording ought to be "translated" so the audience can readily understand what you are writing about.

EXAMPLE OF JARGON

Soon Dorothy Liebes's trademark became her skip dent warp of textured and metallic yarns with unusual weft materials not used before in household fabrics.

REVISION

Soon Dorothy Liebes's trademark became the fabric she designed of unevenly spaced textured and metallic yarns crossed by unusual threads or even by thin strips of wood or metal.

Here are some other techniques you can use to attain good writing through editing sentence structures:

- Use a variety of sentence structures.
- Combine a series of short, simple sentences into a single, more complex sentence.
- Use transitional words and phrases (such as "in addition," "therefore," "equally important," and "nevertheless") to connect ideas smoothly within and between sentences and paragraphs.

- Make sure modifiers are near the words they modify.

- Be sure antecedents of pronouns are clear.

These and many other aids to good writing are explained and developed in composition and rhetoric books; consult them.

Mechanics

A research paper audience expects to find the spelling, punctuation, capitalization, sentence structure, and paragraphing of what they read to look much like what they usually read elsewhere in print. You owe it to that audience to meet those expectations. Any change from the expected is an interference and thus an annoyance to readers. Therefore, help your audience by following the conventions of Edited American English, and present a paper that exemplifies such customs. A check of them is ordinarily the last step in revising and editing your paper.

If you have questions or doubts, a good place to check on the following matters of mechanics is an English handbook or other standard guide.

- Use conventional punctuation.

- Make capitalization accurate.

- Keep verb tenses consistent in accord with what you write.

- Be sure subjects and verbs agree in number.

- Limit abbreviations to accurate ones used only where permissible.

- Adhere to spelling conventions, and check every word whose spelling you're not absolutely sure about. Customarily, keep a dictionary handy, and use it!

In short, do everything you can to be sure your audience focuses on what you have to say rather than on distracting errors of mechanics that could easily have been avoided by careful editing.

REVISING ON A COMPUTER

If you draft your research paper on a computer using a word processing program, you may revise somewhat differently from those who write with pen on paper or with a typewriter. People who compose on computers—which is certainly far superior to writing with another instrument and then simply keying in the text— usually do more revising and editing as they write than they have done in other media. And although various versions of a piece can be saved on disc, almost nobody with a deadline to meet and other interruptions in writing bothers to do so for future comparison.

What is really almost required for people who use computers is to print out a hard copy of the last draft version of a paper already saved on disk and use that for final revisions. Editing on that printed copy has several advantages.

- You can see all at once what was written, and in larger "chunks" than you may be able to see on a computer screen.

- You can turn back and forth to various pages, or even put several pages side by side, to check continuity and prevent repetition.

- You get a better picture of what your final research paper will look like than you can from seeing it on a monitor.

- Seeing your work in a different format (that is, hard copy vs. on-screen) makes you aware of elements, especially mechanics, that you might otherwise overlook because of familiarity or expectations.

Block moves of words are so easy on a computer that you should take advantage of this technology. It enables you to move to different places everything from a few words to a few paragraphs, as a way of finding the best location for some elements of what you write. If any passage doesn't seem to read well, try it in another place; or try revising it or even eliminating it completely. As long as you have a hard copy (or a copy on disc) of the passage before you make the move, you can make a comparison. You can also use the capabilities of some word processing programs to examine different versions of a passage side by side on the monitor screen.

Use the **search** capacity of most word processing programs if you want to make some consistent change not considered during the drafting of your research paper. For example, if you've been writing "on-line" with the hyphen and decide that "online" is more consistent with general use, the computer can make the correction of every instance in far less time than it would take you to search out two examples of what you want to change.

A **spell checker** is one of the most widely used—and most appreciated—editing aids available to those who work on most computers. The program tests your spelling against the conventionally spelled words in its dictionary. Many computer users ask for a spelling check of single words every time they're in doubt while writing; others prefer to wait until a work is finished and then check all the spelling at once. *No* computer will make corrections for you, but most spell checkers will give you choices and make suggestions of how to spell a word it highlights as being spelled incorrectly or unconventionally. Some programs have been touted in ads as knowing whether a word fits into a given context to ascertain its correct spelling (though as this is written, such a program is not yet available for home computers). For example, "red" will be accepted because it's a word in the program dictionary, even though it's erroneous in a sentence such as "I red the book." The watchword for using a spell checker is to accept it as a prompt but not to rely on it blindly.

Many word processing programs have a **thesaurus** built in so that writers can readily search for synonyms. Use it as a revision aid if you have one available. The caution that needs to be observed, however, is the same as in using a print thesaurus you can hold in your hand: don't substitute one word for another without understanding exactly what each word "means" and how each is customarily used. And certainly don't go searching for "big words" in an effort to sound intelligent or mature or sophisticated!

There are also programs that **analyze writing style.** They will perform such functions as spotting passive verbs (and encourage you to change them to active ones), tell you about sentence length and word choice, and give you other information usually helpful in revising the wording and sentence structure of what you have written. One drawback of such programs, however, is that the choices a program recommends are not always those that will improve your own writing. For instance, all passive constructions are not necessarily "bad"; one may be exactly what you mean in a particular spot. You may often need to check a writing handbook or composition text for confirmation of your own—or the program's—choices. Or, as one evaluator of some style analyzers has pointed out, if a writer knows all he or she needs to know to accept or reject the recommendations of such programs, the writer doesn't need the programs.

SELECTING A TITLE

If you haven't already chosen a title for your research paper, you ought to do so by the time you finish writing a draft. Your research paper will be known by its title, so choose one carefully.

Characteristics of a Good Title

A title that **gives readers information** about the contents of the paper is preferable to one that is vague or general.

VAGUE

A Look at William Dean Howells

IMPROVED

The Concept of Work in the Novels of William Dean Howells

Titles don't need to be stuffy or dull, but they should generally give readers some idea at the outset of what the research paper will contain.

Usually, choose a title that is a phrase rather than a complete sentence. The thinking behind such a recommendation probably has its genesis in the recognition that book and article titles are not complete sentences; thus, research paper titles, too, should not be sentences. Besides, a sentence gives so much information away that a reader will look for support of the title rather than allow support for the thesis statement to direct the reading.

LESS DESIRABLE

A Wide Array of Methods for Environmental Activists Makes Violence Unnecessary

IMPROVED

Nonviolent Methods for Environmental Activists

Kinds of Titles to Avoid

As with other aspects of writing, sometimes you get notions about what to do by knowing what you shouldn't do.

1. Cute or coy titles seldom work well.

That's not to say you can't ever use a pun or clever words if they catch the spirit of the paper they name and if they are easily understood by the audience for whom the research paper is written. However, generally choose a straightforward title over other kinds.

COY

Look Who's Pushing the Puffs

IMPROVED

Changing Language in Printed Cigarette Ads

2. Don't use a question in place of a title.

No matter how provocative you think a question will be, it could easily work against you if a prospective reader responds negatively to it. Better to let the title answer the question you thought of posing.

QUESTION

Are Captive Dolphins Worth the Money They Cost to Keep?

IMPROVED

The Case for Captive Dolphins

3. Never use a thesis statement as a title.

It's bound to be too long and tell too much. Besides, it will be a sentence, and a phrase is preferable for a title.

THESIS, NOT TITLE

Intellectual Freedom Is Threatened When School Libraries Ban Books

IMPROVED

Consequences of Book Banning in School Libraries

4. Avoid a long, detailed title that gives too much information.

This is particularly important if you think such a title will make your work sound "academic" or "scholarly." It won't! Rather, a long title is distracting to most readers.

TOO DETAILED

An Examination of the Setting as Metaphor in the Films of John Ford, with Particular Reference to Fort Apache

IMPROVED

Setting as Metaphor in John Ford's Films

Conventions for Titles

The preceding examples of "improved" research paper titles illustrate several conventions you should observe:

- *Use no punctuation at the end of a title.*
- *Capitalize the first letter of each word in a title, except conjunctions, articles, and prepositions.*
- *Do not underline a title or enclose it in quotation marks.*
- *Follow conventions for acknowledging titles within your research paper title.* That is, enclose the titles of other works within quotation marks or underline them as you would normally; note the underlined film title, <u>Fort Apache</u>, in the preceding example. (If you use a word processing program or printer that permits italics, use them in place of the underlining.)

Documenting Your Paper

WHEN, WHERE, AND HOW TO MAKE ACKNOWLEDGMENTS

By now you know that you must tell readers the sources of all material in your research paper that is not original. That means you document all of the following:

- Direct quotations
- Borrowed ideas, including paraphrases and summaries
- Visual materials not your own, such as maps, charts, diagrams, and pictures

Doing so enables a reader to identify and to verify the material, if desired. Furthermore, such acknowledgment establishes your own honesty and scholarly exactness as well as giving support to ideas and conclusions that *are* your own.

The basic or well-known information about any subject that can be ascertained in many sources—what we call "common knowledge" (such as the dates of a person's life, the chemical formula of a substance, or the location of a battle)—does not need specific documentation in a research paper. However, if you have used someone else's words to present the common knowledge, documentation *is* required. If the question of what requires documentation and what doesn't (or what is common knowledge and what isn't) is troublesome, here's a general rule to follow: when in doubt, cite the source. It's better to have too much documentation in your paper than not enough, to be considered overzealous rather than careless.

Acknowledgment means that you must provide documentation in two places:

1. Within the text of the research paper
2. In the Works Cited listing at the end of the paper

The first of these is the subject of this chapter; the second is explained in Chapter 9. Basically, if the resource was in print, you must tell in the text the exact page (or pages) from which you took the information as well as indicate the author and/or the title of the work. (Author, title, and publication information will be contained in the Works Cited.) If the source was not in print and you can provide specifies analogous to a page number about locating the material you used (such as the track on a CD), you should do so.

You also know that documentation must be *in a prescribed form.* In the previous chapter (pages 176–86) you read examples of documentation forms used in the text of a research paper. In this chapter you will find more examples, including details of documentation so that you can apply the conventions to suit your own needs. (When you wrote your preliminary citation cards, you already practiced the punctuation and spacing that are the forms for the Works Cited list.)

Plagiarism—that is, presenting another person's material without documentation and as if it were your own—is less likely if you were cautious about acknowledgment when taking notes than if you were careless in that early part of the research process. But you must remain alert when writing your paper to be sure you don't commit plagiarism by omitting information from your note cards or by failing to include proper acknowledgment in your first draft.

PARENTHETICAL DOCUMENTATION: MLA [MODERN LANGUAGE ASSOCIATION]

Parenthetical documentation is so called because you **enclose the documentation in parentheses at the appropriate place in the text** and give readers information where it is needed without sending them to look elsewhere in the midst of reading. It is the standard in English and other disciplines within the humanities.

Several qualities of parenthetical documentation make it particularly helpful.

1. Typing is easy, because you can put in documentation as you write, without worrying about keeping numbers in order or writing part of the information in one place (the text) and part in another (endnotes).

2. Reading is easy, because the source information is part of the text and doesn't have to be sought elsewhere.

3. Once you learn MLA parenthetical documentation you can readily adapt it to other formats where it is customarily used, albeit with slight differences, such as in the social sciences and natural sciences.

Conventions for Parenthetical Documentation

As with so many other aspects of the research paper, several conventions govern parenthetical documentation.

1. **Do not use the word "page," or any sort of abbreviation for it, in documenting your sources.** A number in parenthetical documentation is assumed to be a page number. Citations in drama or classics are easily recognizable and won't be confused with a page number you are citing.

2. **Omit a page number if the source is complete on a single page,** as in some newspaper and magazine articles.

3. **Omit page numbers in citing alphabetically arranged entries in a reference work** such as an encyclopedia if the entry is complete on a single

page. However, use a page number if what you are documenting is within a multiple-page entry.

4. **If two authors with the same last name are among your sources, you will need to use both given name and surname** in the documentation to differentiate between them.

5. **Shorten any long titles,** if you need to use them, provided they are easily identifiable. For instance, a title such as "Almost 13 Years of Book Protests and Now What?" may be written as "13 Years" because a reader will be able to find the complete title readily in the Works Cited.

6. **Cite act and scene or verse and line of dramatic and classic literary works by using two arabic numerals with a period between them.** Readers will recognize that the first number is that of the larger unit, the act or the verse; it may also refer to the number of the book in certain classical works.

EXAMPLES

```
Tamburlaine, in the play about him, acknowledges his
satisfaction when he crowns himself (2.7).
```

or

```
"Not all the curses which the Furies breathe / Shall make
me leave so rich a prize as this" (Tamburlaine 2.7).
```

or

```
We know a great deal about the battle dress of the early
Greeks by reading a description of Agamemnon (Iliad 11.
15-44).
```

COMMENT

The first two examples refer to Act 2, Scene 7 of the play *Tamburlaine.* The parenthetical documentation for the *Iliad* is to book 11, lines 15 to 44.

Punctuation and Spacing in Parenthetical Documentation

The conventions for documentation dictate that punctuation and spacing must conform to the conventions for writing research papers. Use the following as a guide.

1. **Allow one space before and one after the parentheses that enclose documentation within a sentence.** See especially the examples in this and the previous chapter.

2. **Documentation at the end of a sentence follows the last word or the closing quotation marks by one space. The period marking the end of a sentence is put immediately after the closing parentheses.** This punctuation is illustrated by the next example.

3. **Separate a series of sources by semicolons.**

EXAMPLE

```
. . . even when given the choice of roaming free vs. being
in pens, most who are used to living in the latter
willingly return to them (Borguss; Pryor 246; LaPuzza;
Cousteau 189).
```

Use discretion in the number of items you include in one set of parentheses. If you seem to have a particularly long list of sources to note at once, you may be able to divide the series by grouping them according to content references or by putting the groups in different places.

4. **At the end of a long quotation** (five or more lines and indented ten spaces from the left margin), **put the parenthetical documentation after the period marking the conclusion of the quotation.** (See the quotation by Strauch within the sample research paper on pages 253–54.)

Identifying Sources in Parenthetical Documentation

In Chapter 7 (pages 174–80) you read about integrating resource information smoothly into the text of your research paper as you write it. You also read that the documentation could occur at the beginning, the middle, or the end of a sentence and saw a number of examples of parenthetical documentation. Such variations may serve to maintain reader interest. However, always try to be clear about a source you have used so the reader doesn't confuse what is original with you and what isn't.

1. **Prefer to use an author's last name and a page number in citing a source.** Because the Works Cited list is alphabetized by the last names of authors, you make titles and publication information for sources easy to find by using this method either within a sentence of text or within citation parentheses.

EXAMPLE

```
As Moore suggests (380), "Learning about the dolphins'
natural sonar system . . ."
```

2. **If no author of a work is given, cite it by title and page number. If the source is only one page, title alone is sufficient.**

EXAMPLE

```
Researchers say that each set of answers only raises new
questions ("Dolphin Intelligence") because . . .
```

3. **If you are using more than one work by the same author, indicate which title you are citing.**

EXAMPLE

```
Nathanson notes ("Cognitive Improvement") how remarkably
perceptive dolphins seem to be toward the children.
```

4. **Sources that have multiple authorship show documentation in the order authors appear in the Works Cited listing.** That is, use up to three authors' names in the parenthetical documentation; if there are four or more authors, use the last name of the first person followed by "et al."

EXAMPLE

```
Banned author Kurt Vonnegut referred sardonically to the
First Amendment to the Constitution in his testimony
(Camen, et al. 8).
```

5. **Use an author's last name and/or the title of a work (without page numbers) if you refer to the complete work.**

EXAMPLE

```
Ciardi's translation of The Divine Comedy clearly shows
Dante's rhyme scheme.
```

6. **When citing two or more locations of information within the same work, separate each from the next by a comma and a space.**

EXAMPLE

```
Westin points out the trends and how the speed of a
computer is pushing them toward reality (158-62, 166).
```

7. **If a work you quote from contains a quotation from another work, both sources must be acknowledged.** Try to track down the original quotations. Otherwise, indicate you are quoting from the original speaker or writer and give as much information about the originator as you can.

EXAMPLE

```
"We don't want to make supernatural claims and we haven't
been able to prove what it is about the treatments--the
dolphins themselves, the sea, or the sun. But it works"
(qtd. in Poletz).
```

If the original source appears in quotation marks within the source you used, put that wording in single quotation marks within double quote marks or within the block indentation of a longer quotation.

8. **Use an arabic numeral to refer to the volume if the source you used is part of a multiple-volume series.** Use the abbreviation "vol." if referring to an entire volume. If you identify a page also, write the volume number, put a colon and a space, and then write the page number(s).

EXAMPLE

```
His articles about New York show that he was an inveterate
name-dropper (Huneker, vol. 2).
```

but

```
Antonin Dvorak is called "Old Borax," although the source
of the nickname is never explained (Huneker 2: 65-69).
```

or

`Huneker calls Antonin Dvorak "Old Borax" (2: 65-69),`

`although he never explains the source of the nickname.`

9. **Document nonprint sources as much as possible the way you cite print sources.** Any precise information you can provide to help locate an exact place, such as the side and chapter number of a laser disc or the number of feet or timing on a video or audiotape, or the cut number and timing on a CD will be appreciated by a reader.

EXAMPLES

Documenting an act of an opera:

`When Paolo sees the book Francesca had been reading and`

`asks her to read aloud with him (Francesca da Rimini 3),`

`they are reading a version of the Tristan story that`

`parallels their own lives.`

Documenting a location on a videotape:

`There is ongoing research, readily identified in Dolphins`

`with Robin Williams (at 14:26), about how dolphins in the`

`wild interact with humans.`

DOCUMENTING VISUALS: ILLUSTRATIONS, MAPS, CHARTS, GRAPHS, AND TABLES

If you use any sort of visual within your research paper—a map, chart, table, graph, diagram, picture, or any similar item—you must document it within the paper and show its full source in the Works Cited. However, since you cannot do so in parentheses as part of a text, you *provide a line of acknowledgment below the item and as close as possible to the text it illustrates.*

Figure is the term by which charts, graphs, photos, figures, and drawings are known. Always use the abbreviation "Fig." and give each a consecutive arabic numeral throughout your research paper. Begin the documentation at the left margin and *directly below the figure*; double-space if the label requires more than one line.

In addition to the number of the figure, documentation includes as many items as possible coinciding with those used for written works. That is, include the name of the originator (unless you have created the item for your paper and thus do not credit yourself), a title for the work, and the location of the original.

EXAMPLE

`Fig. 2.  Vincent Van Gogh, Stairway at Auvres, The Saint`

`Louis Art Museum.`

[In this case, the city of location is omitted because it is obvious.]

or

Fig. 3.   How Each Tax Dollar Is Divided by the County.

You must also acknowledge in the Works Cited each visual you didn't develop yourself.

A **table,** whether in words, numbers, or a combination of the two, is so titled and assigned an arabic numeral showing its order in your paper. That designation should be put *above the caption or title of the item,* beginning at the left margin of text. If the table had no title in the source you took it from, or if you originated it, give the table an identifying title.

Below the table, also beginning at the left margin, and double-spacing (if you need to write on more than one line) give needed documentation. That is, after the word "Source" and a colon, cite the place from which you got the table.

EXAMPLE

Table 16-3

The Relative Impact of More Versus Less Developed Nations on the Environment

More Developed Countries (MDCs)	Population (Millions)	Annual Consumption (U.S. $)	Annual Impact
Germany	81.7	$23,560	1,924,852
Japan	125.2	31,450	3,937,540
Switzerland	7.0	36,410	254,870
United States	263.2	24,750	6,514,200
All MDCs	1,169.0	$17,270	20,188,630
Less Developed Countries (LDCs)			
China	1,218.8	$490	592,212
Mexico	93.7	3,750	351,375
Malawi	9.7	220	2,134
All LDCs	4,533.0	$1,030	4,668,990

Note: Consumption is estimated based on a country's per capita GNP. Impact is calculated as the product of population and per capita GNP.

Source: Based on Haub and Yanagishita, 1955. Rptd. in Stockard, Sociology: Discovering Society (Belmont: Wadsworth, 1997) 438.

Because complete information about the source appears in the Works Cited, an alternate form is to use the same kind of documentation you do for text material.

That is, give the source author or authors and page number on which the table appeared.

ALTERNATE FORM

Source: Based on Haub and Yanagishita, 1955 Rptd. in Stockard, 438.

USING COMMENT NOTES IN ADDITION TO PARENTHETICAL DOCUMENTATION

Sometimes you have additional or explanatory material to add to the text or want to make some comment on what you have written in your research paper, but adding to the text would impede the flow of reading. For this reason, as you read in Chapter 7 in the section on "Comment Notes," *comment notes may be used in addition to the parenthetical documentation* in your paper. An example of comment notes is found on page 260 in the sample research paper in Chapter 10.

MLA ENDNOTE DOCUMENTATION

Although parenthetical documentation is widely used and now generally preferred, some instructors may want you to use endnote documentation instead. It is still an MLA-recognized method of documenting sources, so it appears here in case an instructor prefers you to use it. (Footnotes, which have the same format as endnotes but appear at the bottoms of pages on which there is relevant text, are hardly used nowadays for undergraduate research papers. Always difficult to space on a typewritten page, they are even more complicated to manage if the paper is written on a word processor.)

Endnotes are so called because documentation appears *at the end* of the research paper. **Endnotes work in pairs between the text and the page(s) of documentation**; *a superscript number provides the coordination.* Write the superscript (that is, half a line above the normal writing line) in arabic numbers sequentially throughout the paper and immediately after each borrowed idea or quotation in the text (and preferably put at the end of a phrase, clause, or sentence so the flow of thought isn't interrupted). Put the number, *after* a word (without a period or other mark either before or after it) but *before a normal punctuation mark.* Then use corresponding numbers to give the complete documentation on the endnote page(s).

Begin a page of endnotes by typing the word "Notes" at the center of a page, one inch down from the top. (Continue, of course, putting your last name and successive page numbers ½ inch down and ending at the right margin of each page.) Double-space between the heading and the first line of notes, and continue double-spacing throughout the endnotes.

Use paragraph indentation for endnotes, just as you do in ordinary text writing: the first line of each note is indented five spaces from the left margin; succeeding lines each begin at the left margin. Type endnotes **double spaced.**

The **first time** you use an endnote, give four pieces of information about each source: *author, title, publication information, and the actual page or pages used— or other specific location information.* (See page 207.) The **second and subsequent times** you use one of those sources, give *only the author or title and a page number* or an identifying location for nonprint materials. (See pages 209; 210; 213–14.) End each entry with a period. The abbreviations "ibid." (meaning "in the same place"), "op. cit." (meaning "in the work cited"), and "loc. cit." (meaning "in the place cited") are no longer used in research paper documentation.

EXAMPLE (IN TEXT)

This is necessary for them to find food, which they often do cooperatively,[1] as well as for keeping track of others in their group.

EXAMPLE (THE FIRST ENDNOTE)

[1] **Bernd Wursig, "Dolphins," Scientific American 1979: 146.**

EXAMPLE (THE NEXT TIME THAT SOURCE IS CITED)

[4] **Wursig 148.**

Differences Between Endnotes and Works Cited

All the information you need for documenting sources with endnotes is already on your preliminary Works Cited cards; you need only make some alterations. Here are the chief differences between the forms:

Information	*In Endnote*	*Works Cited*
Format	Paragraph indentation	Hanging indentation
Three units: author, title, publication information	Separated by commas or parentheses	Separated by periods
Author's name	Written in usual order	Surname, then given name
Publication information for books	In parentheses	No parentheses
Page numbers or location in nonprint	Given for each note entry	None given

First References in MLA-Style Endnotes: Books

All endnotes are double spaced and have paragraph indentation. The first time you write an endnote listing, give complete information about the source. Always use the full title of a book, including the wording after a colon. Use the following list as your typing guide:

Indent five spaces from left margin, and write a superscript number.

Allow one space after the superscript number.

Write the author's full name in regular order (i.e., first name, then last name).

Put a comma after the name.

Allow one space after the comma.

Write the title of the book (underlined or in italics, of course).

Allow one space after the title.

Enclose the publication information in parentheses:
> the place of publication, a colon, one space, the name of the publisher in the shortened form (as explained on pages 67–68), a comma, a space, and the date of publication.

Allow one space.

Write the exact page or pages from which you obtained the information.

End the documentation note with a period.

EXAMPLE

The same typing conventions prevail for documentation endnotes as you used on the preliminary Works Cited cards and as you will use for the Works Cited listing with regard to using only the names of cities (not states, unless the reader might otherwise not be able to identify the state), using shortened forms of publishers' names, and using abbreviations if you can't find some items of the publication information (see "Conventions for Parenthetical Documentation," pages 199–205).

The following examples show some of the various kinds of first references for books in MLA-style endnotes. A complete list of the Works Cited forms for these and other resources is found in Chapter 9. If what you need isn't shown here, make the necessary adaptations from the Works Cited examples in Chapter 9.

BOOK BY TWO OR THREE AUTHORS

[2] Laura S. Kastner and Jennifer F. Wyatt, The Seven-Year Stretch: How Families Work Together to Grow through Adolescence (Boston: Houghton, 1997) 59.

BOOK BY MORE THAN THREE AUTHORS

[3] James Hiebert, et al., <u>UFO Crash at Roswell: The Genesis of a Modern Myth</u> (Washington: Smithsonian, 1997) 227.

ORGANIZATION OR INSTITUTION AS AUTHOR

[4] Bottom Line Personal, <u>Bottom Line Yearbook/1998</u> (Des Moines: Bottom Line, 1997) 351.

BOOK IN COLLABORATION

[5] Johnnie L. Cochran, with Tim Rutten, <u>Journey to Justice</u> (New York: Ballantine, 1996) 79.

BOOK WITH SINGLE EDITOR OR COMPILER OF A COLLECTION

[6] Michael Hoskin, ed., <u>The Cambridge Illustrated History of Astronomy</u> (New York: Cambridge UP, 1997) 159.

ANTHOLOGY (or COLLECTION) WITH NO EDITOR GIVEN

[7] <u>Heroines: Remarkable and Inspiring Women</u> (Avenal, NJ: Crescent, 1995) 89.

WORK IN AN ANTHOLOGY WITH EDITOR'S NAME GIVEN

[8] Barry Lopez, "A Presentation of Whales," <u>The Presence of Whales</u>, ed. Frank Steward (Anchorage: Alaska Northwest, 1995) 207.

INTRODUCTION, FOREWORD, AFTERWORD, OR PREFACE BY OTHER THAN AUTHOR

[9] Ben Nighthorse Campbell, foreword, <u>Diplomats in Buckskin: A History of Indian Delegations in Washington City</u>, Herman J. Viola (Bluffton, SC: Rivila, 1995) 3.

WORK IN SEVERAL VOLUMES

[10] Mark Twain, <u>The Adventures of Tom Sawyer</u>, The Oxford Mark Twain (New York: Oxford, 1996) 26.

TRANSLATED BOOK

[11] Bronislaw Geremok, <u>Poverty: A History</u>, trans. Agnieszka Kolakowska (New York: Blackwell, 1997) 69.

EDITION OF A BOOK

¹² Audrey J. Roth, <u>The Research Paper: Process, Form, and Content</u>, 8th ed. (Belmont: Wadsworth, 1998) 218.

REPUBLISHED BOOK

¹³ Robert Louis Stevenson, <u>A Child's Garden of Verses</u> (1885; Mineola: Dover, 1992) 32.

First References in MLA-Style Endnotes: Periodicals

The first time you give an endnote reference to a periodical, the form to use is almost exactly like that for a Works Cited entry *except* that commas, each followed by one space, replace periods in the entry and the author's name is given in usual rather than reverse order. Also, *the exact page* you used for specific information is given. This example shows how to record a magazine article by a known author in a publication that is paged by issue:

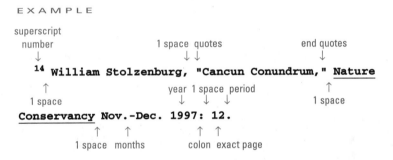

EXAMPLE

The following examples show how to record **MLA-style endnotes for first references** you might use for selected kinds of articles in periodicals. If you don't find models here for the kind of particular endnotes you need, make the necessary adaptations to the examples of periodicals given in the Works Cited listing in Chapter 9.

ARTICLE BY KNOWN AUTHOR IN A PUBLICATION WITH CONTINUOUS PAGINATION

¹⁵ Tom McConaghy, "How Canadian Universities Are Managing Change," <u>Phi Delta Kappan</u> 78 (1997): 660.

BOOK OR FILM REVIEW IN A MAGAZINE OR JOURNAL

¹⁶ Richard Corliss, "These Jokers Are Wild," rev. of <u>The Game</u>, dir. David Fincher, <u>Time</u> 22 Sept. 1997.

The review is on a single page, which appears in the Works Cited and thus is unnecessary in the Notes. If the review is printed on more than one page in the magazine, use a colon (instead of a period) after the date and then write the exact page number used.

NEWSPAPER ARTICLE BY KNOWN AUTHOR

    [17] Nan Chase, "Colors and Crafts," Miami Herald 7 Sept. 1997, final ed.: 4J.

NEWSPAPER EDITORIAL, NO AUTHOR SHOWN

    [18] "China: Rich Without Liberty," editorial, Miami Herald 1 Nov. 1997, final ed.

Because this editorial is on only a single page in the newspaper, which is stated in the Works Cited, giving it again in the Notes would be redundant.

BOOK OR FILM REVIEW IN A NEWSPAPER

    [19] Margaria Fichtner, "A Saga of Regret, Shattered Lives in Old Florida," rev. of Lost Man's River by Peter Matthiessen, Miami Herald 2 Nov. 1997, final ed.

This review appeared on only one page, and that is stated in the Works Cited.

First References in MLA-Style Endnotes: Other Print Sources

When you record pamphlets, letters, and print sources other than books and periodicals, follow the same general rules and conventions that apply to the formats already explained in this section.

The following examples will serve as guidelines for you to record other print sources as first references in endnotes. If you need to acknowledge a source not shown here, adapt it from the Works Cited forms in Chapter 9.

DOCUMENT FROM AN INFORMATION SERVICE

    [20] Robert Freud, "Community Colleges and the Virtual Community," ERIC 1996 ED397871.

PAMPHLET BY KNOWN AUTHOR

    [21] Paula Kurtzwell, Seven Steps to Safer Sunning (FDA Consumer Magazine, 1996) 2.

PAMPHLET BY UNKNOWN AUTHOR

    [22] Air Travel for Your Dog or Cat (Washington: Air Transport Assn., 1991) n.p.

PERSONAL OR UNPUBLISHED LETTER

[23] Sharon L. Wallace, letter to the author, 22 Nov. 1997.

GOVERNMENT PUBLICATION

[24] Subcommittee on the Western Hemisphere, Haiti: The Situation After the Departure of the U.S. Contingent from UNMH, (Rep.) H461-40 (Washington: GPO, 1996) 59.

First References in MLA-Style Endnotes: Electronic Sources

COMPUTER SOFTWARE

[25] GlobalFax® for Macintosh, computer software, Global Village Communications, 1995.

Some computer software is available in different versions or different releases. When necessary, state that information after the title.

CD-ROM

[26] The Story of Glass, Reed Interactive (Oxford, UK, 1995).

PERSONAL E-MAIL

[27] Billy Specht, "dolphin baby!" e-mail to Audrey Roth, 26 Oct. 1996.

ONLINE ARTICLE ORIGINALLY IN MAGAZINE

[28] Richard Blow, "Dr. Dolphin," Mother Jones 1 Jan. 1995, Electric Library.

ONLINE DISCUSSION GROUP

[29] Parker, Stephen, "Exciting Developments," 15 Feb. 1998, Online posting PD Aficionados, 17 Feb. 1998 <http://pdomingo@gte.net>

First References in MLA-Style Endnotes: Nonprint Sources

You may have found information in such nonprint sources as films, paintings, interviews, radio or television programs, CDs, videos, and laser discs that extend the range and kind of resources from which you got information for your research paper. When you quote or borrow ideas from them, readers will want to know the important elements of each source, so you feature them in the documentation for each medium.

Record the necessary information by following the models here, which are based on the Works Cited examples on pages 217–35, or by adapting what you already recorded on your own preliminary Works Cited cards.

PERSONAL OR TELEPHONE INTERVIEW

[26] David Nathanson, personal interview, 15 Sept. 1996.

[27] Lloyd Borguss, telephone interview, 17 Sept. 1996.

WORKS OF ART

[28] Edouard Manet, The Street Singer, Museum of Fine Arts, Boston.

[29] Hanukah Lamp from Poland, Jewish Museum, New York.

[30] Constantin Brancusi, Bird in Space, Museum of Modern Art, New York.

The titles of works of art are underlined or put in italics.

LECTURE, SPEECH, ADDRESS

[31] Carmela Delia Lanza, "Talking with my Hands: Finding a Working-Class Voice in the Classroom," Conference on College Composition and Communication, Hyatt Regency, Phoenix, 14 Mar. 1997.

RADIO OR TELEVISION PROGRAM

[32] Mark Hart, Community Aware, WTMI-FM, Miami, FL, 21 Dec. 1997.

[33] "Nicholas and Alexandra," Biography, A & E, 23 Nov. 1997.

The call letters of radio or television stations are recorded, but if a program is transmitted on cable, use only the cable channel name.

FEATURE-LENGTH FILM

[34] Casablanca, dir. Michael Curtiz, perf. Humphry Bogart, Ingrid Bergman, Warner Bros., 1943, videocassette, MGM/UA Home Video.

- If the version of the feature-length film you viewed was on videotape or laser disc, say so; otherwise, a reel in a projector is assumed.

- It is *not* necessary to give the timing of a feature-length film or to indicate if it is in black and white or color.

SHORT FILM OR VIDEOTAPE

[35] Kim Thompson, filmmaker, <u>All the Great Operas (in Ten Minutes)</u>, Chicago, Picture Start, 1992, videocassette (animated, color, 10 min.).

LIVE THEATRICAL PERFORMANCE

[36] <u>Hair</u>, Book and Lyrics by Gerome Ragni and James Rado, Music by Galt MacDermot, Dir. Patricia Dolan Gross, Jerry Herman Ring Theater, Coral Gables, FL, 14 Nov. 1997.

LIVE MUSICAL PERFORMANCE

[37] Enrique Iglesias, <u>Vivir 1997</u>, Miami Arena, 13 Dec. 1996.

MUSICAL SOUND RECORDING

[38] Dimitri Hvorostovsky, "For the Shores of Your Distant Homeland," by Alexander Borodin, <u>My Restless Soul</u>, Philips, 1995.

A CD recording is assumed unless noted before the recording company is audio-cassette, LP, or other form.

Subsequent References in MLA-Style Endnotes

Once you have recorded the full information about a source in the first endnote documentation, you can shorten the citation the next time you refer to the work. In subsequent endnotes, **give only the author or title and a page number for printed sources. Author or title and any identifying location suffices for nonprint and electronic materials.**

You may make as many references as needed to a work once the first documentation is made in endnotes; the order of doing so is dictated by the use of the source in the text of your research paper. Simply continue the superscript numerals in order.

A Series of First and Subsequent References

[1] Karen Pryor, "The Domestic Dolphin," in <u>Dolphin Societies: Discoveries and Puzzles</u>, eds. Karen Pryor and Kenneth S. Norris (Berkeley: U of CA Press, 1991) 345.

[2] Whitlow W. L. Au, and Charles W. Turl, "Material Composition Discrimination of Cylinders at Different Aspect

Angles by an Echolocating Dolphin," **Journal of the Accoustical Society of America** 89 (1991) 2449.

[3] Au and Turl 2450-451.

[4] Pryor 346.

Two or More Subsequent References by Same Author

Pryor, "Domestic."

Pryor, "Mortal Remains."

Besides using the author's last name, give an indication of each title in the subsequent reference.

CHAPTER 9

Preparing the Works Cited List (MLA Format)

WHAT TO INCLUDE

Academic research papers formerly relied almost entirely on printed sources of information. Therefore, the word *bibliography* (meaning a list of written sources) was commonly used to head a list at the end of a paper showing readers the researched material on which the paper was based. But then students, as well as other researchers, began using such nonprint resources as films, videotapes, and audio discs. Today, preparing a research paper without consulting some of the multitude of electronic resources available is almost unheard of. So the literal meaning of "bibliography" no longer applies.

Works Cited is the term that fits with the parenthetical documentation you read about in the last chapter. The sources you used have already been acknowledged within your paper, so at the conclusion you provide *complete citations for the works you have already referred to*—author, title, publication information, production details, document number, internet address, or whatever else is applicable to enable a reader to locate those sources.

Remember that **a Works Cited list may include only materials you actually documented within the text of the paper.** Most of the details will be on your preliminary works cited cards; some of them you may have to add as a result of having consulted the resources themselves. For instance, most periodical indexes give only the initials of authors, yet you are required to give full names in the Works Cited. Remember, too, that in the Works Cited you need to show the edition and section of a newspaper in which an article appeared; however, you only cite the volume number of a periodical if it is paged continuously throughout a year. There is some leeway in recording nonprint resources, depending on the emphasis in your research paper. For example, for a feature-length film you might list first its director or the leading performer or its writer or cinematographer or the title, depending on the focus of your research.

Unless specifically requested by an instructor to provide a list of Works Consulted at the end of your research paper, you *cannot* list material that you merely discovered was available or that you looked at but found irrelevant, repetitive, or insufficient for your purposes.

Occasionally, an instructor may request an **Annotated List of Works Cited.** This is explained in Chapter 10 on pages 241–42.

Conventions to Follow

Some conventions you have already read about and incorporated into your preliminary citation cards, such as how to record the title of a film included in the title of a book, or not distinguishing a hardbound from a softbound book. Remember to **use hanging indentation for each entry**—that is, *the first line of an entry begins at the left margin, and subsequent lines are each indented five spaces from that margin.* Here are some other important conventions. Many of them are illustrated on pages 261–63, immediately after the sample research paper in Chapter 10.

1. **Start the list of Works Cited on a new page at the conclusion of the text of your research paper.**

2. **Number the Works Cited page(s) successively following the text of your paper.** That is, if the last page of the text was 12, the first page of the Works Cited will be 13. Follow the custom of previous pages by putting the numeral after your name and ½ inch down from the top right-hand corner of the page.

3. **Center the heading Works Cited** (or "Annotated List of Works Cited," if that is what you are required to compile) **1 inch down from the top of the page.**

4. **Double-space between the heading and the first entry—as well as throughout the list.**

5. **List entries alphabetically by the last name of the author** or by that of the first author given if there is more than one author. Do *not* use titles (such as Dr.) or honorifics (such as Sir or O.B.E.), even if they are shown with the author's name in the source you used.

6. **If no author is shown, begin with the title of a work as part of the alphabetized list,** but omit the article *A, An,* or *The* if it is the first word of a title.

7. **If there are several entries by the same author, use the person's name in the first entry only. Substitute three spaced hyphens in place of the name for subsequent works** by that person. Within such a grouping, **alphabetize the works by their titles** to determine the order in which each will be listed.

8. **Use one space after a comma or colon and two spaces after a period within each entry.**

9. **The title of a long work** (book, magazine, film, etc.) **may be printed in italics *or* underlined—*never both.*** Titles of shorter works (poems, newspaper articles, etc.) only appear in quotation marks. Follow the conventions given in Chapter 4.

10. **Do not use page numbers within a book *unless*** your source is a work in an anthology or collection or is only a specific part of the book, such as an Introduction or Afterword.

11. ***Never*** **use the word "page," or an abbreviation of it, in the Works Cited.**

12. ***Never*** **number the entries in a list of Works Cited.**

STANDARD FORMS FOR WORKS CITED

The entries that follow are examples of various books, periodicals, nonprint sources, and electronic research sources, to serve as guides to your Works Cited listing. The examples are divided into six sections (Entire Books, Portions of Books, Periodicals, Other Print Sources, Electronic Sources, and Nonprint Sources); within each section are a variety of samples that progress from the simplest and least complex to those that may be less likely to be used. Look particularly at the punctuation, spacing, and formatting of those examples that are applicable for your purposes.

Entire Books

The author, title, and publication facts are those needed by readers of your research paper. The examples that follow are guides to the forms, most of which should already be noted in these ways on your preliminary works cited cards.

BOOK BY SINGLE AUTHOR

> Diamond, Jared. Why Is Sex Fun?: The Evolution of Human
> Sexuality. New York: HarperCollins, 1997.

- If the main part of the title ends with punctuation (as here with a question mark), show that before the colon that marks a subtitle.
- If an author uses a middle initial, the period after it serves as the period ending the author unit, for example: **Auden, W. H.**

BOOK BY TWO OR THREE AUTHORS

> Kastner, Laura S., and Jennifer F. Wyatt. The Seven-Year
> Stretch: How Families Work Together to Grow through
> Adolescence. Boston: Houghton, 1997.
>
> Saler, Benson, Charles A. Ziegler, and Charles B. Moore.
> UFO Crash at Roswell: The Genesis of a Modern Myth.
> Washington: Smithsonian, 1997.

- Only the name of the first author shown on the title page of the book is given in reverse order (that is: last name, a comma, and then the first name).
- The "and" before the name of the second or third author is preceded by a comma, and those names are in the usual order.

BOOK BY MORE THAN THREE AUTHORS

> Hiebert, James, et al. <u>Making Sense: Teaching and Learning</u>
>   <u>Mathematics with Understanding</u>. Portsmouth: Heinemann,
>   1997.

- The Latin abbreviation *et al.* (for *et alii* or, in English, "and others") is used in place of the string of names.
- The period after the abbreviated word suffices as the period to end the author unit.

ORGANIZATION OR INSTITUTION AS AUTHOR

> Bottom Line Personal. <u>Bottom Line Yearbook/1998</u>. Des Moines:
>   Bottom Line, 1997.

BOOK IN COLLABORATION

> Cochran, Johnnie L., with Tim Rutten. <u>Journey to Justice.</u>
>   New York: Ballantine, 1996.

If the title page shows that the book is "as told to" or "with the collaboration of" another person, use those words rather than the "with" as in this model.

ANONYMOUS BOOK

> <u>Heroines: Remarkable and Inspiring Women</u>. New York:
>   Crescent, 1995.

AUTHOR'S NAME ABSENT FROM BOOK BUT KNOWN FROM ANOTHER SOURCE

> [Dynner, Eugene.] <u>Taking Travel Photos</u>, 3rd ed. Miami:
>   Travelogue, 1996.

The square brackets indicate interpolation by the author of the research paper. In this case, the person who prepared the list of Works Cited was able to determine the actual or probable author, although that name wasn't on the title page of the book.

BOOK BY PSEUDONYMOUS AUTHOR BUT REAL NAME SUPPLIED

> Bachman, Richard [Stephen King]. <u>The Regulators</u>. New York:
>   Dutton, 1996.

Note that the author's real name is in usual first-name–last-name order and that the period concluding the author unit is after the brackets containing the real name.

BOOK IN WHICH ILLUSTRATOR OR PHOTOGRAPHER IS IMPORTANT

Fodgen, Michael and Patricia. Photos. <u>Snakes: The Evolution</u>
<u>of Mystery in Nature</u>. by Harry W. Greene. Berkeley: U
of California P, 1997.

If visuals, such as photographs or drawings, are primary in a book and are the work
of persons whose names appear on the title page, show that information first.

Verner, Elizabeth O'Neill, illus. <u>Porgy</u>. Text by DuBose
Heyward. Charleston Ed., Charleston, SC: Tradd Street
Press, 1985.

Use this abbreviation for "illustrator" if that person is featured on the title page of
the book or if your research paper centers on a book illustrator or on a work of art.
Otherwise, acknowledge the illustrator after the usual author-first citation but before the publication information.

BOOK CONDENSATION OF A LONGER WORK

Crichton, Michael. <u>Airframe</u>. Cond. from <u>Airframe</u>.
Pleasantville: Digest, vol. 4, 1997.

- Give the name of the author of the original book first.
- The word "Condensed" is abbreviated as shown. If the name of the person
  who wrote the condensation is available, write it after the word "by" following the second appearance of the title.

BOOK WITH SINGLE EDITOR OR COMPILER OF A COLLECTION

Hoskin, Michael, ed. <u>The Cambridge Illustrated History of</u>
<u>Astronomy</u>. New York: Cambridge UP, 1997.

- Put a comma after the editor's name, and let the period after the abbreviation for "editor" stand as the period concluding the author (that is,
  editor) unit.
- Use the abbreviation *comp.* if "compiler" or "compiled by," rather than
  "editor," appears on the title page of the book. If there is a different, but
  similar, word on the title page, use it in the citation.

<u>Unsuitable for Ladies: An Anthology of Women Travellers</u>.
Selected by Jane Robinson. New York: Oxford UP, 1995.

BOOK WITH TWO OR MORE EDITORS OR COMPILERS

Applebaum, Paul S., Lisa A. Uyehara, and Mark R. Elin, eds.
<u>Trauma and Memory: Clinical and Legal Controversies</u>.
New York: Oxford UP, 1997.

or

Brown, Michael E., et al., eds. <u>Nationalism and Ethnic
     Conflict</u>. Cambridge: MIT Press, 1997.

The plural of "ed." is "eds." Follow the convention for multiple authorship of a book.

ANTHOLOGY [OR COLLECTION] WITH NO EDITOR GIVEN

<u>Heroines: Remarkable and Inspiring Women</u>. Avenal, NJ:
     Crescent, 1995.

<u>Guys and Dolls: The Stories of Damon Runyon</u>. New York:
     Barnes, 1997.

The second of these examples shows the author of the anthology's contents in the subtitle.

BOOK EDITED BY OTHER THAN AUTHOR OF CONTENTS

Elbert, Sarah, ed. <u>Louisa May Alcott on Race, Sex, and
     Slavery</u>. Boston: Northeastern UP, 1997.

BOOK BEARING AN IMPRINT OF A PUBLISHER

Wright, Richard. <u>Eight Men</u>. New York: HarperPerennial,
     1996.

- An *imprint* identifies a group of books a publisher brings out under a name different from its own.
- If the imprint is listed separately from the publisher, separate the two names with a hyphen.

SEVERAL-VOLUME WORK UNDER GENERAL TITLE BUT WITH EACH VOLUME HAVING SEPARATE TITLE

Stanik, Joseph T. <u>"Swift and Effective Retribution"</u>: The
     U.S. Sixth Fleet and the Confrontation with Qaddafi.
     Washington: Naval Historical Center, Dept. of the
     Navy, 1966. Vol. 3 of <u>The U.S. Navy in the Modern
     World Series</u>, Gen. Ed. Edward J. Marolda.

BOOK IN SERIES EDITED BY OTHER THAN AUTHOR

<u>American Book Collectors and Bibliographers</u>, 2nd series.
     Ed. Joseph Rosenblum. 187 vols. Detroit: Gale, 1997.

WORK IN SEVERAL VOLUMES

Twain, Mark. <u>The Oxford Mark Twain</u>. Ed. Shelley Fisher
     Fishkin. 29 vols. New York: Oxford UP, 1966.

TRANSLATED BOOK BY KNOWN AUTHOR

> Geremek, Bronislaw. Poverty: A History. Trans. Agnieszka
>   Kolakowska. New York: Blackwell, 1997.

- List the book by author if references in your paper are to that person or work.
- The abbreviation *Trans.* is capitalized if it appears before the translator's name.

> Kolakowska, Agnieszka, trans. Poverty: A History. By
>   Bronislaw Geremek. New York: Blackwell, 1997.

- If the translator is the subject of your paper or figures importantly in it, put that person's name first, as in this example. Then put *trans.* (not capitalized) after the person's name.
- "By" precedes the author's name when it appears after the title.

TRANSLATED BOOK WITH AUTHOR'S NAME INCLUDED IN TITLE

> Memoir in Two Voices: Francois Mitterand, Eli Wiesel.
>   Trans. Rich Seaver, and Timothy Bent. New York:
>   Arcade, 1996.

EDITION OF A BOOK

> Roth, Audrey J. The Research Paper: Process, Form, and
>   Content, 8th ed. Belmont: Wadsworth, 1998.

or

> Northrup, Christiane. Women's Bodies, Women's Wisdom, rev.
>   ed. New York: Bantam, 1998.

or

> The Pocket Oxford Dictionary of Current English, 8th rev.
>   ed. Della Thompson, ed. New York: Oxford UP, 1996.

Editions that carry a designation such as Revised (Rev.) or Alternate (Alt.) appear in the Works Cited with whichever wording is on the title page of the book.

PRIVATELY PRINTED BOOK

> Environmental Law Foundation of Vermont, and Rachi Farrow.
>   Good Sneakers and All About Mercury. Montpelier: ELF/
>   VT, 1997.

- The organization appearing as coauthor of this book would make no sense if written in some sort of reverse order.
- Some privately printed books are self-published by the author(s), as in this designation.

- If the book is privately printed by contract with a publishing company (a so-called "vanity press"), write the publication information as you would for any commercially printed work.

REPUBLISHED BOOK OR MODERN REPRINT OF OLDER EDITION

> Stevenson, Robert Louis. A Child's Garden of Verses. 1885.
>
> Mineola, NY: Dover, 1992.

The date of the original publication stands by itself after the title. The name of the original publisher, even though different from the new one, is not shown.

Portions of Books

If your reference source was only part of a book—a poem in an anthology or an introduction, for example—rather than the complete book, the author of just that section begins the Works Cited entry, because to show only the book information would be misleading to anyone trying to locate the source material you used. Also, in addition to the author, title, and publication information, *the page numbers on which this part appears* are added to the citation, beginning two spaces after the copyright date. Do *not* use the word "page" or any abbreviation of it.

POEM IN ANTHOLOGY

> Nye, Naomi Shihab. "Famous." An Introduction to Poetry, 9th
>
> ed. Eds. X. J. Kennedy, and Dana Gioia. New York:
>
> Longman, 1998. 69-70.

ARTICLE, CHAPTER, STORY, OR ESSAY IN A COLLECTION EDITED BY OTHER THAN AUTHOR

> Lopez, Barry. "A Presentation of Whales." The Presence of
>
> Whales. Ed. Frank Stewart. Anchorage: Alaska
>
> Northwest, 1995. 205-22.

INTRODUCTION, FOREWORD, AFTERWORD, or PREFACE BY OTHER THAN AUTHOR OF BOOK

> Campbell, Ben Nighthorse. Foreword. Diplomats in Buckskins:
>
> A History of Indian Delegations in Washington City. By
>
> Herman J. Viola. Bluffton, SC: Rivila, 1995. 3-5.

- The name of the person who wrote the Introduction or other such section should come first if that person is more important than the author of the book itself or is someone of importance in your research paper. Otherwise, begin with the author's name and show the name of the other person after the book title.

- Though the state in which a publisher is located is not usually included in a citation, it may appear if the city alone might not be readily recognized or if the publisher is not well known.

SIGNED ARTICLE IN REFERENCE BOOK

    Celpi, Albert. "Emily Dickinson." Academic American
        Encyclopedia. 1994 ed.

or

    Stead, Christian Karlson. "New Zealand Literature." New
        Encyclopaedia Britannica. Macropaedia. 15th ed.

- Volume and page numbers are omitted from alphabetically arranged reference sources. If an author's initials, but not whole name, appear with an article in a reference book, look for a list of names that the initials stand for; often this list is near the front of a volume. (In the *Encyclopaedia Britannica* it is in a separate volume in the "Propaedia.")
- If both the year of publication and the edition are shown for a reference work, use only one of them. For this source, the edition is usually used.

UNSIGNED ARTICLE IN REFERENCE WORK

    "Dolphins." Encyclopedia Americana. 1995 ed.

Some reference works are designated only by the year of the edition you used, so that's the only information you can record.

Periodicals

The three units of information recorded for each periodical article are author, title, and publication information—including the page numbers on which the article appears. **The headlines of newspaper articles are considered their "titles."** Authorship is shown in a byline, unless the article you are citing is a letter to the editor, in which case the author is the person who signed at the end. **A wire service,** such as AP or UPI, **is never considered an author.**

Your preliminary works cited cards will also show a volume number for continuously paginated journals and magazines, an edition for a newspaper, or other information particular to periodicals. The examples that follow are guides to the forms, most of which are probably already on your preliminary works cited cards. Since **spacing after periods, commas, and colons is important,** use these sample entries as a check on your own work.

ARTICLE BY KNOWN AUTHOR IN MAGAZINE WITH PAGINATION BY ISSUE

    Stolzenburg, William. "Cancun Conundrum." Nature
        Conservancy Nov.-Dec. 1997: 10-17.

This article appears on successive pages in the magazine and so the listing shows the inclusive pages.

> Thigpen, David E. "Still Knocks'em Out: LL Cool J. Has a
>   Book, a CD and Crossover Dreams." <u>Time</u> 3 Nov. 1997:
>   121.

This article is complete on the page named. The parenthetical documentation does not need to give a page, though the page number must appear in the Works Cited.

> Kellow, Brian. "Bus and Truck Boheme: On the Road with New
>   York City Opera's National Company." <u>Opera News</u> Nov.
>   1997: 16+.

A "+" symbol after the first page of an article shows that there are other, but not successive, pages to the article. This one, for example, begins on page 16 but is continued on pages 17, 18, 20, 22, and more.

ARTICLE BY KNOWN AUTHOR IN JOURNAL WITH PAGINATION BY ISSUE

> Uchmanowicz, Pauline. "Lessons from the Margins of the
>   Academic Grove, or 'Hoop Deams'." <u>Writing Program
>   Administration</u> 20.3 (1997): 31-43.

Numerals after the journal title show the volume and issue number within that volume.

ARTICLE BY KNOWN AUTHOR IN MAGAZINE OR JOURNAL WITH CONTINUOUS PAGINATION

> McConaghy, Tom. "How Canadian Universities Are Managing
>   Change." <u>Phi Delta Kappan</u> 78 (1997): 660-61.
> Bloom, Lynn Z. "Why I (Used to) Hate to Give Grades."
>   <u>College Composition and Communication</u> 48 (1997):
>   360-71.

- Because both this wide-readership publication and the academic journal number their pages successively throughout a publishing year, the citation for each shows both the volume and the year in parentheses after the title. Although each has an issue number and month, neither is necessary because of the continuous pagination through the volume year.
- Note, also, that the hundreds digit in page numbering is not repeated.

MAGAZINE ARTICLE BY UNKNOWN AUTHOR

> "One of Our Fifty Is Missing." <u>New Mexico Magazine</u> Nov.
>   1997: 92.

MAGAZINE OR JOURNAL EDITORIAL

> Sawhill, John C. "The President's View." Editorial. <u>Nature
>   Conservancy</u> Sept.-Oct. 1998: 5.

- The editorial is designated as such in order to distinguish it from other articles within a publication.
- If an editorial has a title and the author is stated, use that information in the usual places and ways.

MR [Mark Reynolds]. Editorial. <u>Teaching English in the Two-</u>
   <u>Year College</u> 24 (1997): 183.

- This editorial is signed by initials, but the name of the author is supplied in square brackets.
- Because this scholarly journal is paged by volume, only that information appears in the Works Cited.

BOOK, FILM, VIDEO, OR CD REVIEW IN MAGAZINE

Shenitz, Bruce. Rev. of <u>The Price of a Dream: The Story of</u>
   <u>the Grameen Bank and the Idea That Is Helping the Poor</u>
   <u>to Change Their Lives,</u> by David Bornstein. <u>Smithsonian</u>
   Sept. 1997: 115-17.

If the review is given a title by the publication, it appears in quotation marks after the author's name, as follows:

or

Corliss, Richard. "These Jokers Are Wild." Rev. of <u>The</u>
   <u>Game,</u> dir. David Fincher. <u>Time</u> 22 Sept. 1997: 93.

- The name of the person writing the review comes first in this citation.
- "Rev. of" is followed by the title of the work being reviewed.
- If the review has no title and shows no authorship, begin the citation with: **Rev. of**.
- Directors are usually named in film reviews, but if another element is the focus of the research or is important in the paper—for instance, the writer(s) or the cast—give that information with, or in place of, the director.

NEWSPAPER ARTICLE BY KNOWN AUTHOR

Chase, Nan. "Colors and Crafts." <u>Miami Herald</u> 7 Sept. 1997,
   final ed.: 1J+.

- Show the edition of the paper you used, if possible, because sometimes an article is moved from one location to another in different editions of a newspaper. Therefore, the more specific you are about the location of an article you used, the easier it is for someone else to locate it.
- Record the section of the paper as well as the page number as it appears in the newspaper; a letter designating the section may appear either before or after the page number. If the section number or letter is not part of the pagination, write the abbreviation "sec." preceded by a comma and a space;

follow "sec." with a space and the section number, preceding the colon that shows the page number.

NEWSPAPER ARTICLE BY UNKNOWN AUTHOR

"Nanny Verdict Outrages Britons." <u>Miami Herald</u> 1 Nov. 1997,
    final ed.: 1A+.

To show the page number, follow the same convention as for articles by known authors.

NEWSPAPER EDITORIAL

"China: Rich Without Liberty." Editorial. <u>Miami Herald</u> 1
    Nov. 1997, final ed.: 24A.

If the editorial is signed, begin the entry with the author's name.

BOOK OR FILM REVIEW IN A NEWSPAPER

Fichtner, Margaria. "A Saga of Regret, Shattered Lives in
    Old Florida." Rev. of <u>Lost Man's River</u>, by Peter
    Matthiessen. <u>Miami Herald</u> 2 Nov. 1997, final ed.: 1L.

or

Rodriguez, Rene. "Gere, Film Guilty of a Patronizing
    Smugness." Rev. of <u>Red Corner</u>, dir. Jon Avnet, writer
    Robert King. <u>Miami Herald</u> 31 Oct. 1997, Weekend: 5G.

- This film review appeared in a special section of the newspaper called "Weekend," so that designation is given in place of either a "final" or "late city" or other edition.
- If the title of a film appears in a headline review of it, put the film title in single quotation marks within the double quotation marks of the article title.

MUSIC, RECORDING, THEATER, OR DANCE REVIEW IN A NEWSPAPER

Cohen, Howard. "Spice Girls Strike Again." Rev. of
    "Spiceworld" <u>Miami Herald</u> 31 Oct. 1997, final ed.:
    24G.

or

Dolan, Christine. "Playhouse Presents the Playwright's Love
    Letter." Rev. of <u>The Sisters Rosensweig</u>. <u>Miami Herald</u>
    23 Nov. 1997, final ed.: 11I.

ARTICLE IN NEWSPAPER SUPPLEMENT IN MAGAZINE FORM

Matz, Judith. "Exodus" <u>Tropic</u> in <u>Miami Herald</u> 20 July 1997:
    10-11.

Other Print Sources

DOCUMENT FROM INFORMATION SERVICE

> Freud, Robert. "Community Colleges and the Virtual
>
>   Community." ERIC, June 1996. ED397871.

- The name of the information service and an accession number is added to the usual citation form.
- The service is assumed to be the publisher if the material was not published before, except that it is unnessary to state a location for ERIC (Educational Resources Information Center) or other government information services.

UNPUBLISHED THESIS OR DISSERTATION

> Trout, Ann. "Early Indicators of Learning Disabilities
>
>   Using the Brigance K & 1 Screen for Kindergarten and
>
>   First Grade." Thesis. Middle Tennessee State
>
>   University, 1996.

- Even though a thesis or dissertation may be book length, the title is put in quotation marks rather than being underlined.
- Allow two spaces before and after the designation of the degree it earned (abbreviate a dissertation as "diss."), and name the degree-granting institution before the date.

> Jordan, Janis Evelyn. "In Support of Learning: Mission of
>
>   Community College Library/Learning Resource Centers
>
>   (Academic Libraries)." Diss. Indiana U, 1997. DAI 58
>
>   (1997): 2890.

This entry shows that the work cited is an abstract from *Dissertation Abstracts* (DA) or *Dissertation Abstracts International* (DAI). The granting institution and year follow the title. Leave a space after that designation and before the volume number. The page on which the abstract is recorded follows the colon.

MIMEOGRAPHED, DITTOED, OR PHOTOCOPIED REPORT

> Sears, William T. "Excavations at Kolomaki; Final Report."
>
>   Photocopy. U of Georgia Press, 1956: n.p.

- If no publisher is given, "n.p." appears after the colon citing the location.
- If the date of the printed material does not appear on it but is known, it is put in square brackets.
- The letters "n.p." following the colon indicate that there is no page numbering to this document.

PAMPHLET BY KNOWN AUTHOR

> Kurtzwell, Paula. Seven Steps to Safer Sunning. FDA
>
>   Consumer Magazine, 1996.

PAMPHLET BY UNKNOWN AUTHOR

<u>National Gallery of Art</u>. Washington: GPO, 1965.

PERSONAL OR UNPUBLISHED LETTER

Wallace, Sharon L. Letter to the author. 22 Nov. 1997.

A personal letter is presumed to be in the possession of the person to whom it is addressed. If not, the name of the museum or archives where the unpublished letter is located must be given.

Nightingale, Florence. Letter to Sir Arthur Landrow. 3 Feb.

1898. Sheffield Historical Society, Sheffield,

England.

LETTER PUBLISHED IN NEWSPAPER, MAGAZINE, OR JOURNAL

O'Neill, James R. "Been There, Seen That." Letter. <u>AARP</u>

<u>Bulletin</u> Oct. 1997: 13.

- Letters from readers to editors are often given a "title" or heading when they are published; if so, the heading may be treated as an article title in your Works Cited entry.

- Except for identifying the material as a letter, such an entry follows the usual format for articles in periodicals.

Belanoff, Pat. "Optimism, Writing, Teaching." Letter.

<u>College Composition and Communication</u> 48 (1997):

410-14.

This example illustrates an entry for a letter published in a periodical with continuous pagination.

GOVERNMENT PUBLICATION

<u>Cong. Rec.</u> 30 Oct. 1997: S11449.

Only the date and page number are required for citations from the *Congressional Record*. The "S" preceding the page number shows that it is a record of the Senate. An "H" before the page number signifies it is the record of proceedings of the House of Representatives.

Subcommittee on the Western Hemisphere. Haiti: <u>The</u>

<u>Situation After the Departure of the U.S. Contingent</u>

<u>from UNMH</u>. (Rep.) H461-40. Washington: GPO, 1996.

- If there is no person's name designated as author, show as author the title of the government agency issuing the document.

- The number and session of Congress are listed, and publications are abbreviated according to whether they are resolutions (Res.), reports (Rep.), or documents (Doc.) emanating from the Senate (S) or the House of Representatives (H), together with the number of the document.
- GPO means "U.S. Government Printing Office," the federal printer of all official documents and listed as publisher of some of them.
- Use these examples as a guide to citing publications by state governments, the United Nations, or other countries.

PUBLISHED INTERVIEW

> Hofler, Robert. "Wesley Snipes." Interview. Miami Herald.
>
> Tropic Magazine 16 Nov. 1997: 10.

If an interview has no title in the publication, or if no writer-interviewer is given, use the name of the interviewee as if it were the title, as in this example.

> "Toward the 21st Century." Interview with Bruce Crawford.
>
> Opera News 6 Dec. 1997: 44-45.

- If the interview was published in a newspaper or magazine, indication that the piece is an interview is the only variation from the usual periodical publication information. Lacking an interviewer's name, begin the entry with the title of the piece.
- If the interview was published in a book, treat it as if it were a chapter in the book; if the entire book is an interview, put the title and publication after the interviewer's name.

ELECTRONIC SOURCES

COMPUTER SOFTWARE

> GlobalFax® for Macintosh. Sunnyvale: Global Village
>
> Communications, 1995.

- As versions or releases of the software are changed, put the one used immediately after the title.
- If available, the Internet address (within angle brackets) is the final item in an entry.

CD-ROM

> The Story of Glass. CD-ROM. Oxford, UK: Reed Interactive,
>
> 1995.

PERSONAL E-MAIL

> Specht, Billy. "dolphin baby!" E-mail to Audrey Roth. 26
>
> Oct. 1996.

ONLINE ARTICLE ORIGINALLY IN MAGAZINE OR NEWSPAPER

> Blow, Richard. "Doctor Dolphin." <u>Mother Jones</u> 1 Jan. 1995.
>
>   Electric Library. 20 Oct. 1996.

- After the familiar publication information used for print, give the online source you used and the date you viewed the article.

- Provide the online reference database or source if available. Enclose its URL (uniform resource locator) information, if available, within angle brackets.

ONLINE DISCUSSION GROUP

> Parker, Stephen. "Exciting Developments." 15 Feb. 1998.
>
>   Online posting PD Aficionados. 17 Feb. 1998 <http://
>
>   pdomingo@gte.net>.

End the item with the URL (uniform resource locator), which will include the relevant path name (such as *telnet* or *http*) and, after the first slash, its file names (which may include a Web site indication).

Nonprint Sources

CARTOON OR ILLUSTRATION

> Schulz, Charles. "Peanuts." Cartoon. <u>Miami Herald</u>, final
>
>   ed. 16 Nov. 1997.

- This cartoon panel was on the front page of the comics section, but carries neither page nor newspaper section designation; thus, neither appears in the citation.

- Put the title of a cartoon or illustration in quotation marks. Consider the text or comment line, as in the following editorial cartoon, as the title.

> Herblock. "Unfortunately, I've found this nominee for an
>
>   important civil-rights position to be in favor of
>
>   civil rights." <u>Miami Herald</u>, final ed. 17 Nov. 1997.
>
> "Searching? Look Here." <u>Miami Herald</u>, final ed. 22 Jan.
>
>   1998: 2F.

Consider the caption of a newspaper picture, or the part of it that may appear in boldface type, as its title.

PERSONAL OR TELEPHONE INTERVIEW

> Borguss, Lloyd. Telephone interview. 17 Sept. 1996.
>
> Nathanson, David. Personal interview. 15 Sept. 1996.

RADIO, TELEVISION, OR RECORDED INTERVIEW

> Schmidt, Charles. Interview. <u>Larry King Weekend</u>. CNN. 22
>   Nov. 1997.
>
> Michele Passoff. Interview with Maggie Pelleya. <u>Latin Jazz</u>
>   <u>Quarter</u>. WDNA, Homestead, FL. 1 Apr. 1998.

- The name of the interviewee goes first.
- If the interview is on a local station, put a comma after the call letters of the radio or television station, and then put the city from which the program originated.
- If the interview was heard (or seen) on an audio or video source, provide that information in standard format.

QUESTIONNAIRE, SURVEY, OR POLL

> Dana Earl. "Survey on Necessity of Gun Control."
>   Questionnaire. 1996.
>
> Tori Trevor. Survey Response. 26 Jan. 1997.

- A large-scale survey and/or its responses is cited by surveyor and title, if there is one. Give the name of the particular respondent from whom information used in the research paper came, if you know it. Otherwise, your reader will assume that the questionnaire or survey was answered anonymously. If you had a number of signed responses to an inquiring document, arrange them alphabetically by surname, and use only the first one plus *et al.*, as in **"Adams, Pat, et al."**

WORKS OF ART

> Manet, Edouard. <u>The Street Singer</u>. Museum of Fine Arts.
>   Boston.
>
> Hanukah Lamp from Poland. Jewish Museum. New York.

References to an original work of art tell where it's located.

> Manet, Edouard. <u>The Street Singer</u>. Museum of Fine Arts,
>   Boston. Illus. in <u>Manet</u>. By Lesley Stevenson. New York:
>   Smithmark, 1992.

For photographic images of a work consulted in the course of writing your research paper, give location information, if available, but then cite the illustration number (if there is one), slide number, or page number of the place (or book) where you saw the picture.

> Kazuo, Hiroshima. "Basket for Holding Live Eels." Illus. 9
>   in <u>A Basketmaker in Rural Japan</u>. By Louise Allison
>   Cort and Nakamura Kenji. Washington: Smithsonian, 1994.

The citation is of a basket by a known artist and thus includes the name of its maker, although its present location is not immediately available. Because the item was a numbered illustration in a book, the research paper author must give information about the book in which the illustration was found, as here.

SPEECH OR LECTURE

> Lanza, Carmela Delia. "Talking with my Hands: Finding a
> Working-Class Voice in the Classroom." Conference on
> College Composition and Communication. Hyatt Regency.
> Phoenix, AZ. 14 Mar. 1997.

RECORDED SPEECH OR LECTURE

> Lacey, Walt. Effective Public Speaking. National Seminars.
> Audiocassette. National Press Publications, 1987.

RECORDING OF THE SPOKEN WORD

> Angelou, Maya. Gather Together in My House. Narr. Lynne
> Thigpen. 5 audiocassettes. Prince Frederick, MD:
> Recorded Books, 1994.

RADIO OR TELEVISION PROGRAM

> "Nicholas and Alexandra." Biography. A & E. 23 Nov. 1997.

The quotation marks indicate the title of a single program within a series, which name is underlined. The program appeared on cable, so the cable channel is named but not individual station call letters or the city of viewing.

> Hart, Mark. Community Aware. WTMI-FM, Miami. 21 Dec. 1997.

- Were the scriptwriter or director important in the research paper in which this citation appears, it would be appear before the title of the program, as with a film.

- If the program was not seen on a cable channel, give the local radio or TV station on which the program was heard or seen.

FEATURE-LENGTH FILM

> Casablanca. Dir. Michael Curtiz. Perf. Humphrey Bogart,
> Ingrid Bergman, Paul Henreid, and others. Warner
> Bros., 1943. Videocassette. MGM/UA Home Video.

- If the author of the screenplay, an actor, the cinematographer, or another person connected with the film is of major importance in your research paper, put that name first and give the name of the director after the title of the film. Otherwise, the order is usually: title, director, actors, production company, and year of release.

- Note if the film you consulted for your research was on videocassette or laser disc (and if it is on more than one video or disc).
- Add the date the video was first made available as the final item in the entry, if it is available.

Bergman, Ingrid, perf. Casablanca. Dir. Michael Curtiz.
     1943. Videocassette. 1988.

Epstein, Julius J., Philip G. Epstein, and Howard Koch,
     screenwriters. Casablanca. Prod. Hal G. Wallis. Warner
     Bros., 1943. Videocassette. MGM/UA Home Video.

SHORT FILM OR VIDEOTAPE

Thompson, Kim, filmmaker. All the Great Operas (in Ten
     Minutes). Chicago: Picture Start, 1992. 10 min.
     animated, color. Videocassette.

FILMSTRIP OR SLIDE PROGRAM

"IFR Clearance Shorthand." Advanced Pilot Series. 1
     filmstrip, 1 audiocassette. Englewood, CO: Jeppesen,
     1981. 90 fr. color.

Filmstrips and slide programs are hardly used since the advent of videocassettes. However, many libraries and media centers still have series of some materials or even single items you may have occasion to use and thus to cite. Take these two examples as guides for the content of titles and production information.

National Defense. 2 filmstrips, 2 audiocassettes. Written
     by Kate Griggs. Photo ed. Wendy Davis. Prentice-Hall
     Media, 1982. Each 84 fr., color, mono, 27 min.

Write the medium after the title and before other information.

LIVE THEATRICAL PERFORMANCE

Hair. Book and lyrics by Gerome Ragni, and James Rado,
     Music by Galt MacDermot. Dir. Patricia Dolan Gross.
     Jerry Herman Ring Theater. Coral Gables, FL. 14 Nov.
     1997.

LIVE MUSICAL PERFORMANCE

Iglesias, Enrique. Vivir 1997. Miami Arena. 13 Dec. 1997.

Fedora. By Umberto Giordano. Prod. by Beppe de Tomasi.
     Cond. Roberto Abbado. Perf. Mirella Freni, Placido

> Domingo, Ainhoa Arteta, Dwayne Croft. Metropolitan
>
> Opera. New York. 17 Oct. 1996.

Information about an opera generally lists principal singers according to vocal range: soprano, mezzo, tenor, baritone, bass. However, if the research work you prepare is about a performer or other member of the production team, you may put that person's name first, as you might in writing about an individual involved in a film.

> Domingo, Placido, tenor. <u>Fedora</u>. By Umberto Giordano. Cond.
>
> Roberto Abbado. Metropolitan Opera, New York. 17 Oct.
>
> 1996.

BROADCAST OR TELECAST OF MUSICAL PERFORMANCE

> <u>Billy Budd</u>. By Benjamin Britten. With Philip Langridge,
>
> Dwayne Croft, James Morris. Cond. Charles Mackerras.
>
> Metropolitan Opera. WTMI, Miami. 18 March 1997.

- The radio station call letters and city identify this as a performance heard on the radio.
- Placing the title of the work first shows its importance in this research paper. Otherwise, a different element would be listed initially, such as the composer or a featured singer or the conductor.

SOUND RECORDING

> Gomes, Antonio Carlos. <u>Il Guarany</u>. Perf. Veronica
>
> Villarroel, Placido Domingo, Hao Jiang Tian. Cond.
>
> John Neschling. Sony, 1996.

- If the paper emphasized one of the performers, the conductor, or another element of this opera, that information would be shown first.
- Recordings are assumed to be on CD. If that is not so for a particular work being cited, name the medium—audiocassette, audiotape (i.e., reel-to-reel), LP—before the recording company.

> <u>The Best of Greece</u>. Various performers. Audiocassette.
>
> Atoll/Paris, 1989.

> Stravinsky, Igor. <u>Le Sacre du Printemps</u>. Cond. Bernard
>
> Haitink. Concertgebouw Orchestra. LP. Philips, n.d.

> Hvorostovsky, Dmitri. "For the Shores of Your Distant
>
> Homeland." By Alexander Borodin. <u>My Restless Soul</u>.
>
> Philips, 1995.

An album by one performer (or group) begins with that person's (group's) name. If it contains different works, show individual titles in quotation marks, with the composer's name before the title of the album.

Midori. Niccolo Paganini. <u>24 Caprices for Solo Violin</u>. CBS
Records, 1989.

The name of a soloist, if there is one, will appear before that of the composer or conductor, depending on which is basic to the research paper.

Brahms, Johannes. Symphony #3 in F Major., Op.90. Cond.
Georg Solti. Decca LP, 1978.

Although record titles are generally underlined, that is not done if the composition is identified by form and key.

Final Presentation—MLA Style

MANUSCRIPT PREPARATION AND PROOFREADING

After your paper is written and the revisions are finished, you are ready to do the last few tasks: making a final copy of your paper and putting it in presentation form. Follow the few guidelines in this chapter and your paper will make the best possible impression on any audience, including the instructor who will grade your work.

Check the sample research paper at the end of this chapter, if you are working with MLA style. In it, you will see examples of the details that have been explained throughout the book, so you can use it as a model for your own paper.

Later in this chapter is a section entitled "Other Options," on proposals, abstracts, and other such optional sections of a paper. However, they are more common in business, technical, and scientific research papers, which are more likely to adhere to the APA style. (If you are working with APA style, turn to Chapter 11 for documentation specifics and a different sample research paper.) If you read through this entire chapter, you will see what possibilities exist for various kinds of research papers.

Two kinds of commentary appear in the the margins of both sample papers:

- Information about **form** is in color.
- Comments about **content,** substance, and organization of the papers are in **black.**

Proofread your entire paper carefully when you finish writing the final draft. An author is responsible for the accuracy of all work, so even though spelling and punctuation variations may be typing errors, they will not be excused as such when people read your paper. Therefore, *it's imperative to correct any errors,* especially when going over a final draft.

Most writing nowadays seems to be done on word processors and computers, so final preparation is easy. First, run off a hard copy of your paper, because then typos (typing mistakes) and other errors will be more apparent than they are on the computer screen. If you have a spell checker and a grammar checker, be sure to use them so appropriate corrections are made. Afterward, transfer spelling, punctuation, and grammar corrections (or any last-minute revisions, including additions and deletions) to the on-screen work, and save them to the disc.

If you are using a typewriter, read each page carefully before removing it from the machine. You may be able to white-out minor errors and retype letters or words as needed and still keep lines in place. Short omissions may be typed in directly above the line where it should have been, if you insert a caret (∧) to mark where they belong. Retype pages on which there are long insertions or changes. Don't crowd lines so much that they're unreadable. And never write in the margins.

Take time to proofread your entire research paper before turning it in, because you may catch additional errors when you look at the whole work. If you find any previously overlooked mistakes, make the corrections—very carefully and neatly—in black ink.

WORD PROCESSING/TYPING

Use a standard serif or sans-serif typefont for your research paper, *never* a script or other fancy typeface. Use a laser printer, if possible, or an ink-jet printer for your work, because that will make it more readable than a dot matrix printer. If you use a typewriter or dot-matrix printer, be sure the ribbon is fresh and the type clean. *Use only black ink,* never any color, for the text of your paper. Plain white 8½ × 11 paper of good quality will enable your work to create the best impression. (White pin-feed paper is also acceptable, provided you tear off the perforated edges cleanly after your work is printed.) *Never* use "erasable" paper, because type on it smudges and becomes hard to read; it's also hard for your instructor to write comments on. Onionskin (or other thin paper) is hard to handle and makes reading difficult, so never use it, either.

Accent marks or other symbols you can't type or print should be added afterward in black ink using a fine- or medium-point pen.

Follow these spacing customs for final typing or printing. They are illustrated in the sample papers in this chapter and Chapter 11.

- Type or print on only one side of each page.
- Leave one-inch margins at the top and bottom as well as on the sides of all text.
- Double-space all parts of the research paper, including long quotations and Works Cited entries.
- Indent the beginning of each new paragraph five spaces from the left margin.
- Long quotations (five or more lines of prose, four or more lines of poetry) are indented ten spaces from the left margin and shown *without quotation marks.*
- Prefer to set a computer to print ragged right (rather than with justified-right margin) to make for easy reading.

PAGE NUMBERING

Number all pages consecutively in arabic numerals throughout the research paper, beginning with the first page of text and including appendixes and Works Cited.

Number *front matter pages,* such as the outline, preface, or other material, consecutively in small roman numerals.

Page numbers should be set ½ inch down from the top of each page and aligned at the right-hand margin of the text—that is, one inch in from the right-hand edge of the paper. Do *not* use periods or abbreviations for "page" with the number. However, *do* put your last name (and first initial, if there is more than one person with the same last name in your class) immediately before the page number. (See the sample research paper at the back of this chapter for examples.)

FIRST PAGE OF THE RESEARCH PAPER TEXT (MLA)

MLA style *does not have a separate cover page.* Therefore, **all the necessary identification for you and your research paper goes on the first page of the text.**

One-half inch down from the top of the paper and ending at the right-hand margin one inch in from the edge of the paper, put your last name (and first initial, if needed) and the arabic numeral "1," as noted in the preceding section (and shown on page 246).

In the upper left-hand corner of your paper, one inch down from the top and one inch in from the left side of the paper, type the following **personal identification information** in double spacing:

- Your full name
- The name of your instructor
- The course abbreviation and number for which you wrote the paper (and the sequence number of your section, if so requested by the instructor)
- The date the paper is due

Allow a double space, and **center the title** of your paper. Use capital letters to begin all words except articles, conjunctions, and short prepositions. But *do not* put the title in all capitals, enclose it within quotation marks, underline it, or put a period at the end. However, if the titles of books, films, short stories, poems, or other pieces that are usually underlined or put in quotation marks are part of the title of your paper, write them in an appropriate way,

EXAMPLES

The Case for Captive Dolphins

and

The Book Schindler's List **and Spielberg's Film**

about Schindler

If the title of your paper requires more than one line, use standard double spacing.

Before beginning the text of your paper, use a double space to separate it from the title. Therefore you can keep your typewriter or computer set to double spacing throughout the paper.

Begin the text with the usual five-space indentation from the left margin for the first paragraph. If you begin with a long quotation without introduction, however, follow the customary ten-space indentation from the left margin that you would use anywhere else in the research paper.

OUTLINE

The outline from which you wrote your research paper is often included with the presentation text so an instructor can see the content and organization of your paper before reading it. Because it is preliminary to the research paper, it is usually put before the text of the paper itself but is given the same kind of spacing, personal information heading, and identification as on the first page of your paper. However, use lowercase roman numerals to number pages in an outline, even if there is only one such page.

Double-space all typing or printing in the outline, and adhere to the same margins as in the text of the paper.

Center the title of your paper, and follow it with a double space, just as you do on the first page of the text itself. Usually, begin the outline with the thesis statement of the paper, so labeled and double spaced; then begin the outline. As an example, see page 245 for the outline of the sample research paper in this chapter. You do not need to label this page as an outline, because anybody looking at it can see what it is.

THE TEXT (MLA STYLE)

Follow the information in Chapter 7 about writing your paper and the conventions for documenting it that you read in Chapter 8. Take a last look before submitting your work to make sure that you have acknowledged all material that isn't original, that pages are numbered consecutively, and that you have been consistent in using the preferred documentation system.

Underlining in typing or word processing means that if the words were set in printer's type they would be italicized—the custom for the titles of many works, for foreign words and phrases, and for words you want the reader to note particularly. If your word processing program and the printer you use have italics capability, you may use them instead of the underlining, provided your instructor approves.

If you are printing your research paper from a computer disc, don't get fancy with boldface. Especially, don't try to make multiple typeface changes just because they're available. And definitely *don't* use various colors, even if you have a color printer. Keep the text simple and readable, in black type on white paper.

ILLUSTRATIVE MATERIALS: CHARTS, TABLES, GRAPHS, AND OTHER VISUALS

Illustrative materials may make parts of your paper easier to understand than words alone. If you use them, put such materials as close as possible to the portion of the text they illustrate or refer to. If you haven't included them while you were drafting the text but find, upon rereading, that some would be helpful, add them before the final printing or typing of the text. Use only what you genuinely believe will be helpful to a reader's understanding: a map to show population change, a graph to illustrate the relation between interest rates and stock market prices, a table to show attendance at Superbowl games over the years, some bars of music, an original drawing or photograph. By all means, though, avoid using visuals just to be using them!

Consider creating your own visuals if you haven't found any that are suitable. You can draw, photograph, or create a montage of cutouts. Many computer programs can also accommodate visuals, format them for you, or help you to draw them yourself. Some computer programs are particularly suitable for a variety of charts, graphs, and other visuals.

Follow instructions for labeling tables or figures and citing those you borrow from other sources, as explained in Chapter 8 on pages 203–05. For instance, Figures are labeled below visuals and Tables above. As a final check, be sure all components of illustrative materials are clearly labeled.

COMMENT NOTES

Comment notes are brief elaborations, statements about the text, or a series of sources that would interrupt the text if written as parenthetical documentation. As explained in Chapter 7, such comments are conveniently placed at the end of the text of your paper—if you find the need to use them at all. Begin them on a new page immediately after the text and two spaces below the centered title "Notes" (without the quotation marks) typed one inch from the top of the page. Continue your name and consecutive page numbering as throughout the text.

Begin each comment note indented five spaces from the left margin and with the consecutive superscript (or superior) arabic number that is its designation and is coordinated with the appropriate place within the text. Skip one space and then type the required information. Second and subsequent lines of each comment note begin at the left margin to maintain the *paragraph indentation* used in notes.

Comment notes are double spaced. See an example of them as part of the sample research paper in this chapter, on page 260.

ENDNOTES

Some instructors still prefer that students cite sources at the end of the research paper text as endnotes rather than follow the current MLA style that calls for parenthetical documentation. If you are asked to use this stystem, you can read about it in Chapter 8 on pages 205–14. You may use documentation notes interspersed with comment notes by following the page setup described in the preceding section, provided you begin presenting the information on a page headed Notes.

WORKS CITED

The Works Cited listing follows any Notes and concludes the research paper. The forms to use for this listing were described in Chapter 4 so you could record the information accurately on preliminary citation cards. The **conventions** for the Works Cited list are detailed in Chapter 9. They are illustrated as part of the sample research paper in this chapter, on pages 261–63.

Notice that in your research paper you will be using a **composite list of all sources cited** within the paper. They are typed double spaced with hanging indentation and shown as a single, alphabetized list of works, beginning with the last name of each author, if known, or by the title of the work.

If you require more than one Works Cited page, continue with the sequential page number next to your name at the top right corner, but do not repeat the heading. See pages 261–63 of this book, which are sample research paper pages 16–18.

ANNOTATIONS

An annotation is a short statement that tells what is important or characteristic about a source. It is particularly helpful to any reader trying to decide whether or not to consult a source you have used in preparing your research paper. Because annotations tell something about the contents of a source or make some other comment, they enable a reader to tell what is of special interest.

Keep annotations brief; one or two remarks suffice. Annotations are not usually full sentences, though they customarily begin with a capital letter and end with a period. Begin each annotation two spaces after the period ending the citation.

Head the page on which they begin "Annotated List of Works Cited" rather than simply Works Cited. Otherwise, follow all the conventions you have already read about in Chapter 9 and immediately before this section.

If you know you will have to supply annotations to the works you cite in your paper, you should write comments on the preliminary citation card for each source as you consult it. The questions you answer in evaluating source materials (see page 114–18) will also help you think of comments you might want to make in annotations.

The following list shows the kinds of comments you might want to make in annotations and gives examples of each.

1.   **State the general content of a source.**

     `Shows that the comedian can be serious and literate rather`
     `than always clowning around.`

2.   **Make a judgment about the source.**

     `Makes difficult scientific concepts available to the`
     `layperson.`

3.   **Point out valuable properties or qualities of the source.**

     `Contains photographs by the author.`

4. **Note the viewpoint or bias of the author.**

   `Author asks reader to take much of theory on faith, not`

   `evidence.`

5. **Tell something helpful about the author of the source.**

   `Editor is former dolphin trainer who served on Marine`

   `Mammal Commission.`

Look at the annotated bibliographies in some of the sources you use for your research work and you may discover additional kinds of information an annotation can contain.

Although the Works Cited listing in the sample research paper in this chapter is not annotated, here are some examples of what a few of the entries would be like if it were.

EXAMPLE ANNOTATIONS

`Borguss, Lloyd. Telephone interview. 17 Sept. 1996. Owner`

   `of Dolphins Plus in Key Largo, so gave helpful cost`

   `information.`

`Herman, Louis M., Adam A. Pack, and Amy M. Wood.`

   `"Bottlenose Dolphins Can Generalize Rules and Develop`

   `Abstract Concepts." `Marine Mammal Science` Jan. 1994:`

   `70-80.  Dolphin behavior described almost as if it`

   `were human actions that show learning.`

`Wexler, Mark. "Thinking About Dolphins." `National Wildlife`

   `1 Apr. 1994: n.p. Electric Library 10 Oct. 1996.`

   `Suggests extent of information still not available`

   `about dolphins.`

APPENDIX

An appendix contains additional illustrations or other materials that amplify the text without interrupting it. It is that addition to your research paper where you might put charts or tables useful to readers' understanding, but without breaking their concentration as they read the text of your paper. This book has two appendixes: one gives a selected list of reference works so you can see the extent and variety of library materials you might use, and another shows you words and abbreviations commonly used in academic research. Both are supplemental to the text, so they contain the sort of information that can safely be put in appendixes. (An alternate form of the plural word is "appendices.")

If your paper requires an appendix, or several of them, give each a sequential designation using capital letters. Put them immediately after the text and before the Notes or Works Cited in a research paper, because, strictly speaking, appendixes are supplements to the text. Head the first one Appendix A, give it an identifying title, and center that unit one inch down from the top of the paper. The next one will be labeled Appendix B, and so on.

Continue successive page numbers next to your name as you do throughout the text and other material in your research paper.

OTHER OPTIONS: PREFACES, STATEMENTS OF PURPOSE, PROPOSALS, SYNOPSES, AND ABSTRACTS

Few undergraduate papers require any of these options. Nor will you usually be asked to include more than one of them in the final presentation of your research work. Each precedes the paper itself (or the outline) and is typed in double spacing; the pages are numbered consecutively in lowercase roman numerals, just as all other material ahead of the text is.

A preface is a brief introduction telling the audience what it can expect to find in the paper. Most prefaces are no more than half a page long. If you are asked to include a table of contents with your paper, the preface follows it.

A statement of purpose tells what you propose to do or show in the text that follows. Sometimes it also tells the reason you undertook the research being reported—that is, it tells the purpose you hope to achieve by having done this project. Papers on scientific or science-related subjects often begin with a statement of purpose.

A proposal also tells what you plan to do or show, though often in some context outside the research paper. It is frequently included in business or social science papers if there is a problem to be solved.

A synopsis (the plural is "synopses") **or abstract distills details of the content of a research paper.** Both differ from the preface because they give more information about the content and are also likely to stress the purpose for which the research was undertaken. Neither is longer than one page.

Center the heading telling what is on the page (that is, "Synopsis" or "Abstract" or other—but without the quotation marks shown here) in capital and lowercase letters, one inch down from the top of the paper. Then double-space, before beginning the writing, which is also double spaced. Observe the same one-inch margins around the material as you do in typing the text.

FASTENING PAGES

Use a paper clip at the top left-hand corner to fasten together the pages of your completed research work. The clip is easy for a reader to remove and thus frees the pages to turn. Or a reader may want to put the Works Cited list alongside the text for handy reference. Because all pages are numbered and have your name on them, the paper can be reassembled readily.

Some instructors may want to have papers submitted in one of the many kinds of inexpensive covers or binders that protect the work as well as hold it together. Others may even prefer to have papers stapled together.

Ask your instructor which method of fastening pages is preferred.

SAMPLE RESEARCH PAPER IN MLA FORMAT

On the following pages is a research paper written by a student who followed the process described in this book. It includes an outline, the paper itself with parenthetical documentation, an example of Comment Notes, and a Works Cited listing. You may recognize some parts from having read them as examples throughout this book.

Remember that in the margins of each page are comments: comments about form are printed in color, and comments about content are printed in black. Use these sidebar comments as a guide to preparing your own research paper for final presentation.

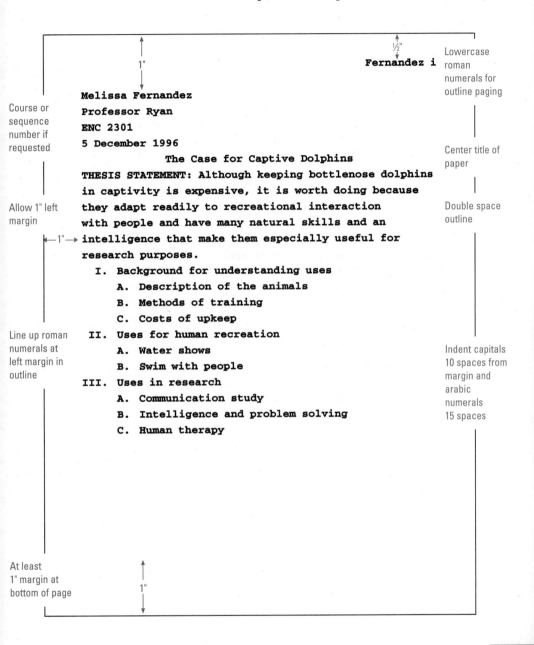

½"

Lowercase
roman
numerals for
outline paging

1"

Melissa Fernandez

Course or
sequence
number if
requested

Professor Ryan

ENC 2301

5 December 1996

The Case for Captive Dolphins

Center title of
paper

THESIS STATEMENT: Although keeping bottlenose dolphins
in captivity is expensive, it is worth doing because

Allow 1" left
margin

they adapt readily to recreational interaction

Double space
outline

with people and have many natural skills and an

←—1"—→ intelligence that make them especially useful for

research purposes.

   I. Background for understanding uses

      A. Description of the animals

      B. Methods of training

      C. Costs of upkeep

Line up roman
numerals at
left margin in
outline

  II. Uses for human recreation

      A. Water shows

      B. Swim with people

III. Uses in research

Indent capitals
10 spaces from
margin and
arabic
numerals
15 spaces

      A. Communication study

      B. Intelligence and problem solving

      C. Human therapy

At least
1" margin at
bottom of page

1"

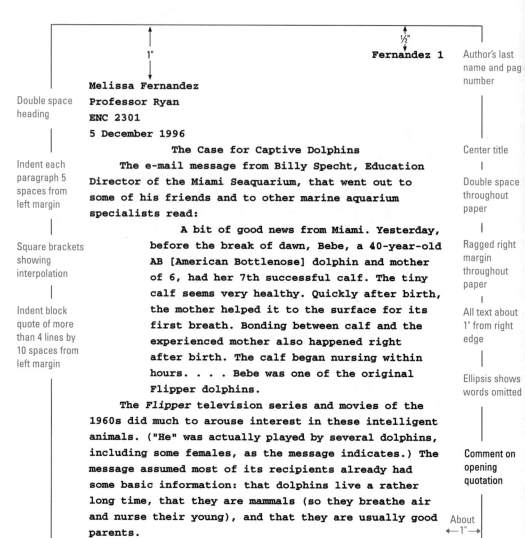

½"

Fernandez 1   Author's last name and page number

1"

Melissa Fernandez

Double space heading

Professor Ryan

ENC 2301

5 December 1996

The Case for Captive Dolphins   Center title

Indent each paragraph 5 spaces from left margin

The e-mail message from Billy Specht, Education Director of the Miami Seaquarium, that went out to some of his friends and to other marine aquarium specialists read: Double space throughout paper

Square brackets showing interpolation

A bit of good news from Miami. Yesterday, before the break of dawn, Bebe, a 40-year-old AB [American Bottlenose] dolphin and mother of 6, had her 7th successful calf. The tiny calf seems very healthy. Quickly after birth, the mother helped it to the surface for its first breath. Bonding between calf and the experienced mother also happened right after birth. The calf began nursing within hours. . . . Bebe was one of the original Flipper dolphins.   Ragged right margin throughout paper

Indent block quote of more than 4 lines by 10 spaces from left margin

All text about 1" from right edge

Ellipsis shows words omitted

The *Flipper* television series and movies of the 1960s did much to arouse interest in these intelligent animals. ("He" was actually played by several dolphins, including some females, as the message indicates.) The message assumed most of its recipients already had some basic information: that dolphins live a rather long time, that they are mammals (so they breathe air and nurse their young), and that they are usually good parents.   Comment on opening quotation

About ←1"→

Although dolphins usually live free in the temperate, subtropical, and tropical oceans of the

1"

1"

Consecutive
arabic page
numbers
throughout

world (there are also a few freshwater species), some,
especially among members of the American Bottlenose
group, are kept in captivity. Keeping them in
artificial habitats such as cement tanks or fenced-in
sections of free-flowing water is not cruelty to
animals, for even when given the choice of roaming
free vs. being in pens, most who are used to living in
the latter willingly return to them (Borguss; Pryor
in "Domestic" 346; LaPuzza; Cousteau 189). Watching
these penned dolphins, and especially their trained
performances, gives people pleasure. So does swimming
with them. Also, dolphins are being used for several
kinds of live research projects. They may earn their
own way as entertainment, but keeping dolphins for
other purposes, though it may seem to be expensive, is
well worth whatever costs are involved because
researchers are constantly gaining information that
can be used to better understand human beings and our
society.

Related
references are
grouped

Thesis
statement
delayed until
now because
of unusual
opening
quotation

   The bottlenose dolphin (*Tursiops Truncatus*), the
subject of this paper, is easily recognized
by its seemingly perpetual smile (see Fig. 1).
Bottlenose dolphins usually grow up to 12 feet long
and weigh about 400 pounds. In addition to their
"smiling" face, they are easily recognized by a long,
sharp snout that is somewhat flattened like a beak
and, if you get close enough, by their cone-shaped
teeth, which are used to grab their food of fish and
squid or other invertebrates. Their sleek form and
front flipperlike fins together with the horizontal
tail help propel dolphins at speeds clocked at 25 mph

Text gives
background
information

Photo
illustrates text

Fig. 1. Photo of bottlenose dolphin. Courtesy of Miami Seaquarium.

in the open sea. Dolphins need that physical structure
in order to surface and breathe through the blowhole
on top of their heads. Sometimes they leap from the
water in an arc while breathing, a behavior that
occurs in the wild but often is demonstrated by one or
several animals in unison during performances for
which they are trained.

They have been studied extensively because they
adapt readily to contact with humans, and there is
now a body of information about dolphins because they
have been trained since just before World War II. As

Fernandez 4

Author of quote identified in text

Karen Pryor, herself a former trainer and later Commissioner of the Marine Mammal Commission, writes,

> Techniques for the maintenance and training of dolphins were being developed during roughly the same decades in which experimental psychologists were teaching an understanding of the laws of operant conditioning, and the ways in which behavior could be modified by using positive reinforcement. ("Reinforcement" 254)

Block indent of more than four lines

Article title shortened in citation

Quotation marks show familiar words used in special sense

No wonder, then, that dolphins are usually trained by the behavioral method we call "positive reinforcement." To do otherwise would be impractical because, as Pryor points out ("Reinforcement" 253), dolphins will just swim away from anyone who attempts to train them by coercion or restraint. In fact, once accustomed to human contact, most dolphins seem to enjoy and even thrive on it, trying to please their trainers. [1]

Parenthetical documentation

Superscript number coordinates with notes

The chief characteristic of dolphins, and the one that is exploited for entertainment and research, is echolocation. That is, by emitting sounds (which are described as clicks and whistles) and attending to the returning "message," which is a natural form of sonar, dolphins can locate and determine the shapes of what is around them. This is necessary for them to find food, which they often do cooperatively (as pointed out by Wursig 146), as well as keeping track of other members of their group, especially in deep water and at night; it is also the way they identify dangers, such as sharks, to each other (Tyack and Sayigh 82).

Author and page number are documented

Fernandez 5

Sound travels 4-1/2 times faster through water than it does on land, so it is a quick method of communication (shown mathematically in Strauch 112). Echolocation has been especially helpful to researchers, although the learning ability and good memory of bottlenose dolphins also make them good subjects for both training and study.

Neither activity is inexpensive for the owners and/or keepers of these mammals. Besides the cost of building and keeping up a healthful environment for captive dolphins (which Specht estimates may be $12,000 to $20,000 a year for the Miami Seaquarium to clean its several tanks but is obviously less for pens within open water areas), they require food, medical care, and training or research facilities. Full-grown, adult dolphins eat about 25 pounds of food a day, primarily table-quality fish, that in summer 1996 cost an average of $.73 a pound, according to Lloyd Borguss, owner of Dolphins Plus on Key Largo, FL. (The amount of food and prices are likely to vary with different animals and at different locations.) In addition, each dolphin receives vitamins costing at least $2 a day. Borguss pointed out that the dolphins he cares for are seen regularly by a veterinarian, and he must carry insurance on the animals, their trainers, and visitors at his research and education center; his trainers are paid anywhere from $300 to $1000 a week. (Salaries are similarly variable at other training and research facilities, according to interviews with both Spencer and Nathanson.) Further, dolphins are highly social animals, so they are

Period after parenthetical documentation in text

Transitional word

Author's comment in parentheses

Source citation is part of text sentence

Citation begins sentence

Transitional word

Fernandez 6

unlikely to survive comfortably unless in groups. All
in all, costs are such that not every researcher wants
to or can afford to own the animals. For example, Dr.
David E. Nathanson, whose Dolphin Therapy Research
facility is located next to Dolphins Plus, said in an
interview that he contracts with that organization to
use some of the dolphins it owns for his own work.

Research grants support the work of many groups.
For instance, scientists at the Kewalo Basin Marine
Mammal Laboratory of the University of Hawaii in
Honolulu have been learning from dolphins since 1969,
mostly supported by various kinds of grants. According
to Thomas Vosmer, one project in 1995-96 at KBMML cost
$370,975, a grant supplemented by accepting paying
volunteers, recruited through Earthwatch since 1981,
for two-week or four-week stints of work for which
each individual contributes; in 1995-96, the amount
was $2,295 to $2,595 for two weeks, depending on the
time of year. (See also Causey) (Such temporary help
from laypeople has been customary at this research
location.) The U.S. Navy, which formerly kept,
trained, and researched with up to 100 dolphins at the
Navy Command Control and Ocean Surveillance Center in
San Diego ^{2}, also regularly made grants available to
researchers, as did the National Science Foundation;
funding from such sources is acknowledged in published
journal articles. (See Herman, Pack, and Wood; Mackay)

Entertaining visitors at marine parks and
aquariums is probably the context in which most people
first encounter dolphins (aside from television

Specifics help
reader
understand
expense of
research

Superscript
number
coordinates
with Notes

Transitional
sentence

Sources for
information in
preceding
paragraph

programs and videos such as <u>Dolphins with Robin
Williams</u> that may be shown in schools). There, they
are usually visible as they swim and are fed by divers.
Mostly, though, the dolphins go through routines they
have been trained to do, such as jumping through
hoops, throwing rings and balls, finding objects on or
in water, and "tail walking" across an enclosure.
(Trainers usually use a form of American Sign
Language.) Such activities in these locations are
unnatural, but they do provide enjoyment for countless
people.

    Another form of entertainment in which humans can
participate is to actually swim with dolphins at a
number of places around the world. Among them in south
and central Florida alone are four locations in the
Keys (Dolphins Plus, the Dolphin Research Center,
Theater of the Sea, Hawk's Cay Resort) and one,
Seaworld, near Orlando. At these places, people who
want to swim in enclosures with the dolphins must have
preparation, in addition to swimming and/or snorkeling
skills, and pay for the privilege.

    According to the U.S. Marine Mammal Protection
Act, dolphins can only be kept for public display,
national defense, or research--and it is in that last
capacity that many kinds of studies continue. Some are
designed to learn about how the animals live and about
how they communicate. Many are designed to test the
intelligence and learning capacity of the animals.
There is also ongoing research, readily identified (at
about 14:26 and ff.) in <u>Dolphins with Robin Williams</u>,
about how dolphins interact in the wild with humans.

Clarification given within parentheses

Videotape location according to timing

Fernandez 8

Dolphins in the open sea live in pods, or groups,
that usually seem to consist of five or six adults
and some young calves. Wursig points out that even
in captivity, they set up their own hierarchical
relationships, usually with the older and/or larger
animals as leaders, for they are basically very social
animals who need the stimulation of interaction with
others of their kind. Simple observation of their
behavior together (aided by radio transmitters
strapped to particular animals in the open sea, as
Wursig describes) is one kind of research that helps
people learn more about these animals. Also, Spencer,
chief dolphin trainer at the Miami Seaquarium, pointed
out that the attitudes of individual dolphins toward
different trainers or those who go into tanks to feed
the animals are recorded and also provide research
information.

How dolphins communicate has been the subject of
many studies and may be one of the most important
things learned from the cost of keeping dolphins for
research. Basically, they make sounds described as
clicks and whistles, as mentioned earlier. Strauch
(112-13) goes so far as to say that because a dolphin
has "two separate sound-producing organs which it can
use together as well as independently," each animal
can both send and receive in stereo. He then writes
that dolphins can therefore communicate with each
other by what he calls mind-to-mind transmission,
"directly transmitting imagery to another dolphin."

> Think about a dolphin that has been
> to the underwater equivalent of over the

Short quotations as part of text

Block indent of long quotation

Fernandez 9

mountains and wishes to tell its peers about
the experience. . . . By stereophonically
reproducing the waveforms it received
while it was echolocating, the dolphin can
communicate the full acoustic image of what
it "saw," placing it directly in the minds
of those it is communicating with. It could
also selectively filter and interpret that
experience, highlighting aspects that it
wished to emphasize and playing down aspects
it wished to de-emphasize. (114)

Documentation after period ending block quotation

Strauch does not know that dolphins actually
do what he has described, but the possibility is
intriguing. In fact, the abstract of a National
Science Foundation Standard Grant awarded in 1992
to Prof. Louis M. Herman of the University of of
Hawaii, Manoa, sought to answer questions about the
relationship of visual and echolocation information
obtained from a study of bottlenosed dolphins. The
grant proposal even suggests that on an applied level,
such "echoic 'visualization'" by dolphins could "offer
fresh insights into the construction of intelligent
sonar apparatus." This, in turn, could have other
uses. As Moore suggests (380), "Learning about the
dolphin's natural sonar system helps us build better
sonar hardware to study the seas and aid in navigation.
Understanding dolphin sonar may also help reduce the
problems of dolphin entanglement in fishing gear"
[such as tuna nets].

Citation begins sentence

The kinds of whistles that dolphins use for
communication are different enough for each other that

Author's explanation in square brackets

they have been called "signature whistles." Tyack writes (82) that a mother and her calf can locate and identify each other by this method. There are also whistles that imitate the signature whistles of other dolphin in a group. This author further speculates:

> Perhaps untrained dolphins imitate the signature whistle of another group member to initiate a social interaction with that dolphin. Perhaps the males imitate the signature whistles of their partners in order to maintain contact with them or even to call them. . . . [observations show that] the males tend to imitate the whistles of animals with which they already share a strong bond. (83)

Hearing all the unusual things about the ability of dolphins to communicate, the question invariably arises: "How smart *are* dolphins?" If not necessarily "smart" in the way we might expect humans to be, at least dolphins can be trained to make various kinds of fine discriminations. For instance, in one experiment described by Au and Turl, the dolphins were trained (taught?) to tell the difference between identical hollow aluminum and stainless steel cylinders suspended in the water at different angles. They could also differentiate between "a hollow stainess steel cylinder . . . and a cylinder consisting of coral rock aggregates encapsulated in degassed epoxy with the same outer diameter and length. . ." (2448).

Herman, Pack, and Wood have reported (and the video <u>Dolphins with Robin Williams</u> shows) their

(margin note left) Author suggests alternate wording

(margin note right) Ellipsis shows wording omitted at end of sentence

Fernandez 11

experiments in having dolphins respond to signals in which the arm/hand configuration represents a word or idea, much as American Sign Language does. The dolphins are able, almost every time, to respond to the trainer's questions about the sameness or difference of objects or even of shapes.

Even more surprising is the ability of dolphins to respond to what amount to sentences of instruction. For example, when signed to put a frisbee on a surfboard, the animal in the tank picked up the frisbee, but since there was no surfboard in the water, she carried it to a place where she pushed a floating paddle that signified "no." That is, she realized that she could not carry out the complete assignment (Wexler).

Author of information in paragraph is credited

While most of these and similar experiments represent dolphins carrying out tasks essentially dictated to them by people. Pryor tells a true story communicated to her by another researcher who said that after making many correct responses, one day the dolphin being studied "made a long series of completely wrong responses. The animal was being reinforced by fish dispensed from a feeding machine; examination revealed that the fish in the machine had dried out and become unpalatable. When the fish were replaced, the / dolphin resumed making correct responses" ("Reinforcement" 255-56). There can be no doubt that the dolphin was telling its trainer something--communicating something for which it had no precedent and certainly no training.

Short quotation is part of text

First of 3 digits omitted rather than repeat it

The research involving dolphins and humans that may be most interesting to the general public, and in the long run the kind that no price tag can be put on, is that involving human therapy, primarily with disabled children. In the Ukraine, dolphins at Sevastopol that used to work for the Soviet Navy are now almost having to earn their own keep, and some of them are helping children as young as two years old who have neurotic disorders such as phobias, neuroses, nightmares, and bedwetting (Poletz). One dolphin, named Diana, has been trained to let the children hold her dorsal fin, and she guides them around her net cage. Dr. Ludmila Lukina says that she doesn't know why this therapy works, but after studying dolphins and collecting research information for twenty years, she knows it does. "We don't want to make supernatural claims and we haven't been able to prove what it is about the treatments--the dolphins themselves, the sea, or the sun. But it works" (qtd. in Poletz).

Nor are others sure what there is about dolphin-human interaction that seems to help others. In 1971 Dr. Betsy Smith of Florida International University was studying such interaction when she let her brother, who was mentally retarded, wade into the water with two dolphins whom she described as "pretty rough." But she reported that in this circumstance, "'The dolphins were around him [the brother], still, gentle, rubbing on him.' Somehow they knew he was different" (qtd. in Blow). A similar phenomenon was described by Chris Connell of the Dolphin Human Therapy and Research Program in Key Largo, FL, who

Single page source needs only author's name

Indirect source cited

Words in square brackets explain pronoun

Quotation within source

Single marks for quote within quotation

Fernandez 13

said, "I remember a boy whose leg had been badly
damaged by cancer. Almost as soon as he got into the
water, a group of dolphins began to softly rub against
his wounded leg" (qtd. in Halls). Such initial study
has expanded until, when Blow wrote in 1995 there were
150 dolphin-assisted therapy research projects around
the world. Furthermore, as Blow summarized, ". . .
there seems little doubt that dolphin swims can help
humans with disabilities such as Down's syndrome,
autism, depression, attention deficit disorder,
muscular dystrophy, and spinal cord injuries."

> **Indirect quotation**

In 1989, David E. Nathanson published the results
of his work with six mentally retarded boys showing
that they "learned two to ten times faster and with
greater retention when working with dolphins" (233).
He believes that dolphin intelligence and being in the
stress-reducing environment of water are responsible.
Nathanson is now director of the Dolphin Human Therapy
in Key Largo, FL, where he continues his work with
special-needs children. However, for a family to
accompany a child to a facility for such special help
is very expensive, for it includes transportation,
food, and lodging, usually for at least two to four
weeks (Personal interview).

> **Author and date cited**

> **Interview is source cited**

There may eventually be an alterate way to achieve
similar results. David Cole, a computer scientist, who
became interest in dolphin-human therapy while a
graduate student, is working on something he calls
Cyberfin, a sort of virtual reality system that can
simulate swimming with dolphins without actually
having captive dolphins present. Cole has done much

Fernandez 14

research on dolphin-assisted therapy and he has come
to believe--as do many other researchers in the field--
that just as the dolphins' echolocation abilities seem
to be able to distinguish between healthy and damaged
parts of the body, they are also responsible for
any "healing" taking place. The theory is that the
dolphins' echolocation energy causes "cavitation, a
ripping apart of molecules" that happens inside soft
tissue in the body (Blow). Cole believes that if the
same process happens with cellular membranes, which
are the boundaries between cells, they could change
cell molecules and thus assist the production of
T-cells, which in humans are the cells that fight
infection. If this is true, it might even offer hope
for conquering AIDS, which is the result of lowered
T-cell counts in the body.

Because of the success with dolphin-assisted
therapy with the mentally and physically disabled so
far, the method holds out hope "for patients with head
and spinal injuries, cancer and other conditions"
(Kalfrin). Obviously, in order to provide such
therapy, some dolphins need to be kept captive in
order to be available to help humans.

Transitional
sentence

Therefore, considering all the recreational
pleasure that captive dolphins give as well as their
contributions to both theoretical and practical
science, paying for the upkeep of these animals seems
a small price, and it, as well as the effort of people
who work with them, is well worth the costs.

Conclusion is
summary

Page numbers
continue
sequentially

1"   **Fernandez 15**

Center heading

Notes

Superscript
number begins
5 spaces from
left margin

[1] Mike Spencer, Supervisor of Dolphin Training at the Miami Seaquarium, talks about how the various dolphins discriminate among the humans who work with them and respond differently to the different people.

Succeeding
lines begin at
left margin

Pryor writes ("Domestic" 346) "When the U.S. Navy released the news that it was using dolphins to search for mines in the Persian Gulf [during the so-called Gulf War], a reporter asked me if I thought the dolphins would find the work arduous or unpleasant. Knowing the character of the animals and the skills of the navy trainers, I could answer instantly, 'Are you kidding? They love it.'"

Double space
throughout

Also, there is ample visual evidence of dolphins responding to signals from researchers, and from visitor Robin Williams, in the video <u>Dolphins with Robin Williams In the Wild</u>.

Cousteau (189) tells how 12 dolphins who lived and trained at Santini's (in the Florida Keys) returned even before rebuilding of their hurricane-destroyed pens was completed and played with workers doing the building.

[2] The dolphins had been trained to signal humans, often on land, about the presence of intruders or mines, and they saw service in Vietnam in 1970 and 1971 as well as in the Persian Gulf in 1986 and 1987. In 1994, Congress authorized release of some of its trained dolphins to marine theme parks and other locations where they might be used for entertainment or research, including breeding (LaPuzza).

Fernandez 16

Center heading

Works Cited

Double space
all items

Au, Whitlow W. L., and Charles W. Turl. "Material
    Composition Discrimination of Cylinders at
    Different Aspect Angles by an Echolocating
    Dolphin." <u>Journal of the Accoustical Society of</u>
    <u>America</u> 89 (1991): 2448-451.

Hanging
indentation
for all items

Blow, Richard. "Dr. Dolphin." <u>Mother Jones</u> 1 Jan. 1995:
    n.p. 15 Oct. 1996. Electric Library.

Borguss, Lloyd. Telephone interview. 17 Oct. 1996.

Interview

Causey, Nathanael. "Dolphin Intelligence." <u>Earthwatch</u>
    1 May 1995: 37. Electric Library.

Cousteau, Jacques-Yves, and Philippe Diole. <u>Dolphins</u>.
    trans. J.F. Bernard. Garden City: Doubleday,
    1975.

Video source

<u>Dolphins with Robin Williams in the Wild</u>.
    Videocassette. Dist. Turner Home Entertainment
    and PBS. 1995.

Halls, Kelly Milner. "'Dolphfriends'." <u>U.S. Kids</u> June
    1996: 6.

Multiple
authorship

Herman, Louis M., Adam A. Pack, and Amy M. Wood.
    "Bottlenose Dolphins Can Generalize Rules and
    Develop Abstract Concepts." <u>Marine Mammal Science</u>
    Jan. 1994: 70-80.

Article from
Internet
source

Kalfrin, Valerie. "Calling Dr. Flipper." <u>Ladies' Home</u>
    <u>Journal</u> 1 May 1996: 92. 15 Oct. 1996. Electric
    Library.

Printed
interview from
radio

LaPuzza, Tom. "U.S. Navy to Retire 25 Dolphins
    Due to Budget Cuts." Interview. <u>All Things</u>
    <u>Considered</u>. Noah Adams, Host. PBS 15 June 1994.
    Transcript. 2 Oct. 1996. Electric Library.

Sequential
page numbers

Mackay, R. Stuart. "Dolphin Interaction with
    Acoustically Controlled Systems: Aspects of
    Frequency Control, Learning, and Non-food
    Rewards." Cetology 41 (1981): 1-12.

Moore, Patrick W. B. "Dolphin Psychophysics: Concepts
    for the Study of Dolphin Echolocation." In Dolphin
    Societies: Discoveries and Puzzles. ed. Karen
    Pryor, and Kenneth S. Norris. Berkeley: U of CA
    Press, 1991: 365-82.

Article within
book

Nathanson, David E. "Using Atlantic Bottlenose
    Dolphins to Increase Cognition of Mentally
    Retarded Children." Clinical and Abnormal
    Psychology 1989: 233-42.

3 hyphens and
period signify
same author as
previous item

---. Personal interview. 15 Oct. 1996.

National Science Foundation Standard Grant 9121331.
    "Integration of Visual and Echoic Information."
    Louis N. Herman, investigator. Univ. of Hawaii,
    Manoa. Aug. 1992-July 1994. 24 Oct. 1996 <http://
    www/ref.gov/flp/awards91/awd912/9121331.txl>.

Internet
accessed entry

Poletz, Lida. "Ex-Soviet Navy Dolphins Undergo
    Military Conversion." n.p. 30 Aug. 1995: n.p.
    28 Oct. 1996. Electric Library.

No page
numbers
shown for
article

Pryor, Karen. "The Domestic Dolphin" in Dolphin
    Societies: Discoveries and Puzzles. ed. Karen
    Pryor, and Kenneth S. Norris. Berkeley: U of CA
    Press, 1991: 345-47.

---. "Reinforcement Training as Interspecies
    Communication" in Ronald J. Schusterman, Jeanette
    A. Thomas, and Forrest G. Wood. Dolphin Cognition
    and Behavior: A Comparative Approach. Hillsdale:
    Earlbaum, 1986: 253-60.

Fernandez 18

Specht, Billy. "Re: dolphin baby!" E-mail to Audrey
    Roth. 26 Oct. 1996.

---. Personal interview. 3 Oct. 1996.

Spencer, Mike. Personal interview. 3 Oct. 1996.

Strauch, Ralph. "Do Dolphins Think Without Language?"
    Sea Frontiers 30.2 (1984): 110-15.

Tyack, Peter L., and Laela S. Sayigh. "Those Dolphins
    Aren't Just Whistling in the Dark." Oceanus, n.d.:
    80-83.

Vosmer, Thomas. "Dolphin Intelligence." Earthwatch 1
    July 1995: 41. 17 Oct. 1996. Electric Library.

Wexler, Mark. "Thinking About Dolphins." National
    Wildlife 1 Apr. 1994: n.p. 17 Oct. 1996. Electric
    Library.

Wursig, Bernd. "Dolphins." Scientific American 240.3
    (1979): 108-19.

APA and Other Styles

"APA" stands for American Psychological Association; its widely used **research paper format is set forth in its** *Publication Manual of the American Psychological Association,* **4th ed.** (Washington: APA, 1994). It is the standard style for writing in most of the social sciences as well as in some other fields, including research in the humanities. APA citations within the text follow an author and date system; that is, they acknowledge the author(s) of a particular work and the date it was published. Although the APA system differs somewhat from the MLA system, you will find it easy to use and comfortable to make the transition if called on to do so. This chapter highlights and illustrates some characteristics of the APA format system and then notes elements of other research styles and documentation systems, should you need to use one of them. A student-written research paper in the APA style concludes this chapter.

APA FORMAT AND PAGE NUMBERING

Follow these conventions in typing or word processing your research paper.

1. **Margins should be 1½ inches at the top, bottom, left, and right of each page in an APA-style research paper.**

2. **Use double spacing throughout** the text of the paper itself and on other pages that go with it.

3. **Prefer to use a ragged right margin for readability** rather than a justified right.

4. **Indent the beginning of each paragraph by five spaces** from the left margin, and **indent each line of a long quotation** (that is, more than 40 words) **by ten spaces** from the left margin.

5. **Use this order of pages for the research paper:**

    -   title page
    -   outline (if requested by instructor)
    -   abstract (if requested by instructor)

- text

- references (sources used in paper)

- appendixes—if required for the paper

- notes—if citations are not included as parenthetical documentation

   Put visuals wherever they relate most easily to the text, even though papers submitted in APA style for publication will have tables and figures each on a separate page and grouped at the end of the article.

6. **A shortened form of the title is placed flush with the right margin** at 1½ inches from the edge **and 1½ inches down** from the top of the paper. **Write the page number a double space below the title** and end flush with the right margin.

7. **Number pages, beginning with the title page, consecutively with arabic numerals.** (APA recommends lowercase roman numerals for pages before the text, such as an outline that must be turned in, but many teachers will accept arabic numbers throughout.)

8. **Endnotes, as an alternative to in-text citations, are often permitted** by instructors whose students prepare undergraduate research papers.

APA-FORMAT TITLE PAGE

   Prepare a separate title page for the beginning of your research paper. Center the title of your paper on the page. Ideally, it will not be very long, but if it is, double-space between the lines. Allow a double-space below the title and center your complete name and after another double-space put the title and/or number of the course for which you are submitting the paper. Use capitals and lower case letters on each line.

   Begin paging the research paper with this title page, so put the number "1" and a short form of the title at the top right and use the spacing for page numbering described in the previous section.

   Some instructors may also request that you write their name and/or the due date of the research paper below the other information. Such recommendations differ in a few respects from what the APA *Publication Manual* suggests, but the information given in that book presupposes manuscripts submitted for publication in refereed journals, not classroom submissions. See the title page of the sample research paper in this chapter (page 277) for an example of a title page.

CONVENTIONS FOR APA CITATIONS IN THE TEXT

   The APA system calls for documentation within the text of the research paper. For the convenience of readers, cite sources of information you used where they are referred to in the text. (Full publication information for both print and non-print sources, except personal communications, is given in a listing titled References, which goes at the end of the research paper.) You can use either parenthetical, partially parenthetical, or in-text wording for citations. Variety in the ways you cite these sources will maintain liveliness in your writing.

1. **Author surname (or publication title if a name isn't available) and publication date are key items;** more complete information is shown in the References. However, if there is more than one reference to the same material in a paragraph, you need not repeat the year.

    EXAMPLE

    ```
    . . . Marc Cooper's article (1996). . . . Cooper further
    states . . .
    ```

    An anonymous article is recorded in the References by its full title, such as "Casino to protect children, animals," but appears in the in-text citation with a short form of the title.

    EXAMPLE

    ```
    The newspaper article "Casino" (1996) states that . . .
    ```

    The title of a book, periodical, or report is underlined. So is any legal material, such as a statute, a court case, or legislation.

2. **Cite specific parts of a source if they are immediately helpful to the reader.** Use abbreviations for page (p.) or chapter (ch.), but write out the words "Figure" and "Table" (without quotation marks) if any of these is your specific reference.

    EXAMPLE

    ```
    The newspaper article Casino (1996, p. A8) states that . . .
    ```

3. **E-mails, phone calls, electronic discussion groups, letters, and other similarly personal communications to the author are cited only within the text,** because it is assumed they are not available directly to readers of the research paper.

4. **Only the first word of a title is capitalized.** Other words, except proper nouns, are all lowercase.

5. **The names of all months are spelled out in full;** none is abbreviated.

6. **If a work has two authors, give both names every time the work is referred to in the text.** However, if there are **three to five authors,** name all of them in the first reference and in later citations use only the last name of the first author followed by "et al." Should you cite a source that has **six or more authors,** give only the surname of the author listed first followed by "et al." for all references to it. Use the word "and" when the names are given in the text, but use an ampersand (&) in parenthetical citations and in the Reference list.

7. **If you used material by two authors with the same surname, distinguish between them by always using the initials of each one, even if the years of their publications are different.**

    EXAMPLE

    ```
    J.R. Aldama (1995) and M.F. Aldama (1997) studied the
    comparative development of . . .
    ```

8. **When citing two or more publications by the same author or authors within the same parentheses, put the dates of publication in chronological order.** Give the name(s) only once.

E X A M P L E

```
Staging variations (Domingo, 1988, 1995, 1996) are well
documented.
```

9. **Two or more works by the same author(s) published in the same year are shown by assigning each a lowercase letter, alphabetically by title, to distinguish them in parenthetical documentation.** Use the same letters when you cite those works in a Reference listing.)

E X A M P L E

```
C. Matz describes computer-generated musical notation in
several publications (1996a, 1996b, 1996c) addressed to
those not in the music business.
```

Quotations Acknowledged in the Text

In addition to the author (or title) and publication date of a work, quotations must show the precise page number on which the words appeared in their original source. Separate each of the three units from those that follow by commas, and use the abbreviation "p." before the page number.

E X A M P L E

```
Hornblower, 1996, p. 50
```

The APA format uses the number of words in a quotation to distinguish between short and long quotations. **A short quotation contains 40 or fewer words,** enclosed, of course, within quotation marks. Just as in acknowledging borrowed ideas, the source of a short quotation may be recognized anywhere within a sentence. If the quotation to be cited occurs *at the end of a sentence,* put the documentation *before* the period. If the quotation is *in the middle of a sentence,* put the documentation immediately after what needs to be cited, and then continue the sentence. You may also put the documentation as an *introductory notation.*

More than 40 words is considered a long quotation and follows the convention of block indentation. That is, omit quotation marks, begin the quotation on a new line from the text, and indent the entire passsage five spaces from the left margin. If the source is not identified in a lead-in line as part of the text, do so in parentheses one space after the period marking the conclusion of the quotation.

COMMENT AND DOCUMENTATION NOTES

Content or commentary notes supplement the text, tables, or other visuals in the research paper without interrupting them. You can also use such notes in individual cases where parenthetical documentation would be unduly long. Therefore, you may list content notes separately just after the text of the paper.

In the text of the paper, use a consecutive superscript arabic numeral to mark each place at which you want to make a comment note. The numeral may be either within or at the end of a sentence before the period. Allow a space after the numeral and before continuing with what you write. Each note must be matched with its explanation on the note page.

Begin the notes on a separate page—still numbered consecutively—that you head "Notes" (without the quotation marks, of course) in the center of the page and 1½ inches down from the top of the paper. Double-space after that, and, beginning five spaces in from the left margin, put the matched superscript number for each note. Begin the note immediately after that number, without allowing any additional space. Since notes are written in paragraph indentation, second and succeeding lines will be at the usual left-side margin of the paper. All text for notes is typed double-spaced.

APPENDIXES AND OTHER MATERIALS

Follow the format and typing instructions already given for the MLA style ancillaries on pages 242-43 if you need to set up these possible additions to an APA-style research paper. Of course, retain the page heading and numbering system of APA.

REFERENCES IN APA FORMAT

The resources you actually used and acknowledged within the text of your paper are called "References" and need to be listed at the end of your work. Center the word (without the quotation marks) 1½ inches down from the top on a new page. Type all information in the References with double spacing. Allow *one space* after periods and commas, none after closing parentheses.

The References are presented in *hanging indentation* format. That is, start the first line of each entry at the left margin, and indent succeeding lines of each entry *five spaces* from that margin.

Put all references in alphabetical order by author's last name. If no author is given, alphabetize the entry by title. Titles beginning with *A, An,* or *The* are typed that way, but alphabetizing is by the next word.

Each entry in the References list contains four units, in the following order, and each unit ends with a period:

- author
- date of publication
- title of work
- publication information: location and name of publisher for books; volume and page numbers for periodicals. *Electronic media show the online source after the title.*

Variations for nonprint references, should incorporate as much of these units of information as possible.

The following list summarizes some of the other customs you are expected to adhere to in the APA style for References.

1. **The Author(s)**

   1.1 **Give the surname followed by a comma and the initials of each author,** no matter how many there are. Use commas between the names and an ampersand (&) between the final two.

   EXAMPLE

   `Kaufman, I.S., & Nimar, S.`

   1.2. **One or more editors of a book are indicated by the abbreviation Ed. or Eds. in parentheses** after the name of the last editor shown. Editors' names are placed in the position that authors would be, but they are shown with surname *after* the initials for given name.

   EXAMPLE

   `Roberts, J., & Ryan, J. (Eds.)`

   1.3. **If there is no author's or editor's name available, move the title of the work to this first spot.**

2. **The Date of Publication**

   2.1. **Enclose in parentheses the year of publication of a book.** Put a period immediately after the close of the parentheses.

   2.2. **Put a comma after the year of publication of a magazine or newspaper, then give the month—written out in full—and the date. Enclose the whole in parentheses.** End this part of the entry with a period.

   EXAMPLES

   `Roth, R. N. (1994).`

   `(1996, July/August).`

   `(1992, August 11).`

3. **The Title**

   3.1. **Capitalize only the first word of a title, the first word after a colon, and all proper names; the remainder is written in lowercase.** No quotation marks are used unless they are part of the title.

   3.2. **Titles of books, periodicals, films, and brochures are underlined** and conclude with a period.

   3.3. **Needed identification of a form is enclosed in square brackets after the title.**

   EXAMPLES

   <u>The story of glass</u> `[CD-ROM].`

   `Cars and clean air [Letter to the editor].`

   <u>Dolphins in the wild with Robin Williams</u> `[videotape].`

   3.4. **Two or more works by the same author(s) are listed in the order of publication. Repeat the name of the author(s) for each entry. If the**

works were published in the same year, assign each a lowercase letter based on alphabetizing the titles, and put it next to the date of each piece of work.

EXAMPLE

```
Michaels, D. (1994a). Living in the 21st century . . .
Michaels, D. (1994b). Mastering model making . . .
```

3.5. **Notation of a special edition of a book,** such as revised (rev.), alternate (alt.), subsequent (8th ed.), and so on, **is enclosed in parentheses after the title.** End that unit of information with a period.

4. **Publication Information**

4.1. **Unless the city in which a book publisher is located is well known, show the state where the publisher is located.** Use standard two-letter Postal Service abbreviations. If a book was published outside of the United States, abbreviate the name of the country, unless the city is well known (such as London, Athens, Rome). Separate the location from the name of the publisher with a colon. End the unit with a period.

EXAMPLE

```
Belmont, CA: Wadsworth.
New York: McGraw-Hill.
```

4.2. **An article or chapter within a book** is treated as an article through the first three units of author, date, and title. Then, add the word "In" and give the author's or editor's name, the title of the book in which it is found, and then parentheses enclosing the abbreviation "pp." with the page numbers on which it appears. Finally, give the publisher's location and name, followed by a period.

EXAMPLE

```
Pryor, K. (1991). The domestic dolphin. In K. Pryor, &
     K. S. Norris (Eds.), Dolphin societies: Discoveries and
     puzzles (pp. 346-397). Berkeley: University of
     California Press.
```

4.3. **Omit such words as "Company" and "Incorporated,"** but keep *Press* and *Books* if they are part of the name, and spell out the names of university presses and of publishing companies. (See example at 4.2.)

4.4. **A journal article in a periodical** shows the name of the publication and volume number (both underlined, but separated by a comma) and then a comma and the page numbers of the article, followed by a period.

EXAMPLE

```
Gebhardt, R. C. (1997). Scholarship, teaching, and the
     future of composition studies. Writing Program
     Administration, 20, 7-16.
```

4.5. Newspaper articles show all the page numbers on which the entry appears, preceded by an abbreviation of either "p" (if the article is on only one page) or "pp." (if it is on several, even discontinuous, pages). If pages are not continuous, show all pages but separate them by commas in this way:

EXAMPLE

pp. 12, 25, 30-32.

Print Resources

The following are some selected examples of the APA system for noting reference works. If you do not find a model in this brief section of a source that you need to list, consult the *Publication Manual of the American Psychological Association* (4th ed.). (1994). Washington, DC: APA.—which is how the entry for that book would appear in an APA References listing.

BOOK BY SINGLE AUTHOR

Diamond, J. (1997). Why is sex fun?: The evolution of human sexuality. New York: HarperCollins.

BOOK BY TWO OR MORE AUTHORS

Kastner, Laura S., & Wyatt, J. R. (1997). The seven-year stretch: How families work together to grow through adolescence. Boston: Houghton.

BOOK EDITED OR COMPILED

Hoskin, M. (Ed.). (1997). The cambridge illustrated history of astonomy. New York: Cambridge University Press.

EDITION OF A BOOK

Roth, A. J. (1998). The research paper: Process, form, and content (8th ed.). Belmont, CA: Wadsworth.

CHAPTER IN A BOOK OR ARTICLE IN A COLLECTION

Lopez, B. (1995). A presentation of whales. In F. Stewart (Ed.), The presence of whales (pp. 205-222). Anchorage: Alaska Northwest.

This entry illustrates that when the names of editors are not in the author position, they are preceded by the word "In" and *are not inverted.* Because the reference is to only a portion of a book, the pages on which it appears are shown after the title of the book and with the abbreviation that indicates they are pages within a work.

ARTICLE IN A MAGAZINE OR JOURNAL WITH CONTINUOUS PAGINATION

> McConaghy, T. (1997). How Canadian universities are
>   managing change. Phi Delta Kappan, 78, 660-661.

MAGAZINE ARTICLE WITH PAGINATION BY ISSUE

> Stolzenburg, W. (1997, November-December). Cancun
>   conundrum. Nature Conservancy, 10-17.

NEWSPAPER ARTICLE BY KNOWN AUTHOR

> Witt, A. (1997, November 18). Church dies, leaving case,
>   questions. Miami Herald, pp. 1B, 6B.

- Page numbers for newspaper articles are preceded by "p" (for a single page) or "pp." (for several pages).
- Separate by commas the several, though not continuous, pages on which an article appears.

Nonprint Resources

FEATURE-LENGTH OR SHORT FILM OR VIDEOTAPE

> Thompson, K. (Prod.). (1992). All the great operas (in ten
>   minutes) [animated; color; videotape]. Chicago: Picture
>   Start.

> Welles, O. (Producer & director & actor). (1941). Citizen
>   Kane [film]. Hollywood: RKO.

- If the producer and director are different people, show the function of each in parentheses after the name. If the director, actor, writer, or title of the film is most important for purposes of your research paper, put that designation first in the entry.
- In the square brackets after the title, specify the medium—that is, state if the work is a film or a videotape (or perhaps a filmstrip or a slide series).

> Mankiewicz, J., & Welles, O. (Screenwriters). (1941).
>   Citizen Kane [videotape]. Hollywood: RKO. (1988 Turner
>   Entertainment).

This illustrates how to list a video that was originally made as a film and subsequently bought by a company that then produced the videotape.

CASSETTE RECORDING, CD, AUDIOTAPE, OR RECORD

> Ogbu, J. (Speaker). (1992). Understanding cultural
>   diversity and learning. (Cassette Recording No. 71168-
>   1288). Urbana, IL: NCTE.

ELECTRONIC RESOURCES

CD-ROM

> The Story of Glass [Computer software]. (1995). Oxford, UK:
> Reed Interactive.

PERSONAL E-MAIL

> Specht, Billy (specht@oj.rsmas.miami.edu). "Re: A Name and
> an e-Mail." E-mail to Audrey Roth (ajr@aol.com). 18
> January 1997.

ONLINE ARTICLE ORIGINALLY IN MAGAZINE

> Blow, Richard. (1995, January 1). Dr. dolphin. Mother
> Jones. [Online], 58(15k). Available: Electric Library.

OTHER RESEARCH DOCUMENTATION AND REFERENCE SYSTEMS

Two "general" style manuals are *The Chicago Manual of Style,* which is widely used in publishing, and the Government Printing Office standard *Style Manual.* Most libraries have copies of these volumes for you to consult, should you need to.

Although *The MLA Style Manual* is widely accepted as the source for both student and professional research writing style for the humanities and the *Publication Manual of the American Psychological Association* serves that purpose for writing in the social sciences, many of the natural sciences publish their own style manuals. These include the following: the *CBE* [Council of Biology Editors] *Style Manual: A Guide for Authors, Editors, and Publishers in the Biological Sciences,* 5th ed.; the *Handbook for Authors of Papers in American Chemical Society Publications;* and style manuals for mathematics, geology, physics, and other academic disciplines, though many are meant for manuscript preparation for specific journals rather than for undergraduate papers.

Footnotes

Sometimes comment or information notes are put at the bottom of the page of text on which the information needs to be noted (hence, footnotes). The forms for writing these are the same as for other notes, whether you use MLA, APA, or another style, and the note is coordinated with its reference point in the research paper by superscript arabic numerals. Although a long-standing research technique, they are difficult to space properly and thus are not used very often.

If you use footnotes, separate the beginning of footnotes from the text on a page with four spaces (that is, two double spaces), and type them single space in paragraph indentation format.

Some computer programs are available that allow for footnotes. Or you can preview the setup of a computer-written page and make adjustments for the footnotes before you print.

Between-Line Documentation

One method for citing information that is sometimes used in theses and dissertations—but almost never in undergraduate papers—puts full citation information and notes at the point where the reader needs the information, even though it is in the middle of a page. The arabic superscript number, successive throughout the paper, appears at the appropriate place in the text, then a line from margin to margin is put across the width of the page as soon as possible beneath it. The coordinated superscript information is written double spaced in paragraph indentation, and another margin-to-margin line encloses the information. The text then continues after the usual double space.

Full In-Text Documentation

Another possibility for documenting sources is to give complete information in the text of your paper. Because it is fairly cumbersome and interrupts the flow of reading, this method is seldom used. However, full in-text documentation might be convenient if you have only a few sources to acknowledge.

In this system, enclose within parentheses the documentation information you do not mention in the text, and put the publication information in square brackets within the parentheses.

EXAMPLE

Robert Goodman (**The luck business**, 1995. [New York: Free Press]) is generally critical of gambling, and is especially critical of casino operations.

If you use this full in-text documentation, it may not be necessary to prepare a separate Works Cited list, because the information will be redundant. Check with your instructor for guidance.

Numbering Sources

This system is widely used in the natural sciences, such as medicine and health-related fields, chemistry, physics, computer science, and mathematics, as well as in technological writing. **Documentation in the text is a sequential, underlined arabic numeral followed by a comma, a space, and then the exact page reference.** The whole is enclosed within parentheses.

Each **numeral is then coordinated with a numbered entry in a list of Works Cited at the end of the paper.** Resources, then, are *listed in the order in which they are cited in the text* rather than alphabetically. Note that although there is a period after the number in the Works Cited listing, none is used after the underlined number in the parentheses within the text.

Strauch goes so far as to say that because a dolphin has "two separate sound-producing organs which it can use together as well as independently," (1 114) each animal can both send and receive in stereo.

and

Blow (2 n.p.) suggests this behavior is evidence that the dolphins somehow knew the boy was different.

The Works Cited for these two sources would be written this way:

1.   **Strauch, Ralph. "Do Dolphins Think Without Language?" Sea Frontiers (1984) 30.2 110-115.**

2.   **Blow, Richard. "Dr. Dolphin." Mother Jones 1 Jan. 1995. [Electric Library] 15 Oct. 1997.**

SAMPLE RESEARCH PAPER IN APA FORMAT

On the following pages is a research paper written by a student who used the APA style, as requested by his instructor. It also divides the text into several sections with headings, a common practice in some kinds of writing and as required by this instructor.

Marginal notes point out matters of **form in color** and of **content in black.**

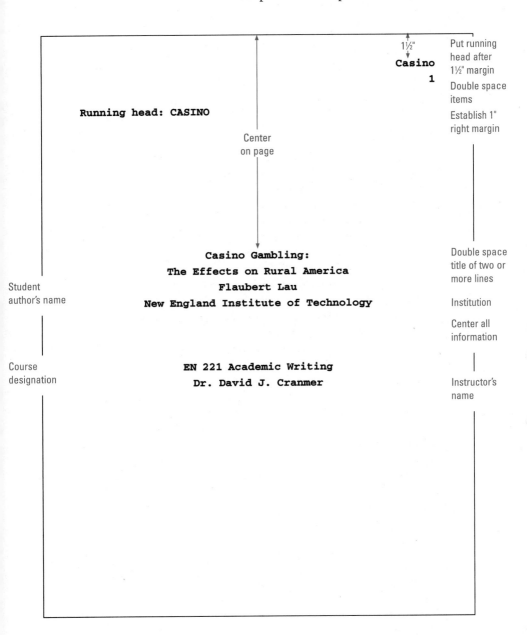

1½"

Put running head after 1½" margin

Double space items

Establish 1" right margin

Casino

1

Running head: CASINO

Center on page

Casino Gambling:
The Effects on Rural America
Flaubert Lau
New England Institute of Technology

Student author's name

Course designation

Double space title of two or more lines

Institution

Center all information

EN 221 Academic Writing
Dr. David J. Cranmer

Instructor's name

Running head
on each page

Number pages
consecutively

Repeat title
and center it

Center section
designation

Casino Gambling: The Effects on Rural America

Introduction

Indent
paragraphs
5 spaces from
left margin

For a long time, casino gambling was located
mainly in Reno and Las Vegas, Nevada, and in Atlantic
City, New Jersey. But now newer casinos are spread
out across the United States, from Connecticut to
California. Most are located on Indian reservations
and the rest in rural areas of the United States.
This paper focuses mostly on Foxwoods Casino in
southeastern Connecticut as one example of casino
gambling in rural America where casinos are very
profitable. According to Shapiro (1996), "People
wagered $482 billion in 1994 on all forms of gambling,
85 percent of which took place in casinos in 27 states,
most of them built in the past five years" (p. 53).
However, the casino is a short-term solution for
business in rural areas, not a long-term one.

Allow at least
1" right margin

←1"→

Use ragged right
throughout

Source
introduces
quotation

Short quotation
is part of text

Exact location
of quotation

Center section
designation

Review of the Literature

Among the American public, casino gambling is
controversial and it has created two well-defined
viewpoints, the anti-gambling forces and the pro-
gambling forces. Each side is able to present strong
reasons to support its views. From the local level to
the federal government, research and studies on this
topic have given varying results, and opinions will
depend on who you ask.

Among proponents of casino gambling, Frank J.
Fahrenkopf, Jr., President and Chief Executive Officer
of the American Gaming Association, testified before

Allow 1"
left margin

←1"→

Leave 1½" bottom margin

the House Committee on the Judiciary on 29 September
1995. Fahrenkopf (H.R. 497, 1995) stated that "[t]he
bottom line is there is a net increase in jobs and
tax revenues, two positive economic indicators, when
gaming entertainment [i.e., casino gambling] is
introduced into a community" (p. 138). He said casinos
produce many jobs, from the construction industries
to the support industries, and with them have come
better salaries for those workers. Also, revenue has
increased for the many kinds of businesses that were
associated with the casino.

At the hearing, Jeremy D. Margolis, a former
Assistant U.S. Attorney and Director of the Illinois
State Police, testified on the issue of crime and
casino gambling. Margolis (H.R. 497, 1995) stated,
"With a dramatic increase in gaming, you have a
dramatic decrease in crime, because the crime has
really nothing whatsoever to do with the activity of
the tourists who arrive at that venue" (p. 425). He
used the example of Las Vegas, Nevada, as his proof.
From 1979 to 1990, casino gambling revenue increased
from $1.5 billion to $5 billion. During that same
time span, the crime rate in Las Vegas declined
dramatically (H.R. 497, p. 424).

Also at the hearing was Richard G. Hill, Chairman
of the National Indian Gaming Association. He testified
on how revenues generated from the casinos on Indian
reservations have helped the Indians and the local
economy in the forms of new jobs and businesses. With

Original is a
capital letter,
so lowercase
one supplied
because quote
is in middle of
sentence

U.S. House of
Representatives
document

the Federal government reducing the amount of money set aside for the Indians, the casinos have made the Indians themselves more self-supporting. One of the key statements from Hill's testimony (<u>H.R. 497</u>, 1955) was "without gaming revenues, we [Indians] would have been on the BIA [Bureau of Indian Affairs] waiting list until who knows when" (p. 407).

Wording in brackets is explanatory

On the other hand, Robert Goodman (1995) is very critical on the issue of gambling in general and especially of casino gambling. Zachary Karabell (1995) stated, "Goodman believes the growth of legalized gambling is almost entirely a result of desperate state governments seeking a quick fix for shrinking budgets and growing demands" (p. 50). Hard-depressed cities will turn to casino gambling as a way to revitalize their areas. But Goodman (1995) said, "The sad lesson of gambling as an economic development strategy . . . is that it creates far more problems than it solves" (p. 7).

Ellipsis shows words omitted from original

Rev. Tom Grey, Executive Director of the National Coalition Against Legalized Gambling (NCALG), also testified at the Congressional hearing. Because Grey has won 23 out of 25 legal battles against the casino opponents (Hornblower, 1996, p. 30), Shapiro notes, "that's why one gambling consultant called Grey 'our most dangerous man in America'" (1996, p. 54). In his testimony, Grey (<u>H.R. 497</u>, 1995) reported:

Single quote marks within quotation

- gambling enterprises cost more jobs than they create;

Casino

5

Quotations of
40 or more
words are
block indented

- gambling misdirects prudent government investment away from sound economic development strategies;
- gambling sucks revenues from local economies;
- gambling establishments tend to attract crime; and
- gambling addiction destroys individuals, undermines families, and weakens our business community (p. 352)

Citation at
conclusion of
block quotation

Transitional
word

Overall, Grey says gambling is not a good idea.

Presentation of Issues

Centered
heading begins
another
section of
paper

Jobs and a better economy are two of the usual reasons presented for building a casino anywhere in America. Areas that are hardest hit from factories closing or declining jobs in the defense industries ought to welcome a casino. But the anti-gambling forces counter that the casinos take jobs away from the local community. People that work for the casino may come from out of town, but many of them used to work in the community. Now that they are gone, who will replace them?

Author's
commentary

A casino can be used as a major tourist attraction for some areas. With more people coming in, the better the business is for the local people and for the casino. For example, Foxwoods Casino in Connecticut is the largest and most successful casino in the Western Hemisphere. Lots of people go there every day. With success comes drawbacks. One of the major problems is the increased traffic on the local roads leading to Foxwoods, especially on weekends and holidays.

Stories from the local to the national news have made the general public more aware of the consequences of having a casino nearby. Crimes, compulsive gamblers, and the effect on family life are some of the major issues raised when a casino is nearby. On the issue of crime, the pro-gambling forces say there is no increase in the crime rate with a casino around. Margolis' testimony at the Congressional Hearing stated that conclusion. However, Shapiro (1996) stated that crime rates are higher in places with gambling: 1,092 incidents per 10,000 population in 1994, compared with 593 per 10,000 for the entire nation (p. 58). (For comparisons of certain crime rates see Appendix.) Such statistics do alarm people when they consider having a casino in their town. For example, the crime rate has gone up at the Connecticut Foxwoods Casino and nearby towns. The following statistics have been extracted from the Westerly Sun (Thefts 1995):

- Thefts have doubled in each of the three years since Foxwoods opened;
- There was a $1.5 million nationwide scam that used stolen credit cards to get cash from money machines at Foxwoods;
- Larcenies account for 560 of 574 major crimes reported at the casino during the first six months of 1994;

Statistics to aid reader

Reference to another section at end of paper

- Total crimes, including arrests for forgery, conterfeiting, vandalism, and drunken driving, rose from 299 in 1992, to 496 in 1993, to 1,155 in 1994;
- People leaving places without paying;
- Petty larcenies, bad checks, credit card fraud, and shopliftying have increased in the nearby town of Stonington, Connecticut. (pp. A1, A14)

Corruption, scandals, and organized crime are other things that are related to having a casino. Organized crime groups have managed to infiltrate the casino business through labor unions (Shapiro, 1996, p. 61).

Compulsive gamblers are another concern raised when a town is deciding whether it should have a casino. The pro-gambling forces say the percentage of problem gamblers is small. But the anti-gambling forces say ". . . the rate of problem gambling in a community tends to go up the more gambling is available in that community and the longer it is available" (Goodman, 1995, p. 47).

Casino gambling has a very strong effect on family life. When the Foxwoods Casino opened in Connecticut, it saw such family problems. For example, parents left children in their car so that they could go gamble. Sometimes the parents did not come back until six to twelve hours later (Casino, 1992, p. A1). The same news story notes that in June of 1992, a man was arrested on charges

Transitional wording

Text moves to another point

Transitional wording

No need to repeat citation just given

that he left his two children at a McDonald's restaurant in Colchester, Connecticut, for more than eight hours while he went to the casino (p. A8).

There are many more terrible stories about the effect on the family way of life. For example, a wife in Collinsville, Illinois, unbeknown to her husband and their two children, took the family money and spent it all at the nearby casino boat (H.R. 497, p. 29). One day the husband, who was at work, got a call from the police to come home. When he got there, he found out that his wife had gambled away all the family money and then committed suicide.

As for the issue of job creation, Marc Cooper's article (1996) included job problems in its presentation of gambling in Iowa. The unemployment rate went down in Iowa, but the wages ran 10 percent or more below the national average (p. 18). In other words, the unemployment level was at a low point but the people were not making enough money to support themselves and their families or pay their bills.

Evaluation of Issues

Two major viewpoints have emerged from the casino gambling controversy. Those who support the casino cambling movement cite jobs and a better economy as part of their reasoning for having a casino in a community. Revenue raised by the casinos has been recirculated into the local economies. Casinos on Indian reservations have helped the Indians become more self-sufficient.

Transitional wording

Section title centered

But the anti-casino gambling movement makes a better argument. The social costs from a casino greatly outweigh the benefits of having one. An increase in crime, suicides, compulsive gamblers, family problems, and lost revenues are some of the negative aspects of casinos. People in debt will turn to committing crimes just to support their gambling addiction, in hopes of winning back their lost money. Many families are torn apart when one member becomes addicted to gambling.

Author summarizes content so far

Conclusion

Casino gambling in rural areas of America has two faces. One is that of a savior in the way of creating jobs and a better economy. For many Indians, it is a means to become self-supporting and move away from federal government assistance. A casino can be a major tourist attraction, just like Foxwoods Casino in Connecticut. All this sounds good.

Author states concluding position

But then the other side shows its ugly face. These rural areas do not yet realize the full effects of having a casino nearby. Cooper's article describes the negative effects in Iowa and surrounding states. Family lives are torn apart. Crimes and suicides are increased. The number of compulsive gamblers has tripled or increased up to ten-fold. These facts are enough to recommend rethinking to any town that is considering having a casino facility built in it or nearby. If the town does decide to build a casino, then it should be prepared for the consequences of the decision.

Start references on new page

Continue page numbering

References

Center headir

Hanging indentation with first line at left margin

Casino to protect children, animals. (1992 September 9). <u>Westerly Sun</u>, pp. A1, A8.

Cooper, M. (1996, February 19). America's house of cards: How the casino economy robs the working poor. <u>The Nation, 262</u>, 11-19.

Succeeding lines of each entry indented 3 spaces

Goodman, R. (1955). <u>The luck business</u>. New York: The Free Press.

Book

Hornblower, M. (1996, April 1). No dice: The backlash against gambling. <u>Time, 147</u>, 29-33.

Double spacing throughout

<u>H.R. 497: National Gambling Impact and Policy Commission Act</u> (1995).

Government document

Karabell, Z. (1995, December 12). Casino evil. <u>Village Voice, 40</u>, p. 50. (from: Magazine Article Summary ELITE, Item Number 9512212155).

Siegel, M.A., Jacobs, N.R., and Landes, A. (1966). <u>Information plus: Gambling</u>. Wylie, TX: Information Plus.

Multiple authorship

Shapiro, J.P. (1996, January 15). America's gambling fever. <u>U.S. News & World Report, 120</u>, 53-61.

Thefts at casino, surrounding area on rise. (1995 May 5). <u>Westerly Sun</u>, pp. A1, A14.

1½"

Continue page
numbering

Appendix

Center title of
section

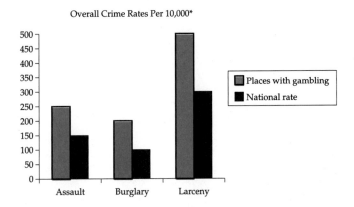

Overall Crime Rates Per 10,000*

Note. A *U.S. News* computer analysis shows that towns
with casinos have experienced an upsurge of crime at
the same time it was dropping for the nation as a
whole. They recorded a 5.8 percent jump in crime rates
in 1994, while crime around the country fell 2
percent. The 31 places that got new casinos just the
year before saw their crime rate jump the most: 7.7
percent. (The crime rate in small cities and towns,
with populations similar to those that have embraced
casinos, rose 1 percent in the same period.) (p. 60).

*Chart extracted from U.S. News & World Report,
January 15, 1996, p. 58.

Source should
be identified
under chart

Selected List of Reference Works Available in Libraries

To list all the reference materials available in even a moderate-sized library is impossible! The addition of computers with access to the Internet, as well as access to many other libraries, makes tabulating such materials as undoable as counting every star on a clear night. Besides, reference materials are constantly being updated and new titles added in all libraries. Periodicals begin or cease publication. New information and retrieval systems are being installed as libraries ceaselessly try to stay up to date with developments in electronic equipment and what it can provide. Whatever might be written down at this moment will be out of date the next.

What follows, then, is a *selected* listing of print sources found in most libraries and likely to help students in preparing research papers. Materials published regularly are followed by the year that publication began. Many of these titles are also available in electronic form, if not in entirety as shown here then probably at least of more recent date.

The titles of most volumes here are self-explanatory, so full citations and annotations are omitted.

Most materials named here either are published as books or are indexes of published periodical articles. If you do your research in a particularly large library or in one devoted to a special subject, be prepared to find many, many additions to this list. Computer information retrieval services can also direct you to hundreds of items in minutes. It is also possible to locate unpublished documents, for example, by consulting the ERIC [Educational Resources Information Center] indexes compiled by government-funded centers that gather, catalog, and reproduce such materials for educators. Furthermore, media centers and audiovisual departments usually have extensive lists of catalogs and sources of information that are not included in this listing; the same is true of computer centers.

Every business, profession, and hobby has at least one journal, magazine, or newspaper published for people concerned with it—publications ranging from *American Waterworks Association Journal* to *Volume Feeding Management*. Obviously, to list every such periodical is impossible! The library where you do most of your research will have a listing of those it subscribes to and facilities for locating periodicals you need to consult. A computer search will also reveal others, many of which you can download to find what is helpful to your needs.

The following, necessarily selected, list is offered only as a guide to the many materials available in some categories often consulted by students. If publication of a title is regular, the beginning date is noted next to it; otherwise, the latest publication date as of this book printing is shown. The list is divided into five main groups with numerous subgroups.

I. GENERAL REFERENCE WORKS
   A. General
   B. Atlases
   C. Biographies
   D. Dictionaries
   E. Encyclopedias
   F. Periodical Indexes

II. SCIENCE AND TECHNOLOGY
   A. General
   B. Agriculture
   C. Biology
   D. Chemistry
   E. Computer Sciences
   F. Electronics
   G. Energy
   H. Engineering
   I. Environmental Studies
   J. Geology
   K. Health and Physical Education
   L. Mathematics
   M. Medicine
   N. Physics

III. SOCIAL SCIENCES
   A. General
   B. Business
   C. Criminology
   D. Economics
   E. Education
   F. Ethnic Studies
   G. Geography
   H. History
   I. Political Science
   J. Psychology
   K. Social Work
   L. Sociology

IV. HUMANITIES
   A. Art and Architecture
   B. Foreign Languages
   C. Language
   D. Literature
   E. Journalism/ Mass Communications
   F. Music and Dance
   G. Philosophy
   H. Religion
   I. Theater and Speech
   J. Women's Studies

V. VOCATIONAL STUDIES
   A. Aviation
   B. Broadcasting and Mass Media
   C. Fashion Careers
   D. Interior Design
   E. Mass Media
   F. Medical and Allied Health Careers
   G. Office Technology
   H. Travel, Motel, Tourism Management
   I. Recreation

I. GENERAL REFERENCE WORKS

A. General

Britannica Book of the Year. Since 1938
Chase's Annual Events. Since 1958
Dissertation Abstracts International. Since 1967 (Formerly
   Dissertation Abstracts. Since 1938)
Europa Year Book: A World Survey. 2 vols. Since 1959
Facts on File: World News Digest. Since 1940 (Now *News Digest*)
Familiar Quotations. 1992
Guide to Popular U.S. Government Publications. 1990
Information Please Almanac. Since 1947
Monthly Catalog of United States Government Publications. Since
   1895
New York Public Library Desk Reference. 1989
The Reader's Adviser. 6 vols. 1988
Statesman's Year-Book. Since 1864
Statistical Abstract of the United States. Since 1878
United States Government Manual. Since 1935
World Almanac and Book of Facts. Since 1868
Year Book of the United Nations. Since 1948

B. Atlases

Atlas of American History. 1987
Atlas of Florida. 1996 (Most states have such atlases)
Doubleday Atlas of the United States of America. Since 1990
The National Atlas of the United States of America. 1970
National Geographic Atlas of the World. 1990
Oxford Atlas of the World. 1992
Rand McNally Cosmopolitan World Atlas. 1994
The Times Atlas of the World, 9th Comprehensive Ed. 1995

C. Biographies

American Men and Women of Science. 8 vols. 1990
Biography Almanac. 2 vols. 1987
Biography and Genealogy Master Index. Since 1980
Biography Index: A Cumulative Index to Biographical Material in Books and Magazines. Since 1946
Chambers' Biographical Dictionary. 1990
Current Biography. Since 1940
Dictionary of American Biography. 1946 (with supplements)
Dictionary of National Biography. 22 vols. 1885–1971
Dictionary of Scientific Biography. 16 vols. 1980
Directory of American Scholars. Since 1942
International Who's Who. Since 1936
McGraw-Hill Encyclopedia of World Biography. 12 vols. 1973. Supplements, 4 vols. 1987
The National Cyclopaedia of American Biography. Since 1888
New Century Cyclopedia of Names. 3 vols. 1954
The New York Times Biographical Service. Since 1970
Twentieth Century Authors. 1942. With supplements, 1955
Who Was Who in America. 1996
Who's Who. Since 1848
Who's Who in America. Since 1899

D. Dictionaries

Acronyms, Initialisms and Abbreviations Dictionary. 1996
American Heritage Dictionary. 1994
Black's Law Dictionary. 1990
Black's Medical Dictionary. 1992
Cancer Dictionary. 1992
The Concise Oxford Dictionary of Proverbs. 1992
Dictionary of Advertising. 1993
Dictionary of Computer Terms. 1992
Dictionary of Economics. 1992
Henderson's Dictionary of Biological Terms. 1989
International Dictionary of Medicine and Biology. 3 vols. 1986
New American Dictionary of Music. 1991

New Palgrave Dictionary of Money and Finance. 1992
Oxford English Dictionary. 20 vols. 1989
Oxford Thesaurus. 1992
Roget's International Thesaurus. 1992
Webster's Third New International Dictionary. 1993

E. Encyclopedias
Academic American Encyclopedia. 1995
Collier's Encyclopedia. 24 vols. 1993
Encyclopedia Americana. 1997
The New Encyclopaedia Britannica. 1987, 1990
Random House Encyclopedia. 1990
World Book Encyclopedia. 22 vols. 1997

F. Periodical Indexes
Applied Science and Technology Index. Since 1958
Art Index. Since 1929
Bibliographic Index: A Cumulative Bibliography of Bibliographies.
    Since 1938
Book Review Digest. Since 1905
Business Periodicals Index. Since 1958
Education Index. Since 1929
General Science Index. Since 1978
Humanities Index. Since 1974
Index to Book Reviews in the Humanities. Since 1960
Industrial Arts Index. 1913–1957. (Superseded by *Applied Science
    and Technology Index* and *Business Periodicals Index.* Since
    1958)
International Index to Periodicals. 1907–1964. (Superseded by
    Social Science and Humanities Index. Since 1965)
International Nursing Index. Since 1966
MLA [Modern Language Association] *International Bibliography.*
    Since 1963
The Music Index. Since 1949
New York Times Index. Since 1851
Nineteenth Centry Readers' Guide, 1890–1899. 1945
Poole's Index to Periodical Literature, 1802–1906. 1945
Public Affairs Information Service Bulletin. Since 1915
Readers' Guide to Periodical Literature. Since 1900
Social Sciences and Humanities Index. 1965–1974 (Superseded by
    Social Sciences Index and Humanities Index. 1974)
Social Sciences Index. Since 1974.
Technical Book Review Index. Since 1917
United States Catalog: Books in Print. Since 1928
Vertical File Index. Since 1935

II. SCIENCE AND TECHNOLOGY

A. General
Great Events from History—Science and Technology Series. 1991
The Great Scientists. 12 vols. 1989
McGraw-Hill Encyclopedia of Science and Technology. 20 vols. 1997
The New Illustrated Science and Invention Encyclopedia. 26 vols. 1989
Science and Technology Desk Reference. 1993
Van Nostrand's Scientific Encyclopedia. 1989

B. Agriculture
Agricultural Handbook. 1988
Agriculture Dictionary. 1991
Biological and Agricultural Index. Since 1916
Yearbook of Agriculture. Since 1894

C. Biology
Atlas of Endangered Species. 1991
Biological Abstracts. Since 1926
Biological and Agricultural Index. Since 1916
Encyclopedia of Human Biology. 1991
Gray's Anatomy. 1994
Grzimek's Encyclopedia of Mammals. 1989
Information Sources in the Life Sciences. 1987
Progress in Biophysics and Biophysical Chemistry. Since 1950
   (Now *Progress in Biophyics and Molecular Biology*)
Visual Dictionary of the Human Body. 1991

D. Chemistry
Chemical Abstracts. Since 1907
Chemical Information Sources. 1991
Dictionary of Biochemistry and Molecular Biology. 1989
The Elements. 1991
Handbook of Chemistry and Physics. Since 1914
Handbook of Industrial Chemical Additives. 1991
Hawley's Condensed Chemical Dictionary. 1993
Merck Manual and Handbook of Chemistry and Physics. Since 1889

E. Computer Sciences
Computer Glossary. 1993
Macmillan Encyclopedia of Computers. 1992
The New Hacker's Dictionary. 1993

F. Electronics
American Electrician's Handbook. 1992
Encyclopedia of Electronics. 1990

G. Energy
Energy Research Abstracts. Since 1976
Energy Update. 1991

H. Engineering
Applied Science and Technology Index. Since 1958
ASM Engineered Materials Reference Book. 1995
Civil Engineers Reference Book. 1989
Engineering Index. Since 1884
Eshbach's Handook of Engineering Fundamentals, 4th ed. 1990
Industrial Engineering Terminology. 1991
Sweet's Catalog. Since 1976
Who's Who in Engineering. Since 1977

I. Environmental Studies
Environmental Abstracts. Since 1971
HarperCollins Dictionary of Environmental Science. 1992
Nature Directory. 1991

J. Geology
Concise Oxford Dictionary of Earth Sciences. 1990
Glossary of Geology, 3rd ed. 1987
Handbook of Minerology. 1990
McGraw-Hill Encyclopedia of the Geological Sciences. 1988
Weather Almanac. 1987

K. Health and Physical Education
Consumer Health and Nutrition Index. Since 1985
Cumulative Index to Nursing and Allied Health Literature. Since 1977
Essential Guide to Vitamins and Minerals. 1992
Marshall Cavendish Encyclopedia of Family Health. 12 vols. 1991
National Health Directory. 1992
Physical Education Index. Since 1978
Sourcebook on Food and Nutrition. 1982
Sports Rule Encyclopedia. 1990

L. Mathematics
A Dictionary of Statistical Terms. 1990
Encyclopedic Dictionary of Mathematics. 1987
Handbook of Differential Equations. 1992
HarperCollins Dictionary of Mathematics. 1991

Mathematical Journals: An Annotated Guide. 1992
The Numbers You Need. 1992

M. Medicine
Glossary of Medical Terminology. 1992
Index Medicus. Since 1927
The Merk Manual. Since 1899
Physicians' Desk Reference. Since 1947

N. Physics
Encyclopedia of Physics. 1996
Handbook of Chemistry and Physics. Since 1914
Macmillan Dictionary of Physics. 1986
Magill's Survey of Science: Physical Science Series. 1992
Reviews of Modern Physics. Since 1929

III. SOCIAL SCIENCES

A. General
Handbook of Research on Social Studies Teaching and Learning. 1991
Public Affairs Information Service. Since 1915
Social Science Encyclopedia. 1996
Social Science Reference Sources: A Practical Guide. 1990
Social Sciences Index. Since 1974

B. Business
Business Information: How to Find It, How to Use It. 1992
Business Information Sourcebook. 1991
Business Periodicals Index. Since 1958
Commodity Year Book. Since 1939
A Concise Dictionary of Business. 1990
Dun's Business Month. Since 1893
Encyclopedia of Business Information Sources. 1992
Foreign Commerce Yearbook. Since 1933
Moody's Manual of Investments. Since 1929
Standard and Poor's Corporation Records. Since 1928
*Standard and Poor's Register of Corporations, Directors and
    Executives, United States and Canada.* Since 1928
Survey of Current Business. Since 1921
Thomas' Register of American Manufacturers. Since 1905
Wall Street Journal Index. Since 1958

C. Criminology
Crime in the U.S. Since 1930
Criminal Justice Abstracts. Since 1977
Criminal Justice Periodical Index. Since 1975

Dictionary of Crime. 1992
Encyclopedia of Police Science. 1995
Encyclopedia of World Crime. Since 1989

D. Economics
Handbook of Economic Cycles. 1991
A Lexicon of Economics. 1991
MIT Dictionary of Modern Economics. 1992
World Economic Survey. Since 1945

E. Education
American Educators' Encyclopedia. 1991
A Critical Dictionary of Educational Concepts. 1990
Current Index to Journals in Education. Since 1969
Digest of Educational Statistics. Since 1962
Directory of American Scholars. Since 1942
Education Index. Since 1929
Encyclopedia of Educational Research. 1992
Encyclopedia of Higher Education. 1992
ERIC Resources in Education. Since 1966

F. Ethnic Studies
Dictionary of American Immigration History. 1990
Dictionary of Race and Ethnic Relations. 1996
Encyclopedia of World Cultures. 1996
Handbook of North American Indians. Since 1978
Hispanic Almanac. 1994
People Atlas. 1991
World Directory of Minorities. 1997

G. Geography
Climates of the States. Since 1974
Concise Oxford Dictionary of Geography. 1992
National Geographic Index. Since 1899
Rand McNally World Atlas. 1992
The Weather Almanac. 1996
Who Was Who in World Exploration. 1992
World Survey of Climatology. Since 1969

H. Health
Cumulative Index to Nursing and Allied Health Literature. Since
    1977
Essential Guide to Vitamins and Minerals. 1993
Home Health Care: An Annotated Bibliography. 1992
Marshall Cavendish Encyclopedia of Family Health. 12 vols. 1991
National Health Directory. 1992
Sourcebook on Food and Nutrition. 1982

I. History
American Destiny. 10 vols. 1975
American Historical Review. Since 1905
Cambridge History of Latin America. 1993
Cambridge Medieval History. 8 vols. 1911–1936
Concise Dictionary of World History. 1983
Dictionary of Amercan History. 8 vols. 1976
Dictionary of Historical Terms. 1990
Encyclopedia of Asian History. 1988
Facts on File Encyclopedia of the 20th Century. 1991
Great Events from History: Ancient and Medieval Series. 1972
Historical Abstracts. Since 1955
History of American Life: A Social, Cultural, and Economic Analysis. 13 vols. 1929–1944
New Cambridge Modern History. 14 vols. Since 1957
Peoples' Chronology. 1992
This Day in American History. 1990
Timetables of History. 1991
The World and Its People. 19 vols. 1988

J. Political Science
American Political Science Review. Since 1906
Atlas of World Affairs. 1991
Congressional Record. Since 1873
Dictionary of Politics. 1992
Facts on File World Political Almanac. 1992
HarperCollins Dictionary of American Government and Politics. 1992
Index to Legal Periodicals. Since 1909
Municipal Year Book. Since 1934
Political Handbook of the World. Since 1928
Public Affairs Information Service Bulletin. Since 1915
Statesman's Yearbook. Since 1964

K. Physical Education
College Admissions Index of Majors and Sports. 1995
Encyclopedia of North American Sports History. 1992
Great Athletes. 1992
Sports Fan's Connection: An All-Sports-In-One-Directory. 1992
Sports Illustrated 1992 Sports Almanac. 1991

L. Psychology
American Journal of Psychology. Since 1887
Encyclopedia of Learning and Memory. 1992
Encyclopedia of Occultism and Parapsychology. 1996
Encyclopedia of Psychology. 4 vols. 1994
Encyclopedia of Schizophreniz and the Psychotic Disorders. 1992

Encyclopedic Dictionary of Psychology. 1991
Marshall Cavendish Encyclopedia of Personal Relationships. 1990
Mental Measurements Yearbook. Since 1938
Psychological Abstracts. Since 1927
Psychological Bulletin. Since 1904

M. Social Work

Adoption Directory. 1989
Assistance and Benefits Information Directory. 1992
Encyclopedia of Child Abuse. 1989
Encyclopedia of Social Work. 1995
Social Work Dictionary. 1991

N. Sociology

American Journal of Sociology. Since 1895
American Sociological Review. Since 1936
Encyclopedia of Sociology. 1992
Handbook of Sociology. 1988
Sociological Abstracts. Since 1953

IV. HUMANITIES

A. Art and Architecture

American Art Directory. Since 1898
Art Index. Since 1929
Encyclopedia of World Art. 15 vols. 1959 (With supplements)
Fine Art Index. 1992
Grove Dictionary of Art. 34 vols. 1996
HarperCollins Dictionary of Art Terms and Techniques. 1991
Illustrated Encyclopedia of Architects and Architecture. 1991
New International Illustrated Encyclopedia of Art. 24 vols. 1967
Who's Who in American Arts. Since 1937

B. Foreign Languages

Facts on File English/Spanish Visual Dictionary. 1992
International Encyclopedia of Linguistics. 4 vols. 1992
Oxford Guide to the French Language. 1992
Random House Portuguese Dictionary. 1991
Vocabulary of Soviet Society and Culture. 1992
Webster's New World Hebrew Dictionary. 1992
The World's Major Languages. 1987

C. Language

Dickson's Word Treasury. 1992
A Dictionary of Linguistics and Phonetics. 1991
Handbook of Good English. 1991
International Encyclopedia of Linguistics. 4 vols. 1992

Linguistics Encyclopedia. 1991
Oxford Companion to the English Language. 1992

D. Literature

Abstracts of English Studies. Since 1958
American Authors, 1600–1900. 1938
American Literature. Since 1929
Black Literature Criticism. 1992
Book Review Digest. Since 1905
British Writers. 8 vols. 1984
Cambridge Guide to English Literature. 1983
Cambridge History of American Literature. 3 vols. 1972
Cambridge History of English Literature. 15 vols. 1907–1933
Columbia Dictionary of Modern European Literature. 1980
Contemporary Authors. Since 1962
Contemporary Literary Criticism. Since 1973
Cyclopedia of Literary Characters. 1990
Dictionary of Concepts in Literary Criticism and Theory. 1992
Dictionary of Fictional Characters. 1991
Dictionary of Literary Biography. Since 1978
Essay and General Literature Index. Since 1900
Fiction Catalog. Since 1908
Granger's Index to Poetry. 1990
Handbook to Literature. 1986
Humanities Index. Since 1974
Macmillan Home Book of Proverbs, Maxims and Phrases. 1965
Magill's Critical Survey of Long Fiction. 8 vols. 1991
Magill's Critical Survey of Poetry. 8 vols. 1982
Magill's Critical Survey of Short Fiction. 7 vols. 1993
Masterplots. 12 vols. 1976
New History of French Literature. 1989
Oxford Campanion to American Literature. 1983
Oxford Companion to Classical Literature. 1989
Oxford Companion to English Literature. 1985
PMLA [Publications of the Modern Language Association]. Since 1921
Poetry Explication: A Checklist of Interpretation Since 1925 of British and American Poems Past and Present. 1980
Short Story Index. 5 vols. 1950, 1973 (Supplements since 1974)
Twentieth Century Literary Criticism. Since 1978
Twentieth Century Short Story Explication. Since 1977
World Literature Criticism. 1992
Writer's Handbook. Since 1936

E. Journalism

Biographical Dictionary of American Journalism. 1989
Journalism: A Guide to the Reference Literature. 1990

The 1992–1993 Guide to Newspaper Syndications. 1992
A Sourcebook of American Literary Journalism. 1992
Ulrich's International Periodicals Directory. Since 1932

F. Mass Communications
Broadcasting and Cable Market Place. 1997
Broadcasting Cablecasting Yearbook. Since 1982
Broadcasting Yearbook. Since 1982
Communication Abstracts. Since 1978
Communications Standard Dictionary. 1989
Facts on File Dictionary of Film and Broadcast Terms. 1991
Longman Dictionary of Mass Media and Communication. 1982
Telecommunications Systems and Services Directory. Since 1983
Television and Cable Factbook. Since 1946
TV Encyclopedia. 1991

G. Music and Dance
Contemporary Musicians. Since 1989
Dance Handbook. 1988
Dance Magazine. Since 1926
Dance World. Since 1966
Great Song Thesaurus. 1989
Illustrated History of Popular Music. Since 1989
The International Cyclopedia of Music and Musicians. 1985
Music Business Handbook and Career Guide. 1990
Music Index. Since 1949
New Grove Dictionary of American Music. 4 vols. 1986
New Grove Dictionary of Music and Musicians. 20 vols. 1980; 1995
New Grove Dictionary of Musical Instruments. 3 vols. 1984
New Grove Dictionary of Opera. 4 vols. 1992
New Oxford Companion to Music. 2 vols. 1983
New Oxford History of Music. Since 1986

H. Philosophy
Concise Encyclopedia of Western Philosophy and Philosophers. 1991
Dictionary of the History of Ideas. 4 vols. 1973
Encyclopedia of Ethics. 1992
Encyclopedia of Philosophy. 8 vols. 1967
Journal of Philosophy. Since 1904
Macmillan Illustrated Encyclopedia of Myths and Legends. 1989
Philosopher's Index. Since 1967
Philosophical Review. Since 1892
World Philosophy. 5 vols. 1982

I. Religion
Bible Atlases and Concordances. (A variety of titles is available)
Concise Dictionary of Cults and Religions. 1991

Dictionary of Judaism and Christianity. 1991
Dictionary of Religion and Philosophy. 1989
Eliade Guide to World Religions. 1991
Encyclopedia of American Religions. 1989
Encyclopedia Judaica. 16 vols. 1972
Encyclopedia of Religion. 16 vols. 1987
Encyclopedia of Relgion and Ethics. 13 vols. 1959
The Golden Bough: A Study in Magic and Religion. 12 vols.
    1907–1915
History of the Church. 10 vols. 1987
International Bibliography of the History of Religions. Since 1954
New Catholic Encyclopedia. 15 vols. 1989
New Schaff–Herzog Encyclopedia of Religious Knowledge. 13 vols.
    1949–1950
Religious Information Sources: A World Guide. 1992
Religious Leaders of America. 1991
Who's Who of World Religions. 1992
Yearbook of American Churches. Since 1916

J. Speech
American Orators Before 1900. 1987
Speeches of the American Presidents. 1988

K. Theater
American Musical Theater: A Chronicle. 1992
American Theatre History: An Annotated Bibliography. 1992
Dramatic Criticism Index. 1972
International Dictionary of Theatre. 1996
Magill's Critical Survey of Drama. 6 vols. 1985
McGraw-Hill Encyclopedia of World Drama. 5 vols. 1984
Play Index. 1992
Theatrical Designers: An International Biographical Dictionary. 1992

L. Women's Studies
Dictionary of Feminist Theory. 1995
Directory of Financial Aids for Women. 1995
Women's Studies Abstracts. Since 1972
Women's Studies Encyclopedia. Since 1989
Women Who Ruled. 1990

V. VOCATIONAL STUDIES

A. Aviation
Aerospace Facts and Figures. Since 1945
Cambridge Air and Space Dictionary. 1990
Dictionary of Aviation. 1991

Jane's All the World's Aircraft. Since 1909
World Aviation Directory. Since 1940

B. Fashion Careers

Conran Directory of Design. 1985
Fashion in the Western World: 1500–1990. 1992
Historical Encyclopedia of Costumes. 1988
Who's Who in Fashion. With supplements. 1992

C. Interior Design

Contemporary Designers. 1990
Encyclopedia of Arts and Crafts. 1989
Interior Design. Since 1932
Penguin Dictionary of Decorative Arts. 1989
Sotheby's Concise Encyclopedia of Furniture. 1989

D. Medical and Allied Health

American Nursing: A Biographical Dictionary. 1992
American Medical Association Encyclopedia of Medicine. 1989
Complete Drug Reference. 1992
Index Medicus. Since 1927
Medical School Admission Requirements. 1996–97.
Merck Manual. Since 1899
Mosby's Medical, Nursing, and Allied Health Dictionary. 1994
Physicians' Desk Reference. Since 1947
Textbook of Medicine. 1982

E. Office Technology

Professional Secretaries International Complete Office Handbook.
   1992
Secretary's Handbook. 1988
Secretary's Standard Reference Manual and Guide. 1978
Van Nostrand Reinhold Dictionary of Information Technology. 1989
Webster's New World Secretarial Handbook. 1989

F. Travel and Tourism Management

Dictionary of Hospitality, Travel and Tourism. 1990
Fodor's Travel Guides. (By country) Since 1936
Hotel and Motel Redbook. Since 1886
Hotel and Travel Index. Since 1938
Travel Dictionary. 1990

G. Recreation

Campground and Trailer Park Directory. Since 1984
Lincoln Library of Sports Champions. 1989
National Parks: The Family Guide. 1991
Parks Directory of the United States. 1994
U.S. Outdoor Atlas and Recreation Guide. 1994

Reference Words and Abbreviations

Searching for and recording information will be easier if you know the words and abbreviations usually found in reference and scholarly materials. You may want to use some of them in your own note taking, and some are appropriate for documentation and citation.

Geographical names have limited use, because the states where publishers are located are not shown in either the MLA Works Cited or text documentation. However, if you use material from outside the United States, whether print or nonprint (such as a film), you must indicate the country of origin. Sometimes that will be shown by a beginning capital letter and an ending period, as in Can. (Canada) and Gt. Brit. (Great Britain). Some countries are shown by only two capital letters: NZ (New Zealand) and UK (United Kingdom). Canadian provinces are also indicated by two capital letters, as in BC (British Columbia) and NB (New Brunswick).

Religious and literary works considered classics are often abbreviated, especially when titles are frequently repeated. Books of the Bible, including the OT (Old Testament) and NT (New Testament) are usually abbreviated; dictionaries often contain such lists. Chief among classical works commonly abbreviated are those by Chaucer and Shakespeare. For example, Chaucer's *CT* (*Canterbury Tales*) and its various sections, such as Pard T (The Pardoner's Tale), MkT (The Monk's Tale), and the WBT (The Wife of Bath's Tale), are often abbreviated in scholarly works. Among Shakespeare's plays, you can easily recognize most of the abbreviations, such as JC (*Julius Caesar*), Oth (*Othello*), Ado (*Much Ado About Nothing*), and H5 (*Henry V*). His sonnets are often referred to as Son., followed by a number or an opening line.

Foreign terms are seldom used. Even the once-popular "ibid." and "op. cit." are no longer recommended for your own documentation, although you may encounter them in your reading of other materials. Also, you will often come across some of these abbreviations for foreign words or phrases that are not put in italics or underlined despite the continuing custom of doing so for some of them in your own writing.

Here, then, are some of the more widely used scholarly and reference words and their abbreviations.

abbr.	abbreviation
abr.	abridged
AD	*anno Domini* ("in the year of our Lord," or after Christ) (used before numerals for a year, as in AD 1776)
adapt.	adapted by or adaptation
anon.	anonymous
BC	before Christ (used after numerals for a year, as in 79 BC)
BCE	before the common era (analogous to BC but used to designate time in calendars, such as the Hebrew calendar, that do not reckon time according to the life of Jesus)
bibliog.	bibliography or bibliographer or bibliographic or bibliographical
biog.	biography or biographer or biographical
©	copyright
c. or ca.	*circa* ("about") (used with approximate dates)
CE	common era (used to describe time in calendars, such as the Hebrew calendar, that do not reckon time according to the life of Jesus; analogous to AD)
cf.	*confer* ("compare with")
ch. or chap.	chapter
chor.	choreographer or choreographed by
col., cols.	column(s)
comp.	compiled by or compiler
cond.	conductor or conducted by
Cong.	U.S. Congress
Cong. Rec.	*Congressional Record*
Const.	U.S. Constitution
dir.	director or directed by
diss.	dissertation
dist.	distributor or distributed by
ed., eds.	edited by or edition or editor(s)
e.g.	*exempli gratia* ("for example")
enl.	enlarged
esp.	especially
et al.	*et alii* ("and others") (always abbreviated)
etc.	*et cetera* ("and so forth")
ex.	example
f., ff.	following page(s)
fig., figs.	figure(s)
fn.	footnote
fwd.	foreword
GPO	Government Printing Office, Washington, DC
H. Doc.	House of Representatives Document
HR	U.S. House of Representatives

ibid.	*ibidem* ("in the same place")
i.e.	*id est* ("that is")
illus.	illustrated or illustrations or illustrator
intl.	international
introd.	introduction or introduced by
l., ll.	line(s)
ms., mss.	manuscript(s)
narr.	narrator or narrated by
NB	*nota bene* ("mark or note well")—take notice
n.d.	no date of publication available
n.p.	no publisher available; no place of publication given
n.p., n. pag.	no pagination shown
op. cit.	*opere citato* ("in the work cited")
orig.	original or originally
p., pp.	page(s)
passim	*passim* ("throughout")—here and there in the work
perf.	performer or performed by
pref.	preface
prod.	producer or produced by
pseud.	pseudonym
pub. or publ.	publisher or published by or publication
qtd.	quoted in
rept.	report or reported by
rev.	revised by or revision; reviewed by or review (spell out the word if confusion is possible)
rpt.	reprint or reprinted by
S	U.S. Senate
S. Doc.	Senate Document
S. Rept.	Senate Report
S. Res.	Senate Resolution
sic	so, or thus (usually within square brackets; otherwise, in parentheses)
supp.	supplement
tr. or trans.	translator or translated by or translation
v.	*vide* ("see," or consult)
viz.	*videlicet* ("namely")
vol., vols.,	volume(s)
writ.	writer or written by

Index

Abbreviations:
  of commonly used terms,
    304–06
  in notes, 119
Abstract, 243
Accuracy in notes, 119–20
Acknowledgments:
  location of, 176–78; 198
  note numbering system,
    186
  of ideas, 107
  of maps, charts, diagrams,
    pictures, 203–05
  of sources, 4; 108; 198
Alphabetizing:
  in library sources, 38–40
  preliminary citations by
    author, 138
  in References (APA), 269
  in Works Cited (MLA),
    216
Analyzing as approach, 51–52
Annotation:
  defined, 241
  examples of, 241–42
  in Works Cited, 241
APA [American Psychological
    Association]:
  appendixes, 269
  citation forms, 268–69
    from electronic sources,
      274
    from nonprint, 273
    from print, 272–73
  documentation forms,
    273–74
  format, 265–66
  in-text citations, 266–68
  page numbering 265–66
  quotations, 268
  sample paper, 277–87
  title page, 266
  typing customs, 265–66

Appendix:
  defined, 242
  place in paper, 242; 269
Approach, finding an, 49–55
  wording an, 55–56
Approaches to subject:
  analyzing, 51–52
  comparing and contrasting,
    53
  criticizing, 52
  evaluating, 52
  examining, 51–52
  persuading, 54–55
  relating, 53–54
  wording of, 55–56
Argument as approach, 54–55
Assigned topics, 15; 20
Audience:
  importance of, 10–17
  writing for, 10; 17; 20; 44
Audiotapes, 104–05
Author:
  of encyclopedia article, 74
  on preliminary citation
    cards, 64–65
  reliability, 115; 116
Author-date system:
  for APA References,
    269–74

Background as opening,
    168–69
Bad endings, 190
Bad openings, 169–70
Between-line documentation,
    275
Bias in writing, 163–64
Bibliography:
  aiding topic choice, 25
  defined, 202
  source of information, 74
  See also Preliminary
    citations; Works cited

Body of paper, 170–86
Borrowed ideas,
  acknowledging, 107–08
Brackets, square, 131; 132
Brainstorming, 33

Catalog systems:
  Dewey Decimal, 34; 36
  Library of Congress, 34–36
  Online, 26–27; 37; 89–90
Cause to effect, organization
    by, 146–47
CD-ROM, 28; 93
CDs, preliminary citation,
    93–95; 104–05
Central idea. See Thesis
    statement
Challenging assumption as
    opening, 166
Choosing a subject. See
    Narrowing topics; Topics
Citations. See Preliminary
    citations
Clarifying subject as opening,
    164
Clustering, 45–46; 143
Coherence in writing, 170–73
Combination notes, 126
Comment notes, 126; 137;
    185–86; 205
  place in paper, 240
Common knowledge, 112–13
Comparing and contrasting:
  as approach, 53
  as organization, 145–46
Completeness in notes,
    120–21
Computer:
  aids to outlining, 158
  as information sources,
    88–97
  catalogs, 27
  databases, 91–92

Computer (*continued*):
 drafting on, 162
 editing, 193–95
 revising, 192–93
 searches, 89; 194
 spell checker, 194
 style analyses, 194–95
 Web searches, 31
 word processing, 155
Conclusion reached as ending,
  186–90
Concrete wording, 173
Content organization. *See*
  Organization of content
Continuous pagination, 69
Controversial topics, 19
Copying without
  acknowledgment, 5
 See also Plagiarism
Critical thinking, 10
Criticizing, as approach, 52

Database:
 choosing topics from
  catalogs, 26–27
 defined, 91
 preliminary citations from,
  91–92
Decimal outline, 154
Dewey Decimal classification,
  34; 36
Discipline, self, 11
Documentation:
 APA forms, 266–74
 author and dates, 268
 between lines, 275
 content of, 268–74
 conventions of, 199–200
 footnotes, 274
 full in-text, 275
 MLA forms, 199–214
 numbering sources, 275–76
 parenthetical, 175
 quantity of, 179
 of quotations, 180–85
 of visuals, 203–05
 work quoted in another,
  129–30
Documented paper, 2
Documented report, 2
Double submission, 40
Drafting paper, 8; 160–62
Drama, quotations from,
  184–85

Editing, 9; 190–93
 for mechanics, 193
Effect to cause, organization
  by, 146–47
Electronic:

aids to choosing topic,
  21–29
 documentation, 229–30
 resources, 60–61; 88–97
Ellipsis, 129
Emphasis in writing, 172–73
Encyclopedia:
 in choosing a topic, 23
 general, 73
 source of research ideas,
  23
 subject, 73–74
 in Works Cited, 74–76
Ending a paper, 186–90
Endnotes, 205–06; 207–13;
  (MLA) 240; 266
 difference from Works
  Cited, 206
 for books, 207–09
 for electronic sources, 211
 for nonprint sources,
  211–13
 for other print sources,
  210–11
 for periodicals, 209–10
 subsequent references in,
  206; 213–14
Evaluating:
 as approach, 52
 information, 7
 notes, 137–38
 source materials, 114–18
Evolution:
 of outline, 142–49
 of thesis statement,
  141–42
Examining as approach,
  51–53

Fact:
 as opening, 167–68
 defined, 119; 120
 marked on note card,
  119–20
Fastening pages of research
  paper, 243
Field-of-study topics:
 aids to choosing, 20–31
 computer links, 33
 course materials, 23
 defined, 15
 encyclopedias, 223–27
 library browsing, 32
 online catalog, 37
 personal interests, 32
 taking stock, 21
 textbook, 21
Figures, 203
Films, 102–03
Filmstrips, 102–03
First page of paper:
 APA style, 265–66

MLA style, 238
Five Ws, 46–49
Focusing on a subject, 44–46
Footnotes, location of, 274
Free association, 44–45
Free choice topics, 31–33
 choosing, 31–33
 defined, 16
Freewriting, 44

General to particular:
 organization by, 146
Good endings, 187–90
Good openings, 164–69
Good writing, 163–64
Government publications:
 sources of information, 86
 Works Cited forms,
  228–29

Handbooks, 76
Hanging indentation form, 63;
  269
Headings on research paper
  pages:
 APA, 265–66
 MLA, 238

Identifying sources on note
  cards, 120–21
Illustrative material (MLA),
  239–40
Importance of research paper,
  9–10
Indentation:
 in APA References, 206–07;
  269
 in endnotes, 207
 in MLA Works Cited, 63;
  241
Indexes:
 as sources of information,
  76–84
 conventions of recording
  information, 78–80;
  81–85
 of journals, 81–82
 of magazines, 80–81
 of newspapers, 82–84
 of periodicals, 78–85
Inferences, 119; 120
Information:
 adequate, 17
 evaluating, 7; 114–15
 integrating in writing,
  174–80
 primary sources of, 57–58
 secondary sources of, 58
Integrating resources,
  173–80

Internet surfing to find topics, 31
  sources of information, 90–91
Interpolations in notes, 131
Interviews:
  as research source, 99–100
  Works Cited form for, 100
In-text documentation, 175
Investigative report, 2

Journals, indexes for, 81–82
  publication information, 69–70

Key words. *See* Slug lines
Known to unknown, organization by, 145

Laserdiscs, 103
Lectures:
  as sources of information, 100–01
  preliminary citation, 101
Legibility of notes, 118–19
Length:
  of outline, 150
  of research paper, 6; 42
Letters, 87
Library catalogs, 34–37
  customs, 37–40
  explained, 34–40
  order of entries, 38–40
Library cataloging customs, 33–39
Library of Congress classification, 34–39
Library report, 2
Limitations of topic, 18–20
Linking as ending, 189

Managing time, 11–12
Manuscript preparation, 236
Mapping, 148–49
Mechanics of writing, 193
Microforms, 87–88
MLA [Modern Language Association] sample paper, 245–63

Names:
  in writing, 163
  order in catalog, 38; 39
Narrowing topics, 42–44; 44–55
"Neutral" subjects, 36
Newspaper:
  indexes, 82–84
  publication information, 84–85

Nonprint media:
  as source of information, 61; 97–105
  preliminary citations for, 97–98
  "publication" information, 98
  Works Cited forms for, 230–235
Note cards:
  abbreviations on, 119
  accuracy of, 119
  combination, 126–27
  comment, 126
  completeness, 120–121
  content of, 118
  conventions of, 128–33
  evaluation of, 137
  identification on, 120–21
  kinds of, 121–27
  legibility of, 118
  number of, 127
  outline symbols on, 158
  paraphrase, 123–24
  personal comments, 126
  poetry, 130
  preview reading for, 119
  qualities of good, 118–19
  quotations on, 125; 128
  source notations on, 120; 121
  summary, 122–23
  words omitted from, 131
Note taking:
  general information, 113–14
  poetry, 130; 183–84
  quotation, 128–30
  quotation acknowledgment, 128–30
  quotation within quotation, 129–30
Numbering sources for documentation, 280–81

Online (computer) catalog, 26–28; 37
Openings of research paper:
  bad, 169–70
  good, 164–69
Opinion, 5; 119
Order of material, 141–46, 150–52
Organization and overall appproach:
  by time, 145
  cause to effect, 146
  comparison and contrast, 145–46
  effect to cause, 146–47
  general to particular, 146
  known to unknown, 145
  of ideas, 8
  particular to general, 146

problem to solution, 146
  question to answer, 146
  simple to complex, 145
  visual, 147–149
Original work, 3; 4–5
  See also Plagiarism
Outline:
  characteristics of, 150–53
  computer aids to, 158
  content of, 150–53
  conventions of, 154–57
  decimal, 154
  defined, 149–50
  evolution of, 142–44
  explained, 149–58
  forms for, 153–54
  indentation system, 156
  information in, 150–53
  in presentation, 238
  length of, 150
  organizing content, 145–47
  paragraph, 154
  punctuation in, 156
  reason for, 149
  relation to thesis statement, 149
  relationship of ideas, 149–53
  revising, 150; 179; 190
  sentences in, 153
  spacing, 152; 156–57
  subordination, 151–53
  symbols on note cards, 158
  symbols used, 152; 155–56
  topic, 153
  typing, 157
Overworked topics, 19

Page numbering in research paper, 237–38
Pagination in periodicals, 69–71
Paradox as opening, 166–67
Paragraph outline, 154
Paraphrase notes, 123–24
Parenthetical documentation, 175; 199
  conventions of, 199–200
  identifying sources in, 201–03
  punctuation and spacing in, 200–201
Particular to general, organization by, 139
Peer evaluation, 158
Periodical articles:
  publication information about, 69–70
  Works Cited forms for, 69–71
Periodical indexes:
  as sources of information, 78, 80–84

Periodical indexes (*continued*):
  conventions of, 69–71
Periodicals:
  continuous paging system,
    69–71
  paging by issue, 69–71
  volume year, 70
Personal comment notes, 165
Personal interest in choosing
  topics, 29
Personal inventory, 29
Personal opinion, 5; 112–13
Persuasion. *See* Argument as
  an approach
Plagiarism, 5; 108–11
  avoiding, 106; 108–11
  in notes, 107
  of words and ideas, 107
  unconscious, 107; 108–09
Plays:
  documentation of, 184–85
  in Works Cited, 181–82
Poetry:
  documentation, 130
  in Works Cited, 182–83
  quotations, 183–84
Polls, 101–02
Preface of paper, 243
Preliminary citations:
  alphabetizing, 138
  author unit, 64–65
  bibliographies, 74
  books, 66–85
  content of, 63
  conventions of, 63–72
  defined, 63
  electronic resources, 88–97
  encyclopedias, 73–74
  forms for, 63–66
  government publications,
    85
  handbooks, 76
  indexes, 76–84
  nonprint, 97–105
  publication information
    unit, 66–72
  radio and TV, 98–99
  reference books, 75–76
  title unit, 65–66
  uses for, 63
Presentation form (MLA):
  abstract, 243
  annotations, 241–42
  appendix, 242–43
  comment notes, 240
  endnotes, 240
  fastening pages, 243
  first pages, 238
  general information,
    236–43
  illustrations, 239–40
  outline, 239

page numbering, 237
preface, 243
proofreading, 236–40
proposal, 242
statement of purpose, 243
synopsis, 243
text, 238
title page, 239; 240
typing, 237
word processing, 237
Works Cited, 241
Preview reading, 113
Primary sources:
  defined, 57
  importance of, 57
  location of, 57
Printed aids to choosing topic,
  21–26
Problem to solution,
  organization by, 146
Process log, 11–14
Process of research paper,
  6–9
Procrastination, 11
Proofreading, 236–37
Proposal, 243
Prose quotation, 182–83
Publication information:
  for books, 66–69
  for electronic media, 72
  for nonprint, 72
  in Works Cited, 66; 105
  magazines and journals,
    69–71
  newspapers, 71–72
Publishers' names:
  in Works Cited, 67–68
  "streamlining," 67–68
Punctuation:
  for quotations, 128–32; 133
  in parenthetical
    documentation, 200–201
  of quotations within
    quotations, 121–30

Qualities of writing, 162–64;
  170–73; 175–80
Question to answer
  organization, 134–36
Questionnaires, 101–02
Quotations:
  acknowledging, 128–30
  as ending, 187–88
  as opening, 167
  do not constitute research
    paper, 5
  of drama, 184–85
  of poetry, 130; 183–84
  of prose, 182–83
  on notes, 125; 128–31
  punctuation of, 128;
    180–85

within quotations, 129–30
words omitted from, 131

Radio and TV programs:
  as source of information, 98
  Works Cited forms, 99
Reading for notes, 113–18
Reference forms, APA,
  269–70
Reference words and
  abbreviations, 304–06
Reference works available in
  libraries, 289–303
  general, 291–93
  humanities, 299–302
  science and technology,
    294–96
  social sciences, 296–99
  vocational studies, 302–03
Relating:
  as an approach, 53–54
  as an opening, 165
Reminder as ending, 187
Reports, 2
Research:
  academic, 2
  applied, 1
  business, 1
  defined, 1–2
  market, 2
  pure, 1
  scholarly, 2
  sources of information,
    57–58; 62–63; 73–105
  technical, 2
Research paper:
  audience, 10; 17; 20; 44
  bases of, 6–9
  characteristics of, 3–4
  comment notes, 126
  defined, 2; 3–4; 4–6
  importance of, 9–10
  length of, 6; 42
  outline of, 142–53
  page numbering:
    APA, 265–66
    MLA, 216; 237–38
  participant in, 10
  personal advantages of, 4;
    9–10
  process log, 11–14
  readers of, 10
  steps to, 6–9
Resource information:
  evaluating for notes,
    115–17
  integration with text,
    174–80
Return to statement, as
  ending, 188
Reusing research paper, 18
Revising:

computer aids to, 158; 193–94
outline, 150–53; 158
writing, 5–6; 191

Sample research paper:
    APA, example, 277–87
        format, 265–76
    MLA, example, 245–63
        format, 236–44
Scanning to take notes, 114
Search strategy, 58–61
Search strategy record, 61–63
Secondary sources:
    defined, 58
    location of, 58
Selecting general topic, 16–20; 29–34
Selecting research subject, 44–55
Sentence outline, 153
Simple to complex organization, 145
Single source topics, 18
Skills from research, 9–10
Skim reading, 114
Slug lines, 121; 137; 158
Sources:
    credibility, 115–17
    evaluating, 114–18
    full identification of notes, 120–21
Spacing in parenthetical documentation, 200–01
Specialized library collections, 87
Specifics in writing, 173
Speeches:
    as source of information, 100–01
    preliminary citations, 101
Spelling, 191; 193
Square brackets, use of, 131–32
Statement of purpose, 243
Stating position:
    as ending, 188–89
    as opening, 165
Statistics as opening, 167–68
Structuring strategies, 142–49
Style of writing, 162–64
Subdividing, 46–47
Subject:
    choosing, 6–7
    defined, 15
    different from topic, 15
    focusing on, 44–46
Subjects. *See* Narrowing Topics; Topics
Subsequent reference forms in endnotes, 206; 213–14
Summary:

in notes, 122–23
is not a research paper, 4
Supporting statements, 172; 178–79
Survey as information,101–02
Synopsis, 243
Synthesis, 3

Tables, 204
Television programs:
    as sources of information, 98–99
Term paper, 2
Text of paper (MLA), 239
Textbook for topic ideas, 21–23
Thesis statement:
    basis of outline, 142
    defined, 138–39; 197
    evolution of, 141–42
    functions of, 139
    not a purpose, 139
    not a question, 141
    not a title, 140
    not a topic, 140
Third person, 163
Time:
    as opening of paper, 168
    management, 10–11
    outline organization by, 145
    studying, 12
    thinking, 12
Title page of paper:
    APA form, 266; 277
    MLA form, 238; 245
Titles:
    conventions of, 197
    for research paper, 56; 195
    in taking notes, 120
Topic outline, 153
Topics:
    assigned, 15; 20
    choosing, 16–20
    controversial, 19
    defined, 15
    field-of-study, 15; 20–30
    free choice, 16; 31–33
    good, 16–17
    narrowing, 42–49
    neutral, 19
    originality of, 16
    sources available, 17
    to avoid, 18–20
    unfruitful, 18; 19
Typing:
    annotations, 241–42
    of endnotes, 205–07
    of outline,154–59
    of quotations, 180–85
    of References, 269–74
    of research paper, 237
    of text (APA), 265–66

of text (MLA), 239
of Works Cited, 241
parenthetical documentation, 175; 199–200; 201

Unity in writing, 170–72

Videocassettes, 103
Visuals, documenting, 203–05

Web sites, 27
Word choices, 191–93
Wording an approach to subject, 55–56
Word processing, 237
Works Cited:
    contents of, 215
    conventions in research paper, 216–17
    defined, 215
    for books, 217–22
    for electronic sources, 229–30
    for portions of books, 222–23
    general information, 202–20
    in periodicals, 223–27
    in research paper, 202–20, 245–46
    MLA style, 217–35
    nonprint sources, 230–35
    other print sources, 227–29
    page numbering, 216
    place in research paper, 241
    typing, 216
Works Cited cards:
    conventions of, 63–66
    for books, 66–69; 77–78
    for electronic transmissions, 72; 89–97
    for encyclopedias,73–74
    for indexes, 76–78
    for magazines and journals, 69–71
    for newspapers, 71–72
    nonprint materials, 96–103
    publication information, 66–69
Writing:
    bias in, 163
    body of paper, 170–90
    coherence, 170–73
    concreteness, 173
    documentation in, 8; 175
    drafting, 8; 170–90
    editing, 9; 191–93
    emphasis, 172–73
    endings, 186–90
    integrating information, 174–80

Writing (*continued*):
  mechanics, 193
  openings, 164–70
  outline forms, 153–54
  the paper, 8; 162–93
  proofreading, 193

qualities of, 162–64;
  170–73; 180
revision, 8–9; 190–91
sentence structure, 177;
  191–93
specificity, 173

style, 162–64; 176
support, 172
unity, 170–72
vary wording, 176
word choice, 163; 173;
  191–93